The English Hero, 1660–1800

Edited by Robert Folkenflik

Newark: University of Delaware Press
London and Toronto: Associated University Presses

© 1982 by Associated University Presses, Inc.

Associated University Presses, Inc.
4 Cornwall Drive
East Brunswick, N.J. 08816

Associated University Presses Ltd
27 Chancery Lane
London WC2A 1NS, England

Associated University Presses
Toronto M5E 1A7, Canada

Library of Congress Cataloging in Publication Data

The English hero, 1660–1880.

Includes bibliographical references.
Contents: England, 1660–1880—an age without a
hero? / James William Johnson—Absalom and
Achitophel and the father hero / Larry Carver—
Dryden's Alexander / W. B. Carnochan—[etc.]
1. English literature—18th century—History
and criticism—Addresses, essays, lectures.
2. English literature—Early modern, 1500–1700—
History and criticism—Addresses, essays, lectures.
3. Heroes in literature—Addresses, essays,
lectures.   I. Folkenflik, Robert, 1939–
PR449.H45E5   820'.9'353   80-53894
ISBN 0-87413-174-X   AACR2

Printed in the United States of America

Contents

For Vivian

Acknowledgments

A collective enterprise of this sort necessarily involves a good deal of help from a large number of people, some of whom I am inadvertently about to overlook. I wish to thank the late Reuben Brower, Brick Frohock, Joel Gold, Bruce Johnson, Carey McIntosh, James Rieger, John Paul Russo, and David Tarbet. Although all of the contributors have been helpful in various ways, I am especially grateful to Rob Hume for reading the full manuscript at an early stage. Anne Hebenstreit, our editor, caught a number of errors. The Research and Travel Committee of the School of Humanities, University of California, Irvine, granted me funds that helped to defray some of the expenses of the volume. I am indebted to the chairman, Franco Tonelli, and to the dean of the School of Humanities, William Lillyman. For help of various sorts, I am once again grateful to my wife, Vivian.

All of the essays were commissioned especially for this volume. Part of "Johnson's Heroes" is reprinted from Robert Folkenflik, *Samuel Johnson, Biographer,* pp. 56–70, copyright © 1978 by Cornell University. Used by permission of the publisher, Cornell University Press. "Wars within Doors" is reprinted with some changes from Peter Hughes's article "Wars within Doors: Erotic Heroism and the Implosion of Texts," *English Studies* 60 (1979): 402–21 by permission of Swets Publishing Service, Lisse, Holland. "'I the Lofty Stile Decline': Self-apology and the 'Heroick Strain' in Some of Swift's Poems" copyright © 1981 by C. J. Rawson.

Abbreviations Used in the Notes

EC	Essays in Criticism
ECS	Eighteenth-Century Studies
ELH	Journal of English Literary History
HLQ	The Huntington Library Quarterly
JEGP	Journal of English and Germanic Philology
JNL	Johnsonian News Letter
JWCI	Journal of the Warburg and Courtauld Institutes
MP	Modern Philology
N&Q	Notes and Queries
PLL	Papers on Language and Literature
PMLA	Publications of the Modern Language Association of America
PQ	Philological Quarterly
RES	Review of English Studies
SEL	Studies in English Literature, 1500–1900
SILI	Studies in the Literary Imagination
SP	Studies in Philology
TSLL	Texas Studies in Literature and Language
UTQ	University of Toronto Quarterly

Introduction

The hero has always compelled attention. William James claimed, while agreeing, that "mankind's common instinct for reality . . . has always held the world to be essentially a theatre for heroism."[1] The fortunes of the hero during the age that runs roughly from the reopening of the theaters to the publication of *Lyrical Ballads,* however, have received only isolated and fragmentary study. And this is the period that, by the testimony of most historians, witnesses the transition from an aristocratic world to the modern world in which we live. Who are the heroes of this age? What are their relations to society? Do they possess virtues that are closed to others or to which others may aspire? Are they the embodiment of the collective will, exemplars, or symbols? Are they different from other men and women in kind or in degree?

A recent book that reprints a number of excellent articles on the hero in literature from classical antiquity to modern times skips suddenly, as it approaches the Restoration, from Milton to Hegel.[2] Perhaps we can account for such a leap by the assumption that an age so patently interested in mock-heroic has little interest in the heroic itself. The eighteenth-century hero, so this line of reasoning might plausibly go, is more likely to be Yorick than Hamlet, Tristram Shandy than Sir Tristram. Indeed, it would seem that we are faced with a *hero absconditus.* Another recent book that deals with heroic themes, Thomas Edwards's *Imagination and Power,* traces the "Disappearance of Heroic Man" to the seventeenth century, and Mario Praz's *The Hero in Eclipse in Victorian Fiction* suggests that he is still to be sought. Victor Brombert can even assume that modern incarnations of the hero "are, of course, paralleled by a steady shrinking of the heroic."[3] This too is plausible, yet we may suspect that the whole story of heroes in this period cannot be so easily summarized. Brombert has in mind the literature of the nineteenth and twentieth centuries, but in the development of modern ideas of the hero, as in so much else, the Restoration and eighteenth century are of crucial importance, and an examination of the period from this perspective may help us to see the sources of our own notions of heroism.

A few distinctions are necessary at the outset. First, although most of these essays deal with the hero in literature, some consider historical figures and "culture" heroes. To look at the literary hero solely risks improper generalizations about the age, a period bracketed by such worrisome examples of heroic greatness as Cromwell and Napoleon. The ghost of Cromwell seems to hover about much thinking on heroism during the eighteenth century. That the graves in Gray's country churchyard may contain "some Cromwell guiltless of his country's blood" may help to reconcile us to the loss of a "mute, inglorious Milton." In addition, some "literary" characters are historical, and a full appreciation of, say, Swift's "On the Death of a Late Famous General" depends to some extent on a knowledge of the figure Marlborough cut in Whig histories. Besides, a broader scope may help to discern anomalies: the same period, for example, to which Praz assigns the decline of the hero in the novel is the heyday of Carlylean hero-worship. Certainly, to take an instance of enduring importance, the rise of literary biography had an influence on that characteristic hero of the mid- and late eighteenth century, the poet.[4]

Second, within literature there is the confusion, which came about during this period and is with us yet, engendered by the use of the word *hero* to signify a protagonist or another character with heroic qualities and also, as a literary convention, to mean simply the protagonist of the work in which he appears. (One of the following essays directly addresses the problems of interpretation that this confusion has caused.[5]) But at the same time there is a tendency during the age for any protagonist by dint of his centrality or exposed position to be measured by heroic expectations of one kind or another. Fielding's sudden shift in the middle of a mock-heroic battle catches the spirit of this transformation:

Reader, we would make a Simile on this Occasion, but . . . we could find no Simile adequate to our Purpose: For indeed, what

Instance could we bring to set before our Reader's Eyes at once the Idea of Friendship, Courage, Youth, Beauty, Strength, and Swiftness?; all which blazed in the Person of *Joseph Andrews.* Let those therefore that describe Lions and Tigers, and Heroes fiercer than both, raise their Poems or Plays with the Simile of *Joseph Andrews,* who is himself above the reach of any Simile.[6]

Fielding plays with and parodies heroic notions, but he also consciously makes heroic claims. In others, the presentation of the protagonist may be left to make its own claim. Therefore, no attempt has been made to restrict the figures discussed only to those who embody traditional ideas of the hero, though all the essays address themselves at one point or another to the problem of heroism.

The hero begins as a ἥρως, a warrior with intimations of immortality. He is either a demigod or at least one of the gods' favorites. The first reference to a hero in English, according to the *OED,* is as an allegorical Christ-figure. In the Renaissance he still maintains his classic pose: "Goddes made of men whom the antiquitie cauled heroes" (1555).[7] Two hundred years later when Samuel Johnson came to publish his *Dictionary,* the two meanings he gives show the break that had come about. The first is "a man eminent for bravery"; the second, "A man of the highest class in any respect." His illustrative quotations under the variations of *hero* and *heroine* are drawn from a fair sampling of the English heroic tradition: Sidney, Chapman, Shakespeare, Waller, Milton, Cowley, Dryden, Addison, and Pope. Johnson's definitions show a shift from Nathan Bailey's more typical single definition earlier in the century in his *Etymological Dictionary* (1721): "A great and illustrious Person, a Person of singular Valour, Worth, and Renown, among the Ancients, who although he was of mortal Race, was yet esteemed by the People to partake of Immortality, and after his Death was reckoned among the Gods." Boswell's choice of heroes for his biographical works could be taken as illustrations of Johnson's two definitions: Pasquale Paoli, a general and head of state, a traditional hero, but so rare by the late eighteenth century that Boswell emphasizes the primitive country he rules and agrees with Chatham that such a man "is no longer to be found, but in the lives of Plutarch," and Johnson himself, the hero as man of letters, a Monarch of Literature.[8] Boswell's description of Paoli also testifies, as do the definitions of Bailey in the early eighteenth century and Eden in the Renaissance, that the "heroic times" maintained their hold on the imagination and that the inhabitants of a postheroic age were hero-haunted by Greek and Roman prowess.

Two different responses to heroism may help to clarify this point. In what was probably intended as part of a "Character of the Hero," Samuel Butler distinguishes the diminished modern "hero" from the ancient version, whose abilities are demythologized to begin with:

A Hero was nothing but a fellow of a greate Stature, and strong Limbes, who was able to carry a heavier Load of Armes on his Back, and strike harder Blows, then those of a lesser Size. And therefor since the Invention of Guns came up, there can be no true Hero in great Fights, for all mens Abilitys are so leveld by Gun-shot, that a Dwarf may do as heroique Feats of Armes that way as a Gyant. And if he be a good Markesman, be too hard for the stoutest Hector and Achilles too.[9]

Elsewhere he claims that "no Age ever abounded more with Heroical Poetry then the present, and yet there was never any wherein fewer Heroicall Actions were performd. . . ."[10] If, according to Bacon, modern man is intellectually a dwarf standing on the shoulders of a giant, the modern hero, thanks to technology, is the dwarf himself.[11]

Butler is a satirist; his great admirer Swift offers the most consistently anti-heroic and debased versions of heroism in the period. Yet throughout Swift's works one can find hints of another attitude. In the *Battle of the Books* the heroic stature of the Ancients is used to measure the Moderns' deviations. In Glubbdubdrib Gulliver asks the necromantic Governor to call up the Senate of Rome and a "modern Representative" (read "The House of Commons"): "The first seemed to be an Assembly of Heroes and Demy-Gods; the other a knot of Pedlars, Pickpockets, Highwaymen and Bullies." And when Gulliver converses with Brutus, he is told "that his ancestor *Junius, Socrates, Epaminondas, Cato* the Younger, Sir *Thomas More* and himself, were perpetually together: A Sextumvirate to which all the Ages of the World cannot add a Seventh."[12] If one is tempted to see in these references the use of an ancient club to brain the moderns, the standard response of the *laudator temporis acti,* the believer in historical decline, such views would distort Swift's position. He has an interest in heroism that can be found in rulers and generals, pagans and Christians, saints and philosophers, even ancients and moderns. His unpublished "Of Mean and Great Figures Made by Several Persons" provides a gloss on this passage. Behaviorist that he is, Swift focuses on "some particular Action or Circumstance of their Lives." Among the twenty listed are four members of the sextumvirate: "Socrates, the whole last Day of his Life, and particularly from the Time he took the Poison to the Moment he expired"; "Epaminondas when the Persian Ambassador came to his House and found him in the midst of Poverty"; "Cato of Utica, when he provided for the Safety of his Friends and had determined to dy"; and "Sir Tho More during his Imprisonment, and at his Execution."[13] Though the two Brutuses are not mentioned, Gulliver says that one could see in Marcus Brutus "the most consummate Virtue, the greatest Intrepidity, and Firmness of Mind, the truest Love of his Country, and general Benevolence for Mankind in every Lineament of his Countenance." And Caesar confesses that Brutus's taking of his life was more glorious than "the greatest actions of his own Life."[14] Swift revered Republican Rome, and in a letter to Pope called "the Caesars and their successors, the most infamous tyrants that have any where appeared in story."[15] What Swift admires is heroic sacrifice and martyrdom (though he is not to be taken as an admirer of philosophic Stoicism). Had he stipulated the greatest action of Lucius Junius Brutus, it would undoubtedly have been his command that his sons Titus and Tiberius be killed for attempting to restore the Tarquins to power. There are no kings among his six, though his "Great Figures made by several Persons" includes "King Charles the Martyr during his whole Tryall, and at his Death."[16] It also includes Cromwell quelling a mutiny and Alexander, following his victory at the Straits of Tarsus, with the queen and princesses of Persia at his feet. Some of his choices are perhaps more surprising: "Virgil, when at Rome the whole Audience rose up out of Veneration as he entered the theatre"; and

Harry the Great [Henri IV] of France, when he entered Paris, and sate at Cards the same Night with some great Ladyes, who were his mortal Enemyes."[17]

There are several other observations to be noted before returning to the fate of ancient heroes in the period. One man's hero may well be another's villain—Marcus Brutus, whose initials may be the source of Swift's use of "M. B." as the signature of the *Drapier's Letters,* winds up along with Judas in the mouth of Satan in the lowest part of Dante's *Inferno.* And although the charismatic hero may attract unquestioning devotion to his whole life (this is the recommended Carlylean posture), Swift does not think that way: both Charles I and Cromwell also show up on the list "of those who have made a mean contemptible Figure in some Action or Circumstance of their Life."[18] This list contains a far greater number of kings than the other—among the English, John and Richard II, the two Charleses, James II, William III and Queen Anne, as well as Spanish and Polish kings.

The heroes of the classical historians, especially those found in Plutarch's pages—those noble Greeks and Romans—would tenuously survive the cultural upheavals of the period. In some cases they even contributed to them. Lee's *Lucius Junius Brutus* (1680) was banned, and Addison's *Cato* (1713) and Richard Glover's *Leonidas* (1737) were praised and damned by different political factions. Johnson tells the famous anecdote of Addison's changing a line in Pope's prologue to his play from "Britons, arise, be worth like this approved" to "Britons, attend," for fear "he should be thought a promotor of insurrection."[19] The reception of these works by contemporaries and in later years signals the last gasps of the heroes of antiquity as the protagonists of those major forms, tragedy and epic. At the end of the century they reached their highest point when Jacques-Louis David, who might in several senses be dubbed a "promoter of insurrection," made such heroes exemplars of revolution in his Neoclassical paintings. That was in another country and another medium, but it is worth noticing that of Swift's six, David painted Socrates taking the hemlock (1787) and Lucius Junius Brutus sitting impassively as the bodies of his sons are brought back (1789).[20]

David's program was the culmination of a number of tendencies. In 1754 La Font de Saint-Yenne disparaged mythological fictions as subjects for painters and recommended instead history painting of "the virtuous actions of great men, exemplars of humanity, generosity, grandeur, courage, disdain for danger and even for life itself, of passionate zeal for the honour and safety of the country."[21] He suggests Plutarchan subjects—Socrates, Epaminondas, Decius, Marcus Curtius, and Lucius Junius Brutus—as appropriate.

This demythologizing had its price. Not many of the figures considered in this volume would score high on Lord Raglan's famous checklist of heroic attributes. Among his twenty-two points are:

(1) The hero's mother is a royal virgin.
(4) He is . . . reputed to be the son of a god.
(11) After a victory over the king and/or a giant, dragon, or wild beast,
(12) He marries a princess, often the daughter of his predecessor, and
(13) Becomes King.
(18) He meets with a mysterious death,
(19) Often at the top of a hill.
(20) His children, if any, do not succeed him.
(21) His body is not buried, but nevertheless
(22) He has one or more holy sepulchres.[22]

Oedipus gets full marks; Arthur nineteen; Hercules seventeen; and Robin Hood thirteen. Some of the heroes of Restoration tragedy can hold their own by such a standard, but the heroes of Pope, Swift, Johnson, and the novelists are nowhere. Yet is this not to say that the hero in the Restoration and eighteenth century has become more typically human than before? This hero may have shrunk, declined, or even been demolished, as some critics have had it, but he has a good deal to tell us of what has become of heroism in this century, when bourgeois heroes and anti-heroes are nauseated, angry, or paralyzed throughout our literature, and the concept of military and political heroism seems at best tarnished or dubious. One should also recognize that the critique of heroism, strenuously mounted during this period, may be as important as heroism itself, and at certain times more important. The tendency of a hero-cult to dichotomize society into the leader and the led, master and slave, is all too evident in the writings of Thomas Carlyle, to say nothing of its horrific role under the Nazis in the twentieth century. Nevertheless, although we cannot live with the hero and we abhor the atrocities commited in his name, we can hardly do without heroes of some sort, for the idea of heroism is a mirror of an age's very conception of itself at its best.

Some of the following essays deal with genres (Hume, Anderson), some with major writers (Rawson, Folkenflik, Hunter) or individual works (Carver, Carnochan, Lindley), while others attempt a synthesis (Johnson, Hughes). Looking closely at the period from the middle of the seventeenth century to the last years of the eighteenth century, the essays comment on and illuminate other ages as well.

James William Johnson, confronting the major problem head-on, discovers a plethora of heroes but a lack of "consensus in Stuart-Georgian England as to the attributes of the hero, the constituent elements of heroism, or even as to whether the heroic concept had any validity." The tensions that arise from such a situation are apparent throughout the studies that follow. Dryden, represented by two essays devoted to different works, has pride of place, as befits the foremost author of this period whose primary concerns from first to last involved the role of the heroic.[23] Larry Carver shows how a domestic metaphor, put in the service of the highest public office, kingship, provides the basis for Dryden's greatest political poem, *Absalom and Achitophel.* The world may have been well lost for Antony; Alexander is a hero who wept that there were not more worlds to conquer. Such at least is one received notion; but W. B. Carnochan, who stresses that "according to the tradition Alexander was a heroic bundle of contradictions," is concerned with Alexander as *victor victus,* a highly problematic and ironic hero, and with Timotheus, the lyre player, forerunner of the musicians, painters, and poets who were to become such important heroes in the second half of the eighteenth century and later. The full title of Dryden's work is, after all, "Alexander's Feast; or, the Power of Musique."

The next writer would purge the comic of a spurious heroism. Robert D. Hume examines the comedies of the Restoration and early eighteenth century with an eye to sorting out modern misinterpretations caused by the assumption that the "heroes" of these plays are offered as exemplary figures, a notion that begins with Steele, whose own comedies are meant to be exemplary and attempt to take over for the protagonist of comedy the heroic ethic formerly the preserve of the tragic hero.

Despite his admiration for heroic acts, Swift was very ambivalent about heroism in general and his own heroism in particular. C. J. Rawson's account of Swift's poetry closely assesses the nature of Swift's engagement with heroic themes, postures, and styles. It concludes with a reading of the *Verses on the Death of Dr. Swift* that subjects the poem to searching criticism while comparing it to poetry by Pope, Pound, and Yeats.

Fielding has links to Steele's Christian Hero, but J. Paul Hunter traces the development of Fielding's early work from its strong engagement with the anti-heroic concepts of Pope, Swift, and Gay to a position, in some ways close to that of Defoe, in which he "could postulate a Christian hero as a modern alternative to Augustan visions of anti-hero." The last part of his account reminds the reader that the whole story of Tom Jones is played out against the background of an authentic national crisis—the abortive revolution of '45—and shows that in Tom Fielding presents "the new man of mid-century English society," a man equipped to deal with the realities of life after the crisis has passed.

Like Swift and Fielding, Johnson attacks traditional notions of the hero, but he is concerned, as I argue in my essay, to substitute in their place a hero at once pious and ambitious, whose relation to the fact of human mortality consists of a Christian patience in the face of adversity and a continuous striving for intellectual achievement.

A very different shift away from heroic action, the movement from battlefield to boudoir, is the subject of Peter Hughes's essay. In this version of the transformation of the hero from public to private, exterior to interior, Hughes details a characteristic metamorphosis during the whole period, when wars of passion replaced heroic fury. By moving freely between France and England he also properly emphasizes that English ideas were not insular at this time.

The battle of the sexes that Hughes discusses serves to remind us that although we may speak of heroes, this is an age distinguished by its heroines as well. The next essay, by Arthur Lindley, deals with those mighty opposites Lovelace and Clarissa and demonstrates that, to establish his own conception of heroism in *Clarissa*, Richardson had to present a critique of some traditional conceptions in the person of Lovelace, much as Milton's critique of the heroes of Renaissance epic is embodied in Satan. Lindley suggests that Lovelace as a role-playing hero has qualities in common with characters from Shakespeare to Mailer, and in the terms of the novel, he derives from the heroes of Dryden, whose dramas Lovelace frequently quotes.

The final essay explores the nature of a hero who comes into being in the later eighteenth century and continues as a major figure to the present, the Gothic hero-villain. Howard Anderson attempts to show that "these characters are authenticated for the reader by a unique—and in the greatest gothic novels, complex—balance between psychological characterization and mythic allusion." These heroes bring back the superhuman (and supernatural) that had disappeared, though in a different key (melodrama) and a different location (interiors)—ruined castles and mouldering mausoleums. The Gothic hero forces the reader to face the evil within the self as well as in the world. And in considering the problem of evil, which is as central to heroic literature and speculation as to theodicies, this collection comes to an end.

To generalize the findings in these essays would inevitably reduce them. But it may perhaps be worthwhile to suggest ways in which important developments of the period relate to the heroes discussed. Take what in one aspect is the Fall of Public Man or the Rise (not of the Middle Class, which was always rising) of Domestication. This major transformation (of central concern to Peter Hughes) from public to private affects mind as well as locale. It leads to an emphasis on psychology over behavior and on interiors over exteriors. In the shift from Dryden's defense of monarchy in *Absalom and Achitophel* to the tensions in his handling of Alexander, we can see some of the changes in value coming about. The rise of the heroine of the "she-tragedies" of Banks and Rowe and in the heroines of Richardson (and of the novel in general) are typical of the shifts in heroism brought about by domestication, as is the move away from the Herculean hero typical of Renaissance and early Restoration drama.[24] J. W. Johnson details some of the cultural signals that point to a shift in heroic conceptions. Thaumaturgic kingship was declining with the last Stuarts. After William's reluctance to touch for the "King's evil," Queen Anne was the last ruler of England to attempt the cure.[25] (The scrofulous infant Samuel Johnson was her best-known suppliant.) With the coming of the Georges, the basis for the inherited sacred power was no longer present. J. W. Johnson notes too that William was the last ruler of England to be painted officially in armor; in the eighteenth century such a warrior-king gives way to "Farmer George." And yet it should be remembered that George II was the last English king to lead his troops in battle (Dettingen, 1743), a fact memorialized in a marble bust of the king in armor by Rysbrack.

In the very notion of a comic hero whose actions can in some way or ways be considered heroic (whether in Steele's plays or Fielding's novels), the stage of heroism has been transformed. Swift's nostalgia for the heroes of Republican Rome and rejection of modern heroes helps to account for his uneasiness in dealing with his own heroism. Johnson's heroes are heroes of mind and, as such, typical of the tendencies throughout Europe in the middle of the eighteenth century that, according to Hugh Honour, brought about "a desire to praise famous men, especially writers and philosophers, in imperishable marble or bronze. . . ."[26] The poet-hero, a special case, takes the world into his own mind and projects it publicly after transforming it by means of his imagination. The difference between the Gothic hero-villain and his counterpart in Restoration tragedy appears in such a perspective by the emphasis of the Gothic novel on the claustrophobic space of the castle and the unknowable mind of the protagonist—hence such a title as *The Castle of Otranto,* a novel named for its setting rather than its protagonist. The middle term between the Restoration tragedy and the Gothic novel is precisely Arthur Lindley's subject, Richardson's Lovelace.

In closing, it may be worthwhile to comment on a work only considered in passing in this volume. Domestication helps reveal the nature of Boswell's epic, *The Life of Samuel Johnson,* which, as Boswell puts it, "may in one respect be assimilated to the *Odyssey.* Amidst a thousand entertaining and instructive episodes the *Hero* is never long out of sight.[27] In this biography the dinner table becomes the battlefield where Johnson "talked for victory," and as such is related to the rather different sort of battle that Peter Hughes discusses, which takes place in other voices and other rooms. The English hero during this period may not have a thousand faces, but as these essays bear witness, he is more abundantly varied than previously had been supposed.

NOTES

1. William James, *Varieties of Religious Experience* (New York: Mentor, 1958), p. 281.

2. *The Hero in Literature,* ed. Victor Brombert (Greenwich, Conn.: Fawcett Publications, 1969). Jenni Calder's popular account, *Heroes: From Byron to Guevara* (London: Hamish Hamilton, 1977), takes the "Romantic Movement . . . and its association with revolution and new ideas about individual and collective possibilities" as her starting point (p. ix).

3. Thomas Edwards, *Imagination and Power* (London: Chatto & Windus: 1971), pp. 7–46; Mario Praz, *The Hero in Eclipse* (London: Oxford University Press, 1956); Victor Brombert, "Introduction: The Idea of the Hero" in *The Hero in Literature,* ed. Brombert, p. 20.

4. I am currently at work on a study of the artist as hero, 1660–1820. Some of my preliminary findings were presented in papers at the Modern Language Association (December 1979) and the American Society for Eighteenth Century Studies (April 1980). For relevant observations see my "Macpherson, Chatterton, Blake and the Great Age of Literary Forgery," *Centennial Review* 18 (1974): 378–91, and "The Artist as Hero in the Eighteenth Century," *Yearbook of English Studies* 12 (forthcoming, 1982).

5. That of Robert D. Hume. Edith Kern deals with the problem in relation to the hero of the novel. See "The Modern Hero: Phoenix or Ashes," in *The Hero in Literature,* ed. Brombert, pp. 266–77.

6. Henry Fielding, *The Works of Henry Fielding,* Wesleyan ed., vol 1, *Joseph Andrews,* ed. Martin C. Battestin (Middletown, Conn.: Wesleyan University Press, 1967), p. 241.

7. Trevisa speaks in 1387 of the Sibylla Erythraea who "wroot moche of Criste an that openliche, as in this vers of heroes." The Renaissance quotation that follows comes from Eden's *Decades.*

8. For a good account of Boswell's heroic themes, see William C. Dowling, *The Boswellian Hero* (Athens, Ga.: University of Georgia Press, 1979).

9. Samuel Butler, *"Characters"* and *"Passages from Note-books,"* ed. A. R. Waller, Cambridge English Classics (Cambridge: At the University Press, 1908), p. 468. And see Michael Seidel, *Satiric Inheritance, Rabelais to Sterne* (Princeton, N.J.: Princeton University Press, 1979), ch. 4, for Butler on heroic issues.

10. Butler, *"Characters"* and *"Note-books,"* p. 442.

11. For the metaphor of the dwarf in armor, see J. W. Johnson, below, p. 28.

12. *Gulliver's Travels 1726,* vol. 1 of *The Prose Writings of Jonathan Swift,* ed. Herbert Davis (Oxford: Basil Blackwell, 1959), p. 196.

13. *Miscellaneous and Autobiographical Pieces, Fragments and Marginalia,* vol. 5 of *The Prose Writings of Jonathan Swift,* ed. Herbert Davis (Oxford: Basil Blackwell, 1962), pp. 83–84.

14. Swift, *Gulliver's Travels,* ed. Davis, p. 196.

15. 10 January 1720. *The Correspondence of Jonathan Swift,* ed. Harold Williams (Oxford: Clarendon Press, 1963), 2:373.

16. Swift, *Miscellaneous Pieces,* ed. Davis, p. 84.

17. Ibid.

18. Ibid., pp. 85–86.

19. Samuel Johnson, *Lives of the English Poets,* ed. G. B. Hill (Oxford: Clarendon Press, 1905), 2:100.

20. For David, see especially Robert Rosenblum, *Transformations in Late-Eighteenth-Century Art* (Princeton, N.J.: Princeton University Press, 1974), ch. 2, "The *Exemplum Virtutis.*"

21. Quoted and translated by Hugh Honour, *Neo-classicism* (Harmondworth: Penguin Books, 1973), p. 44. Secularization also played its part. Honour notes later that "the hero takes the place of the saint in the iconography of death," p. 153. In England Gavin Hamilton painted *Brutus* (1763) and Benjamin West, *Epaminondas* (1771). West's painting might be taken as the fulfillment of Samuel Johnson's recommendation that the history painter would find a suitable subject in Mantinea. See *Idler* No. 45, "*The Idler*" and "*The Adventurer*" vol. 2 in *The Yale Edition of the Works of Samuel Johnson,* ed. W. J. Bate, John M. Bullitt, and L. F. Powell (New Haven, Conn.: Yale University Press, 1963), p. 142. For the hero in art during this period, see Edgar Wind, "Humanitätsidee und heroisiertes Porträt in der englischen Kultur des 18. Jahrhunderts," *Vorträge der Bibliothek Warburg* 9 (1931–32): 156–229, and David Irwin, *English Neoclassical Art: Studies in Inspiration and Taste* (Greenwich, Conn.: New York Graphic Society, 1966).

22. Fitzroy Richard Somerset, Lord Raglan, *The Hero: A Study in Tradition, Myth, and Drama* (New York: Vintage Books, 1956), pp. 174–75.

23. For Dryden, see H. T. Swedenberg, Jr., "Dryden's Obsessive Concern for the Heroic," in *Essays in English Literature of the Classical Period,* ed. Daniel W. Patterson and Albrecht B. Strauss (Chapel Hill, N.C.: University of North Carolina Press, 1967), pp. 12–26, and the fine series of articles by Michael West, "Dryden's Ambivalence as a Translator of Heroic Themes," *HLQ* 36 (1973): 347–66; "Dryden and the Disintegration of Renaissance Heroic Ideals," *Costerus* 7 (1973): 193–222; "Shifting Concepts of Heroism in Dryden's Panegyrics," *PLL* 10 (1974): 378–93.

24. See Eugene M. Waith, *The Herculean Hero in Marlowe, Chapman, Shakespeare and Dryden* (New York: Columbia University Press, 1967) and *Ideas of Greatness: Heroic Drama in England* (New York: Barnes & Noble, 1971).

25. For an account of this development see Marc Bloch, *The Royal Touch: Sacred Monarchy and Scrofula in England and France,* trans. J. E. Anderson (London: Routledge & Kegan Paul, 1973), esp. ch. 6, "The Decline and Death of the Royal Touch," pp. 214–23.

26. Honour, *Neo-classicism,* p. 83.

27. James Boswell, *Boswell's Life of Johnson,* ed. George Birkbeck Hill and L. F. Powell, 6 vols. (Oxford: Clarendon Press, 1934–50), 1:12.

The English Hero,
1660–1800

England, 1660–1800: An Age without a Hero?

JAMES WILLIAM JOHNSON

To ask whether the period between 1660 and 1800 in England was an age without a hero appears, at first blush, rhetorically fatuous, intellectually perverse, or perhaps merely ignorant. Everyone knows the period abounded with those models of admiration and emulation commonly termed "heroes"; and anybody who has read a modicum of the literature of the times can reel off their names. One finds heroes listed everywhere—in Denham's *Cooper's Hill*, Temple's *Of Ancient and Modern Learning* and *Of Heroic Virtue*, Evelyn's *History of Religion*, Swift's *Contests and Dissentions* and *Of Mean and Great Figures, Made by Several Persons*, Steele's *The Christian Hero*, Pope's *Windsor Forest*, Thomson's *Winter*, Gibbon's *Essay on the Study of Literature*. There were the heroes of biblical and Greco-Roman antiquity, the noble founders of a glorious England, and an international array of illustrious monarchs, generals, patriots, even scholars. Furthermore, from 1660 to 1800, eulogists proclaimed the heroism of living contemporaries from General Monck to Queen Anne to Dictionary Johnson. An age without heroes indeed! On the contrary, it seems an age with far too many.

This in fact was the problem. Despite the plethora of great men named in its literature, there was by no means a consensus in Stuart-Georgian England as to the attributes of the hero, the constituent elements of heroism, or even as to whether the heroic concept had any validity. Moreover, an obvious attenuation of beliefs can be seen not only in literary but plastic representations of the heroic from 1660 to 1800. Verrio's painting, the *Sea Triumph of Charles II,* differs vastly from Allan Ramsey's portrait of George III in heroic style as well as in ideological assumptions. Verrio depicts a celestial monarch seated at the apex of a pyramid of lesser deities with his head emanating lambent glory. Ramsey shows a calf-faced "Farmer George," weighed down with ermine at the base of an overshadowing Roman column, framed by a dark, lopsided scalene triangle, toward the lowest point of which he seems to incline. A similar predicative gulf separates Vanbrugh's Blenheim Palace, a monument to a great general paid for (partly, anyhow!) by a grateful nation, and the elegant but small Apsley House, designed by Robert Adam and purchased out of his own pocket by the Duke of Wellington. By the time Dr. Johnson described him, his eyes overflowing with the tears of dotage, the great Marlborough had already descended metaphorically from his plinth at Woodstock; and the redoubtable Cato who inspired Addison and caused Pope to weep in admiration merely evoked Horace Walpole's yawn of bored dismissal. Plainly, something drastic was happening to the heroic ideal in an age thronging with nominal "heroes."

A rapid survey of key writers discloses the general nature of the change, though perforce it must slight many conceptual streakings. As Poet Laureate and chief propagandist for the Stuarts, John Dryden serves as spokesman for the theoretical notion of the hero in the first two decades following the Restoration. In the preface to *Annus Mirabilis* (1667), the dedication to *The Conquest of Granada* (1672), "Of Heroic Plays, An Essay" (1672), and his preface to *The State of Innocence* (1677), Dryden tells the reader that courage and perseverance in war and other disasters, a generous emulation for one's own glory, a piously magnanimous mind are the prerequisites for the heroic. When combined in the person of a single great man, these qualities are magnified to divine proportions, and a superhuman conqueror-administrator stands forth—a Caesar or Alexander the Great. Eulogists then blazon his greatness to compliment the hero and incite him to still more heroic actions, the results of which are immortal fame for the great man and national glory for his subjects.

For five years or so after the Restoration, the Stuarts basked in heroic analogies and hyperboles. Not only the academic contributors to *Britannia Rediviva* saw them in scripturally and classically heroic dimensions; such intellectually assorted types as Clarendon, Pepys, Evelyn, and Anthony Wood all subscribed to the mythic grandeur of Stuart heroism. The royal brothers, ominously enough, had to share the attributes of the totally great man, however. Dryden specified the allotment of virtues when he wrote to the duke of York:

> I have always observed in your royal highness an extreme concernment for the honour of your country: it is a passion common to you with a brother, the most excellent of kings; and in your two persons are eminent the characters which Homer has given us of heroic virtue; the commanding part in Agamemnon, and the executive in Achilles.

Thus it took two Stuarts to equal one Alexander. As the "commanding" half, Charles stressed his divinity mostly by touching each month some 1,500 to 3,000 victims of the King's Evil (scrofula), a remedy that infallibly cured those who accepted His Sacred Majesty's kinship to Christ. Other public demonstrations of his celestial qualities Charles left to writers and painters. Led by the Laureate, a tribe of poets endowed their patron with every sublime quality but incorporeality; and Sir Peter Lely suggested the monarch as God-head by painting Lady Castlemaine and her bastard son in the guise of the Virgin Mary and Infant Jesus. Meanwhile, the commander-hero regularly showed his true, human nature by removing himself and his mistresses away from plagues, fires, battles, sessions of Parliament, and other mundane distractions.

Simultaneously, the duke of York demonstrated other disparities between the real and ideal behavior of the "executive" side of Stuart heroism. Proclaimed by his panegyrists to have won over opposing troops by his very name and to have defeated Spain and caused Dunkirk to fall by the expedient of being present, James soon failed to live up to such verbal laurels. In the naval battle off Harwich in May 1665, the duke displayed an unheroic horror— some said cowardice—when he was splashed with the brains and blood of his young favorite, Lord Fitzhardinge. An ensuing series of routs, defeats, and scandals compounded by corruption in the Navy, which he commanded, soon led Parliament and a disabused public to demand an end, in 1667, to the military and political antics of its erstwhile heroes. When Dryden attempted, in the *Annus Mirabilis* (1666), to give heroic dimension to the fiascos of the previous year, the cynical pointed out that only his impudence and stanzas were heroic. In the five years following, the conventions of heroic literature and heroic posturing became objects of mockery for Andrew Marvell *(Last Instruction to a Painter,* 1667), Buckingham and Butler *(The Rehearsal,* 1671), and many others. When the Third Dutch War was imminent and Dryden tried to refit heroic panoply to the diminished stature of James Stuart, declaring that *The Conquest of Granada* was a "faint representation of York's own worth and valor" in the person of Almanzor, his critics gleefully attacked the hero-manqué. Drawcansir huffed, strutted, and puffed because he dared in Buckingham's *The Rehearsal;* and Buggeranthus, the impotent general in Rochester's *Sodom,* faced a limp defeat in the battle of the sexes. The metaphor of the dwarf in giant's armor proved an effective means of satirizing the puny nature of modern "heroes"; Swift used it most hilariously to satirize Dryden in *The Battle of the Books,* and it eventually found a place in the Gothic, when the fragile Conrad, heir of Otranto, was mysteriously crushed by a gargantuan helmet belonging to the truly heroic founder of the royal line.

By 1675, after fifteen years of Stuart duplicities and disparities, not only was the surface of heroic behavior being openly mocked; its underlying political and psychological motivations were also seriously questioned. The acerbic Lord Rochester, who had distinguished himself for bravery in the naval battles of 1665–66 but had kept removed from everything military in 1673–74, devastated the theoretical postulates of heroism cherished by Dryden and other stay-at-home devisers of "heroic" couplets, stanzas, and dramas. Deftly using their own literary techniques, Rochester declared in the mock-heroic couplets of his *Satire Against Reason and Mankind:*

> For hunger or for love [beasts] fight and tear,
> Whilst wretched man is still in arms for fear.
> For fear he arms, and is of arms afraid,
> By fear to fear successively betrayed;
> Base fear, the source whence his best passions came:

His boasted honour, and his dear-bought fame . . .
Merely for safety, after fame we thirst,
For all men would be cowards if they durst.

In the 1680s, with the heroic drama defunct and the traditional depiction of Stuart heroism laughed away as sycophantic puffery, the basic idea of heroism underwent sharp critical scrutiny. The centuries-old concept began a process of ideological mitosis, its component threads separating from each other.

Both John Evelyn and Sir William Temple, long-time observers of the Restoration scene, retained the aristocratic ideal while de-emphasizing the traditional stress on military conquest. Each began by insisting there are two distinct kinds of heroism: military and civic—or, in broader terms, destructive and constructive. Evelyn, in several essays, praised the hero as a builder, one who fabricates some public work of lasting value, such as a building or constitutional process. Temple, in his influential essay, *Of Heroic Virtue* (published in 1690), enthusiastically concurred. While acknowledging the aristocratic basis of heroism, Temple managed to shift Dryden's heroic thesis in such a manner as to undermine the whole concept. Said Temple:

> Though it be easier to describe heroic virtue by the effects and examples than by causes and definitions, yet it may be said to arise from some great and native excellency of temper or genius transcending the common race of mankind in wisdom, goodness, and fortitude. These ingredients advantaged by birth, improved by education, and assisted by fortune, seem to make the noble composition which gives such a lustre to those who have possessed it as made them appear to common eyes something more than mortals, and to have been born of some divine mixture between divine and human race; to have been honoured and obeyed in their lives, and after their deaths bewailed and adored.

Temple's subtle qualification that the hero *seems*, not is, divine to common eyes drastically alters Dryden's absolute suppositions; so do his statements that "heroic virtue" has been forgotten or unknown in latter ages, and that "the character of heroic virtue seems to be, in short, the deserving well of mankind." Using his own yardstick of the public good, not personal glory, Temple goes on in his essay to criticize the supposed heroes who had supplied the stuff for so many dramas of the 1660s and 70s. Alexander the Great was proud, lustful, intemperate, and wrathful. Julius Caesar had all the qualities of heroism but honor; he overthrew his country's laws and made enemies of his fellow citizens. Atahualpa, Aureng-Zebe, Almanzor, Ibrahim—all were lacking in humanity or justice or honor. Indeed, according to Temple, the greatest heroes were the law-givers, Confucius and Mohammed, not the military conquerors. The exception was Tamerlain, whose character Temple altered so radically through his suppositions as to make him a model of the theoretical fusion of conqueror and legislator. It was this version of the Mongol tyrant that Nicholas Rowe saw fit to dramatize some years later and that eventually drew a wry smile from Edward Gibbon.

But the chief example of Sir William Temple's nondivine, domesticated heroism was William of Orange, the father of the new British king. It was, presumably, to William III that Temple's final evaluation of heroism was directed:

> After all that has been said of conquerors or conquests, this must be confessed to hold but the second rank in the pretensions to heroic virtue, and that the first has been allowed to the wise institution of just orders and laws, which frame safe and happy governments in the world. The designs and effects of conquests are but the slaughter and ruin of mankind, the ravaging of countries, and defacing the world: those of wise and just governments are preserving and increasing the lives and generations of men, securing their possessions, encouraging their endeavors, and by peace and riches improving and adorning the several scenes of the world.

As a longtime soldier, King William could not entirely disclaim all the attractions of military pursuits nor could he disregard the threat to government posed by rebels and insurgents. His campaigns against France and Ireland were lauded, and he chose, like James II, to be painted while wearing his armor. He was the last of the monarchs to do so. The imbecilities of Charles's bastard son, the duke of Monmouth, served as a warning in excess to William. Monmouth had sought to demonstrate that the healing power for the King's Evil descended even through the bar sinister; and his courtship of popular sentiment by stripping off his clothes and running footraces reached its apotheosis when he "invaded" England in June 1685 with eighty-two comrades; he was beaten in battle by Jack Churchill for his pains and subsequently beheaded for treason. King William also rightly reckoned the divine power to heal had outreached credibility; he prudently refused to "touch" so long as he ruled.

The joint reign of William and Mary produced another important alteration in the concept of heroism. Queen Mary was praised for her "virtue," as her husband was for his courage. This virtue came increasingly to be associated with the more humble Christian qualities, such as piety, modesty, charity—in brief, with the "feminine" aspects of Christianity. When Queen Anne replaced her sister and brother-in-law on the throne, it was for eminent piety that she was praised; indeed, it would have been difficult to find much else to praise Anne for. Moreover, during Anne's rulership, the military duties of heroism were delegated to Churchill, who had no royal blood and was thus fair game for Jonathan Swift, whose *Examiner* papers did much to depreciate the martial values of heroism, reducing the ruling passion for glory in battle to ambition, pride, and avarice. Thenceforth, military leadership, aristocratic superiority, and heroism were disjoined increasingly. The Hanovers did little to effect their reunion. George I was too torpid; the only arms that encumbered George II were those of his German mistresses, as Pope archly implied in his *Epistle to Augustus;* and with the confrontation of "Butcher" Cumberland and the idiotic Bonnie Prince Charlie in 1745, both Hanover and Stuart behavior confirmed the impossibility of viewing aristocratic militarism as heroic any longer.

When it became apparent, early in the eighteenth century, that contemporary military leaders had feet—and often brains—of clay, the concept of heroism as physical courage in battle bifurcated. The ideal was transferred to the ancient past; and the Catoes, Epaminondases, and Themistocleses were exhumed from the pages of history to tread the boards of the London stage or to swell the bulk of political pamphlets. As ideals, they came more and more to conform to the judicial and civic aspects of heroism; they also represented the unattainable and thus abstract. As Samuel Johnson remarked, Cato was above all human concern, and it was only a matter of time before the educated populace began to agree with Temple on the one hand and Johnson on the other in finding long-dead heroes either hopelessly remote or impossibly superior. Public school education insured their immortality, however, so that the glorious ancients were jauntily used to puff the self-esteem of British regiments.

> Some talk of Alexander, and some of Hercules;
> Of Hector and Lysander, and such great names as these;
> But of all the world's brave heroes, there's none that can compare
> With a tow, row, row, row, row, row, for the British Grenadier.

While the Grenadiers were boasting their kinship to ancient conquerors, a young Ensign in the Cold-Stream Guards was penning a rhetorical question: "Why is it that the Heathen struts, and the Christian sneaks in our Imagination?" Richard Steele went on to write in the *The Christian Hero:*

> If it be as *Machiavil* says, that Religion throws our Minds below noble and hazardous Pursuits, then its Followers are Slaves and Cowards; but if it gives a more hardy and aspiring Genius than the World before knew, then He, and All our fine Observers, who have been pleas'd to give us only Heathen Portraitures, to say no worse, have robb'd their Pens of Characters the most truly Gallant and Heroick that ever appear'd to Mankind.

The most heroic characters, Steele demonstrated, were Jesus and Paul—not Cato or Caesar or Brutus, all moved by vile Ambition or Pride, the evidence of "our deprav'd Natures." Only through suffering misery with magnanimity, enduring poverty with courage, can one attain "that Sublime and Heroick Virtue, Meekness, a Virtue which seems the very Characteristick of a Christian, and arises from a great, not a groveling Idea of things. . . ." While not without contradictions, Steele's Christian hero, who could assault without passion and stab without hatred, became a popular model of heroism later in the century. He took his most endearing shape in Tristram Shandy's Uncle Toby, who was modest as a maiden, innocent as a child, and too tenderhearted to kill a fly, but was nevertheless a professional soldier.

Not only his gentle nature but his battlewound made Uncle Toby a veritable embodiment of the new kind of heroism, the "hero" having been demasculinized some time earlier. Addison and Steele had long since asserted that one did not have to be a high-born male to be a hero. In *The Spectator,* No. 240 (December 5, 1711), Steele raised the matter of "Heroick Virtue in common Life"; in No. 248 (December 14), he expounded upon the ways that, "actuated by a secret celestial Influence, . . . worthy Minds in the Domestick Way of Life" could perform these heroic acts:

> . . . to give Comfort to an Heart loaded with Affliction, to save a falling Family, to preserve a Branch of Trade in their Neighbourhood, and give Work to the Industrious, preserve the Portion of the helpless Infant, and raise the Head of the mourning Father.

Thus Steele made it possible for many men, many women, and many children to be heroes; and the life of anyone could provide examples of genuine heroism. Thenceforth, the hero of literature might be such a one as Dean Swift, Thomas Gray, or even Colley Cibber, Letitia Pilkington, and Richard Savage. In drama, the common man might provide a greater lesson in humanity and moral improvement than a dozen Catoes; George Barnwell, clerk to a London merchant, being a case in point. Implicit support to the equality of the great man and the lowly one was even provided negatively by Gray's *Lines Wrote in a Country Churchyard* and Johnson's *The Vanity of Human Wishes,* which saw the grave as the common denominator of mankind.

In the emergent fictive genres after 1740, one sees not only the antithesis to the premises of Restoration heroic drama but endless combinations of traits formerly sought in great men only. Defoe's low-born heroes and heroines had struggled through misery with courage. Richardson's anguished heroines proved the transcendent worth of Christian virtue and piety. Fielding's *Jonathan Wild* demolished the Great Man, making Newgate thief, prime minister, and Alexander the Great all such and declaring them all fit for hanging. Parson Adams, Joseph Andrews, and Tom Jones were versions of the Christian hero, Fielding's ready replacement for

great men with good men. Sterne, Smollett, Burney, and Austen
followed suit.

To be sure, with all the other variants, the superman hero
survived in popular English thought of the eighteenth century,
waiting to be resurrected by the Satanists and Imperialists of the
nineteenth century. He was, nonetheless, only one of many heroic
types. Unlike the nut-cracking Elizabethan, who admired the
Scourge of God, or the proper Victorian, who adored both God
and Mammon, the Englishman of the eighteenth century finally
refused to fix on one or even few heroic models. If the century
produced its own special hero, John Bull the Common Man, his
countrymen and women refused to worship that graven image
above the rest. They knew from experience that all that glistered
was not necessarily golden heroism. Thus they avoided crowning a
single hero, leaving it to Thomas Carlyle to categorize and us to
settle the proportion of ubiquity among the heroic contenders of
the age.

Absalom and Achitophel and the Father Hero

LARRY CARVER

> But, knowing that piety alone comprehends the whole duty of man toward the gods, towards his country, and towards his relations, he judg'd that this ought to be his first character, whom he would set for a pattern of perfection.
>
> > Dryden quoting Segrais in
> > *Dedication of the Aeneis*

> . . . here it will be necessary to consider several sorts of Parents, according to which the duty to them is to be measured. Those are these three, the Civil, the Spiritual, the Natural.
>
> The Civil Parent is he whom God hath established the Supreme Magistrate, who by a just right possess the Throne of a nation. This is the common father of all those that are under his authority
>
> > *The Whole Duty of Man* (1658)

IT is no coincidence that *Absalom and Achitophel* was published on or shortly before November 17, 1681 because November 17, the anniversary of Queen Elizabeth's accession day, was also the date of the great pope-burning ceremonies of 1679, 1680, and 1681. A contemporary broadside describes the ceremony held on November 17, 1679. A procession with an effigy of the pope stopped at Temple Bar, and there a mock-papal spokesman appealed to the English people.

> From York to London Town we come
> To talk of Popish Ire

35

> To reconcile you all to Rome,
> And prevent Smithfield Fire.

And the people of England replied:

> Cease, Cease, thou Norfolk Cardinal
> See yonder stands Queen Bess,
> Who sav'd your Souls from Popish thrall,
> O Queen Bess, Queen Bess, Qu. Bess.[1]

Symbolically, the good queen looked on approvingly as the pope burned. A huge statue of Elizabeth stood at Temple Bar, and on this occasion she had been dressed up appropriately

> . . . like an Heathen Idol. A bright shield was hung upon her Arm, and a Speer put in . . . and Lamps or Candles were put about . . . to enlighten her Person, that the People might have a full view of the Diety that, like the Goddess *Pallas,* stood there as the object of the Solemn Sacrifice about to be made.

Elizabeth, transformed into a goddess, became both the inspiration for and the defender of this band of brothers in their overthrow of the pope, the terrible father. Ostensibly, the pope was the sole object of the people's ire. But those of the Court Party, like Dryden, knew better; the ceremonies represented an attack upon another father figure also, the king. As Dryden sardonically observed in his "Prologue to *The Loyal Brother*" (1682): "Kings . . . Are safe—as long as e'er their subjects please / And that would be till next Queen Bess's night."[2] Elizabeth held a high place in the imaginations of those opposed to Stuart rule, and these opponents called upon the matriarch of what by then they conceived to have been a golden age to protect them from tyrannical father kings.[3]

Dryden saw in the pope-burning ceremonies, then, an attack on a social order he held dear. For Dryden, as for men like Bishop Sanderson, Filmer, Temple, and later the third earl of Shaftesbury and Bolingbroke, society is not an intellectual construct of man's own making as Hobbes and Locke would have it. Rather, society is a hierarchical arrangement in which each man is related to others by mutual obligations, duties, and trust. Authority comes from above; it arises not from the consent of the people, but earns the people's consent by being prudently administered. Society may not actually be a family, as man's original social organizations were, but at its best the relationship between ruler and subjects is like that of a father to his children.[4] For Dryden, the patriarchal hierarchy of the family provided an analogy for proper order in politics, religion, and art. He had mocked and in turn held up as a standard familial ties and true succession by ridiculing that poet, priest, and king, Mac Flecknoe. The pope-burning ceremony of 1681 provided Dryden the occasion not only to uphold but to praise the patriarchal ordering of society. Charles-David becomes the father who represents proper order familial, political, and divine and who, as a musician, represents the harmony that should prevail in all three realms.

From the analogy of family and state that informs *Absalom and Achitophel* springs the poem's major thematic concern: whether, in the words of the seventeenth-century pamphleteer Edward Gee, the "rise and right of government" is "natural and native" or "voluntary and conventional."[5] Achitophel, with his derisive contempt for "successive title, long and dark / Drawn from the moldy rolls of Noah's ark," (ll. 301–2) favors contractual government or at least is against government natural and native. As he argues:

> . . . the people have a right supreme
> To make their kings; for kings are made for them.
> All empire is no more than pow'r in trust,
> Which, when resum'd can be no longer just.
>
> (Ll. 409–12)

Achitophel's case for government by consent is countered by the argument that the king holds his power not by election or consent, but by right of successive title passed down through the father. The chief support for this argument is based on Biblical genealogy, those moldy rolls of Noah's ark. As the narrator points out:

> If those who gave the scepter could not tie
> By their own deed their own posterity,
> How then could Adam bind his future race?

How could his forfeit on mankind take place?
Or how could heavenly justice damn us all,
Who ne'er consented to our father's fall?

(Ll. 769–74)

As with sin, so with power; both descend through the father. And *Absalom and Achitophel* concerns the king as father faced with rebellious children attempting to sweep away age-old paternal rights.

As *pater familias*, David faces the potential usurpation of his son Absalom. Absalom's rebellion is in turn motivated by a desire to appear first in his father's eyes. "Scanted by a niggard birth" (l. 369), he longs to replace his rival who is "secure of native right" (l. 354). Absalom is in a difficult situation, one for which the narrator has a good deal of sympathy. He is David's son and he is not, son by nature but not by law and custom. Nevertheless, it is clear he owes a son's obedience to David, and in heeding the advice of a surrogate father, Achitophel, "His old instructor" (l. 971), he violates familial and political bonds.

Achitophel's rebellion is also seen in familial terms. His actions give credence to Norman O. Brown's gnomic statement that "without an understanding of the seamy side of sexuality there is no understanding politics."[6] There is simply nothing natural or native about Achitophel. In a poem whose focus constantly shifts between individual families and that of the state and which suggests that the two are inextricably bound together, Achitophel's politics become a manifestation of his own unnaturalness. As those often-quoted lines point out, he possesses a pigmy body and has engendered

. . . that unfeather'd two-legg'd thing, a son;
Got, while his soul did huddled notions try;
And born a shapeless lump, like anarchy.

(Ll. 170–72)

Like the devil, whose representative he becomes, Achitophel "pimps for ill desires" (l. 81). Furthermore, it is Achitophel who compares politics and "women's lechery" (l. 472) and who suggests that Absalom "commit a pleasing rape upon the crown"

(l. 474). And it is Achitophel who desires to make the potent king impotent by stripping him so that "he shall be naked left to public scorn" (l. 400). Achitophel's dislike of natural and native succession is as natural as his body, offspring, and actions are unnatural.

As *pater patriae,* David faces the rebellion of his subjects or his sons. The rebels are "Adam-wits" who "too fortunately free / Began to dream they wanted liberty" (ll. 51–52). In calling the rebels "Adam-wits," the narrator reminds the reader that in Adam's disobedience, the first son's rebellion against his father in quest of liberty, is found the archetype of all subsequent rebellion. The rebels are also "rasher charioteers" who "like th'unequal ruler of the day / Misguide the seasons, and mistake the way" (ll. 909–11). Like Phaeton, they desire to usurp their father's place.

The role of David as God the Father is so interwoven with his role as *pater patriae* that to speak of one is necessarily to speak of the other. As we have seen, the main argument for David as father king is based on patriarchalism supported by Biblical genealogy. John Figgis has pointed out that "the patriarchal conception of society is far from being of the essence of the theory of the Divine Right of Kings; it is merely the best argument by which it is supported."[7] God granted dominion to Adam who was both father and king. All of Adam's successors, so the argument runs, held their positions by right of this original donation. God is both king and father and so too are His earthly representatives. At the end of the poem, "godlike David" speaks and the people "their Maker in their master hear" (ll. 937–38). Patriarchalism and divine right combine nicely when David refers to his "forgiving right" (l. 944).

That Dryden meant the reader to perceive David as representative of God the Father there can be little doubt, but it is disconcerting when reading the poem's opening lines to think of this king as God's agent. It would seem that the appropriate gloss on these lines is not any concept of divine right but rather the quip in "A History of Insipids": "To say such kings, Lord, rule by thee / Were most prodigious blasphemy." Yet Dryden's fable, as numerous critics have pointed out, allows him to write of the king who, as Lord Rochester put it, "Never said a foolish thing / Nor ever did a wise one." After all, the story takes place "In pious times, ere priestcraft did begin / Before polygamy was made a sin" (ll. 1–2).

Dryden, of course, is having much good fun playing with patriar-chal ideas. David is seen as being literally the father of his subjects. Once when designated the father of his people, Charles himself reportedly said, "Well, I believe that I am, of a good number of them."[8] And one anonymous poet in attacking the idea of a father king accused Charles of being "the truest *Pater Patriae* e're yet / For all, or most of's subjects, does beget."[9] But Dryden, literal and playful, is also deadly serious. David scatters "his Maker's image thro' the land" (l. 10). David is literally the father of all his subjects, for in him the society has its life and well-being. He is the "tiller," the good, royal husbandman who cares for his crops or his offspring even in those days when "the dog-star heats their brains. . . ." (l. 334).

But Dryden relied on more than humor and the distancing force of his fable in order to circumvent the problem of writing of the real king while holding the ideal king in mind. He made use of the concept of the king's two bodies.[10] In writing first of the king's natural body Dryden did not just flash his wit for the knowing. He also struck a blow at the king's enemies, those survivors of the Good Old Cause who had killed the father and now threatened the son. Under the pretense of defending kingship, the enemies of Charles I used the theory of the king's two bodies to attack the king. They objected, or so they said, not to his political but to his natural body. Or as they put it: "We fight the King to defend the King."[11] For Dryden, '81 was '41 all over again. Thus Achitophel advises Absalom to "try your title while your father lives / And that your arms may have a fair pretense / Proclaim you take them in the king's defense" (ll. 462–64). And some of David's enemies are more openly vicious; they "a double danger bring / Not only hating David, but the king" (ll. 511–12). Dryden employs precisely the same theory, only he does so in the king's defense. In thrusting the king's natural body before the king's enemies he reminds them of something they willingly forgot. For one of the main tenets of this theory was that "the king's acts are valid regardless of the personal worthiness of the body natural. . . ."[12] As part of the Restoration settlement, anyone of any position in society had declared "that it is not lawful upon any pretense whatsoever to take arms against the king, and that I do abhor that traitorous position of taking arms by his authority against his person. . . ."[13]

Dryden, like the artful debater he was, put the worst case that could be brought against the king first. And he defeats that case by employing in the king's defense the very arguments used against both Charles II and his father. The point would not have been lost upon commonwealth men of whatever ilk.

The point would have become all the more telling as the poem unfolds and the king's natural body is seen as attached to his political, divinely sanctioned body. According to Ernst Kantorowicz, the theory of the king's two bodies, instrumental among Tudor jurists, had its origins in medieval christological doctrine, the king's two bodies corresponding to the two natures of Christ, the God-man. Dryden, like the Tudor jurists before him, also developed a royal christology. David is the father king and also the Father, both as God the Father and as Christ.

This becomes abundantly clear in the poem when we notice the terms in which both Achitophel and the narrator couch their descriptions of Absalom. Achitophel flatters Absalom by telling him that he is the "Auspicious prince, at whose nativity / Some royal planet rul'd the southern sky" (ll. 230–31). He is the "second Moses" (l. 244), or typologically Christ. Achitophel, becoming more bold, calls him "Saviour" (l. 240). And as Absalom makes his progress through the west, the narrator describes how the people look upon him as their "young Messiah" (l. 728). Yet it is plain that Absalom is the false son theologically as well as naturally. Achitophel tells Absalom at one point that David

> . . . is not now, as when on Jordan's sand
> The joyful people throng'd to see him land,
> Cov'ring the beach, and black'ning all the strand;
> But, like the Prince of Angels, from his height
> Comes tumbling downward with diminish'd light.
> (Ll. 270–74)

It is not David, however, who fails. He is not Satan in rebellion against God the Father. Absalom is the false, would-be Christ. It was upon Charles II's birth, so Stuart legend has it, that a bright star rivaled the noon sun. Ironically, Achitophel himself acknowledged the Christ-like nature of David when he argued, "Better one suffer than a nation grieve" (l. 416). And it is David who is left standing at the end of the poem, the source of order, the promise of "a series of new time" (l. 1028). David is the true Son as Absalom is the false.[14]

This conception of David as Father and Son helps us to understand that otherwise bewildering passage (ll. 757–810) where Dryden appears to nod only to wake up just in time to make a fine muddle. Dryden seems to want his king, as an heir of Adam, to hold his position by divine right but also by consent of the people, government natural and native, but also voluntary and conventional. And so he does, but in a special way. The king is under the law, his rule and power subject to changes in law and custom. How else, Dryden asks, can a people protect against tyranny? This is the king as Christ the Son, under the law. But the king is also the source and foundation of human law, yet above it. This is the king as God the Father, Dryden's ark of government. In this role the king secures "private right" (l. 789) and tempers the people's judgment. As Father and Son, the king embodies both divine and human law, and the people can innovate in the sphere of human law but dare not tamper with the divine.

Perhaps the finest gloss on the role of the divine king in Dryden's poem is not words but a picture. The frontispiece to Dryden's translation of *The History of the League* (1684) depicts Charles upon his throne. A hand from heaven holds a crown from which radiates a beam of light that falls on Charles's head. On the beam are the words *Per Me Reges Regnant*. At Charles's feet rest his temporal realm, the land, the fleet in harbor, justice on his right side, and the lords of the kingdom at whose feet is a scroll with the words *Sibi, et Successoribus suis Legitimis*. This picture, like so many of its medieval predecessors upon which it is no doubt modeled, is an emblem of Christ-centered kingship. The king is both Father and Son. That is, he is above the law (Father), being touched by heaven, and subject to the law (Son), the lower half of his body resting in the temporal sphere. This is an excellent representation of the multiple roles of the father king in *Absalom and Achitophel*.

Like "the sober part of Israel," Dryden "well-knew the value of a peaceful reign" (ll. 69–70). And his numerous poems on the Stuarts testify to his long and abiding concern over the proper role and function of kingship. These poems in their representation of the king reflect not so much the often sordid world of Restoration politics as much as an ideal king ruling in golden times. And for Dryden the golden age was not embodied in the slogan associated with the Levellers: "When Adam delved and Eve span / Who was then a gentleman?" In Dryden's vision of a "series of new time" society is hierarchical, authority is paternal. The father, like Saturn who also had to deal with a rebellious son, comes to set the times right. Dryden, expressing that childhood longing that informs the aristocratic version of the golden age, depicts a father-centered world where the just win out, where caprice and chance are banished, and where the unfortunate event is always rectified.

If in representing the ideal king, Dryden's imagination often resorted, following the dictates of the times, to the idea of a father king, it did so too in imitation of the poet and of the poem Dryden admired most, Virgil and the *Aeneid.* In his *Dedication of the Aeneis* Dryden writes of Virgil:

> Oblig'd he was to his master for his bounty; and he repays him with good counsel, how to behave himself in his new monarchy, so as to gain the affections of his subjects, and deserve to be call'd the father of his country. (P. 495)[15]

As Virgil advised the father of his country, Dryden advised his. Moreover, Virgil, Dryden says, chose "for the groundwork of his poem, one empire destroy'd and another rais'd from the ruins of it" (p. 495). He did so in part so that the situation of Aeneas could parallel that of Augustus. Aeneas could not claim to rule from lineal succession. But with one empire destroyed, the "Trojans chose him to lead them forth, and settle them in a foreign country" (p. 495). Aeneas, therefore, ruled by trust. And Virgil, or so Dryden's argument runs, wanted to represent Augustus as ruling by the trust of his people, not by inheritance from Julius Caesar: "Such a title being but one degree remov'd from conquest, for what was introduc'd by force, by force may be remov'd" (p. 495). Virgil, Dryden believed, "concluded it to be in the interest of his country to be so govern'd; to infuse an awful respect into the people towards such a prince; by that respect to confirm their obedience to him and by that obedience to make them happy"

(p. 494). Dryden chose just such a groundwork for several of his poems in which the father king plays a vital role. Thus, "Astrea Redux," "To His Sacred Majesty," *Annus Mirabilis,* and *Absalom and Achitophel* all begin with a world destroyed or threatened and end with a messianic vision of an ordered world living on into blessed times. Dryden chose such a groundwork not to stress, as did Virgil, disruption, but to stress in the figure of the father king the need and desirability for continuity and stability.

"An honest man," Dryden wrote, "ought to be contented with that form of government, and with those fundamental constitutions of it, which he receiv'd from his ancestors, and under which he himself was born" (p. 493). Born under an hereditary monarchy, Dryden saw that the happiness and well-being of his fellow subjects lay in that

> Succession of a long descent
> Which chastely in the channels ran,
> And from our demigods began
> Equal almost to time in its extent.
> (Ll. 308–11, "Threnodia Augustalis")

He saw that the blessings of a peaceful reign were to be found in the rule of a father king drawing his native right from those moldy rolls of Noah's ark. Dryden's hero was the father king with his ancient origins and his semi-divine powers. And for Dryden, as for the churchmen, the whole duty of man in matters familial, political, and religious was piety.

NOTES

1. Quoted in Sheila Williams, "The Pope Burning Processions of 1679, 1680, 1681," *JWCI* 21 (1958): 116. Much of my information about the pope-burning ceremonies of these years I owe to Williams's article, including Roger North's description of the statue of Queen Elizabeth. The interpretation of this information is, of course, my own.

2. *The Poetical Works of Dryden,* ed. George R. Noyes (Cambridge, Mass.: Riverside Press, 1950), ll. 16–18. All references to Dryden's poetry are to this edition and will be cited by line number in the text.

3. For example, in "The Royal Protestant's Litany," *Bagford Ballads,* ed. J. W. Ebsworth (Hertford, 1878), 2: 660, an anonymous poet wrote:

> From such as presume to speak ill of Queen *Bess,*
> From a Popish Midwife in Sanctifyed Dress,
> Adorn'd with a wooden Ruff or a Crest,
> *Libera nos Domine.*

Roy C. Strong, "The Popular Celebration of the Accession Day of Queen Elizabeth I," *JWCI 21 (1958): 86*–103, has an excellent discussion of the origins of the celebrations of Elizabeth's accession day. He does not, however, carry his discussion beyond the Elizabethan period except to note that November 17 became a day to express opposition to the Stuarts.

4. In "The Development of the Hero in Dryden's Tragedies," *JEGP* 52 (1953): 161–73, John Winterbottom suggested, the first to do so, that Dryden's thought has much more in common with Filmer than with Hobbes. His suggestion about the influence of patriarchal thought on Dryden has been picked up and expanded upon. See Alan Roper, *Dryden's Poetic Kingdoms* (London: Routledge and Kegan Paul, 1965), pp. 52–111, 146–47, and 200–203; Bruce King, *Dryden's Major Plays* (London: Oliver and Boyd, 1966), particularly his section on *The Spanish Fryar;* Bruce King, "Dryden's Ark: The Influence of Filmer," *SEL* 7 (1968): 403–14; and Anne T. Barbeau, *The Intellectual Design of John Dryden's Heroic Plays* (New Haven, Conn.: Yale University Press, 1970), particularly pp. 40–54.

5. Quoted in Peter Laslett's introduction to Robert Filmer, *Patriarcha and Other Political Works of Sir Robert Filmer* (Oxford: Basil Blackwell, 1949), p. 38.

6. *Love's Body* (New York: Random House, 1966), p. 11.

7. John Figgis, *The Divine Right of Kings* (New York: Harper and Row, 1965), p. 150.

8. Quoted in *Roxburghe Ballads,* ed. J. W. Ebsworth (Hertford, 1884), 4: 597.

9. *Roxburghe Ballads,* ed. Ebsworth, 5: 130.

10. So far as I know, Earl Miner, *Dryden's Poetry* (Bloomington, Ind.: Indiana University Press, 1967), has been the only one to take notice of this. In commenting upon the problems Dryden faced in structuring the opening of *Absalom and Achitophel,* Miner writes: "Dryden had to take cognizance of the personal character of Charles II before he could compare him in his political and religious character to David. Or, to use the centuries-old distinction lasting into Dryden's day, he needed to account as well for the king's body natural as for his body politic" (p. 115). Miner's reference to the political theory of the king's two bodies is astute, though he does not go on to develop this idea and to show how the theory underlies the structure and method of the entire poem, as well as how it furthers Dryden's satiric intention in the poem's opening lines.

11. Quoted in Ernst H. Kantorowicz, *The King's Two Bodies* (Princeton, N.J.: Princeton University Press, 1957), p. 18.

12. Ibid., p. 18.

13. *The Uniformity Act 1662,* in *The Stuart Constitution 1603–1688 Documents and Commentary,* ed. J. P. Kenyon (Cambridge: At the University Press, 1966), p. 381.

14. For a discussion based specifically on the typological meaning of characters and episodes in *Absalom and Achitophel,* see Steven N. Zwicker, *Dryden's Political Poetry: The Typology of King and Nation* (Providence, R.I.: Brown University Press, 1972), pp. 83–101.

15. This *Dedication* is included in Noyes, *Poetical Works of Dryden,* pp. 487–521. Page numbers in the text refer to this edition.

Dryden's Alexander

W. B. CARNOCHAN

IT is not likely, perhaps, that Dryden was under the influence of "Dr. Bate's Pacific Pill" or "Venice Treacle" or any other of the opium preparations that were available when he wrote "Alexander's Feast" (1697).[1] Yet the poem has even more in common with "Kubla Khan" than its Eastern setting, its Miltonic overtones, its "symphony and song,"[2] and its ancestral solicitations to violence and war. The familiar story of its composition is recounted by Scott:

> "Mr St John, afterwards Lord Bolingbroke, happening to pay a morning visit to Dryden, whom he always respected, found him in an unusual agitation of the spirits, even to a trembling. On enquiring the cause, 'I have been up all night,' replied the old bard: 'my musical friends made me promise to write them an Ode for this feast of St Cecilia: I have been so struck with the subject which occurred to me, that I could not leave it till I had *completed* it; here it is, *finished* at one sitting.'"[3]

Whatever the facts—and this account, like Coleridge's of his dream, is open to doubt[4]—the sense of Dryden's ode as something struck off in the heat of inspiration (the way odes should be) coincides so well with its rapidity and grandeur as to be one of those truths that at least ought to be true. At the same time this sense of the poem puts critics off, where perhaps they need not be put off.[5] What can be done, so the spoken or unspoken question has been, with an artifact so dazzling and so intuitively arrived at?

Best known about "Alexander's Feast" are its musical intentions (even though the original setting is lost) and its climactic celebration of the untuning of the sky.[6] It would be misguided to try to change that emphasis radically: the ode is for Saint Cecilia. Still, as the title has it, it is Alexander's Feast. One senses the materials of a power struggle. Whose feast is it really? That kind of question touches the aural splendors of "Alexander's Feast" with uncertainty. Looked at more closely, the ode yields another version, among the many that the age provided, of a problematic heroism, well attuned to the problematic character of its hero. According to the tradition Alexander was a heroic bundle of contradictions.[7]

I am not proposing anything radically new. Readers who have not been swept away and have paused to see what actually happens in the poem have agreed, at least lately, that the tone is mixed. Paul Ramsey asks whether "Alexander's Feast" is a mock-opera or a mock-symphony, a question I do not altogether understand but one that raises the issue of verbal as against musical content and assumes that the ode is mocking something.[8] Earl Miner sees "laughing, good-natured, and altogether effective irony."[9] John Heath-Stubbs sees irony in "Alexander's Feast" as well as in the heroic plays.[10] This approach to a new consensus is fairly impressive. In this essay I mean to develop and sometimes qualify. Is the irony, for example, really so good-natured as all that?

Furthermore, the specialized reading of the ode as a satire on William III, a reading that has gained some ground recently, cannot help enforcing the view of Alexander as doubtfully heroic.[11] Support for this reading comes with Earl Miner's conversion from tentative assent to out-and-out acceptance.[12] William III, on Miner's evidence, was endlessly celebrated as the Alexander of his age, and one can readily imagine Dryden wanting to answer the likes of Nahum Tate, who had proclaimed that "the *Boyne,* till now obscure, shall hereafter be Celebrated equally with the *Granicus,* and the Memory of *Europe*'s Deliverer Eclipse what was done by the Son of *Jupiter Ammon.*"[13] Even as dedicatory prophecies go, by poets laureate and otherwise, this is breathtaking. On the other hand, the evidence of direct satire in "Alexander's Feast" is inferential. So it seems more circumspect to begin with what is plain to see: that Dryden's Alexander is from one angle of vision something of a "puppet"; from another, "almost a child."[14] If the shoe fit William III, no doubt there were those ready and waiting to slip it on the royal foot.

Of course even puppets, as well as children, are objects of fondness and affection.[15] And real heroes are not always easy to live with. An essay of Saint-Evremond's, translated as a *Judgment on Alexander and Caesar* (1672), comes close to something essential in the mood of Dryden's times. While on the one hand " 'Tis a consent almost universal, that *Alexander* and *Caesar* have been the greatest men of the world," on the other hand greatness risks self-defeat. "It is a troublesome condition, to depend on men so great, that they may lawfully despise us. However, since there is no reigning in desarts and solitudes, and that there is a necessity of their conversing with us; it should methinks be their interest, to accommodate themselves to our weakness; and we should reverence them like gods, if they would be content to live with us like men."[16] If you want to be a god, so the postheroic (as well as the Christian) paradox goes, you had best come down to earth and accommodate yourself to mortal weakness. If Dryden's Alexander is in fact childlike, so much in some ways the better. Of such ambiguities the poem is made.

As the curtain goes up, Alexander looks like the real thing:

> Aloft in awful State
> The God-like Heroe sate
> On his Imperial Throne.[17]

(Ll. 3–5)

If anything seems ambiguous, it is that the emperor may have a Satanic touch about him ("High on a Throne of Royal State . . . Satan exalted sat" [*Paradise Lost*, 2.1–5]). Yet even in this lofty beginning Dryden's readers might have sensed more comic possibilities. In 1665 Samuel Clarke (1599–1683; not to be confused with his more famous namesake) had published a moralizing *Life & Death of Alexander the Great* and in it retold this story of Alexander's ascent to Darius's great throne; "Here [at Persepolis] it was that *Alexander,* setting himself down upon *Darius* his Throne, it was so high that his feet could not reach the ground, whereupon one of his attendants brought him a little Table, and set it under his feet." At that, another of the Persian attendants wept, explaining that Darius had valued the table highly and now, alas, it had been turned into a footstool.[18] Here, potentially, is material of comedy. What is more, as readers have usually noticed, Thais in real life was no blooming Eastern bride nor even much like one. She was a courtesan or, as Clarke more severely put it, an "infamous Strumpet."[19] The similitude of Alexander as "God-Like Heroe" tarnishes by association. The focus becomes clearer in the second stanza as Alexander is upstaged by Timotheus. Unlike Alexander, Timotheus has a place to stand—not just "aloft," but squarely "plac'd on high / Amid the tuneful Quire" (l. 21). And his superior position marks his precedence. It is as if he were the father and Alexander the offspring of his song: "The Song began from *Jove*; / Who left his blissful Seats above . . . " (ll. 25–26). Timotheus touches the scene into life:

> The list'ning Crowd admire the lofty Sound,
> A present Deity, they shout around:
> A present Deity the vaulted Roofs rebound.
>
> (Ll. 34–36)

And Alexander rather sleepily stirs into motion:

> With ravish'd Ears
> The Monarch hears,
> Assumes the God,
> Affects to nod,
> And seems to shake the Spheres.
>
> (Ll. 37–41)

"The comic effect of the last three lines," as John Heath-Stubbs says, "should be unmistakeable."[20] The effect becomes more comic, though also more sinister, in light of a marginal heading in Clarke's moralistic biography of Alexander: "He affects a Deity."[21]

Quickly Timotheus reveals himself as the demiurge of the passions. The "sweet Musician" singing Bacchus's praises in stanza 3 becomes in stanza 4 the "Master." The master of the king's music becomes master of the king. Pride and pity and love captivate Alexander in rapid succession. Again it is all rather funny, but in the long run the laughter includes some solicitude. The king has had an emotional workout:

> The Prince, unable to conceal his Pain,
>   Gaz'd on the Fair
>   Who caus'd his Care,
> And sigh'd and look'd, sigh'd and look'd,
> Sigh'd and look'd, and sigh'd again:
> At length, with Love and Wine at once oppress'd,
> The vanquish'd Victor sunk upon her Breast.
>
> (Ll. 109–15)

Alexander is at his most boyish here. Poor Alexander, one thinks. He's tired, worn out with all that drinking and feasting, all those emotions, all that sighing and looking. It is time for some rest.

Dryden is playing with the psychological possibilities of an old rhetorical commonplace: "The vanquish'd Victor sunk upon her Breast." As *victor victus* Alexander was a standby for medieval moralists charting the turns of fortune's wheel or the fatal flaws of greatness. "Comments based upon this simple rhetorical pattern," writes George Cary, "were eagerly manufactured by every scribbler who aspired to taste."[22] In Dryden's version, however, the wheel of fortune and tales of the fall of princes are being supplanted, making way for an ironic view of the world as a place in which victors and victims are the same. Alexander sinks on Thais's breast for all the world as if she were his mother, as well as his mistress. It smacks of Oedipal parody.[23]

Indeed the poem, to this point, parodies the hero in his adolescent exertions of feeling and his adolescent helplessness. Heroes, especially tragic heroes, usually have something of the small boy about them, reliving as they do the triumphs and sexual traumas of nursery and schoolyard. Achilles sulks in his tent like the spoiled youth whose favorite plaything has been taken away by a larger and more powerful, if not more aggressive, companion. Odysseus tells some grand fibs. Oedipus goes back to the womb. Hamlet is the perennial student. Lear is in his second childhood. Coriolanus is another mother's boy who wants to be his own father—and, as a case where the symptoms of adolescence are very near the surface, worth pausing over.[24] When Coriolanus invokes the god of war and Aufidius rebukes him—"Name not the god, thou boy of tears" (5.6. 101)—it sends the Roman warrior into spasms of wounded fury:

Measureless liar, thou hast made my heart
Too great for what contains it. "Boy!" O slave!
(5.6. 103–4)

And then, immediately:

Pardon me, lords, 'tis the first time that ever
I was forc'd to scold . . .
(5.6 105–6)

It is as if Aufidius had touched this hero's deepest nerve, maybe
every hero's deepest nerve. And, in doing so, Aufidius draws forth
some of the female sexuality that is part of Coriolanus's psychic
makeup. He imagines himself after his outburst as having played
the exasperated mother scolding her child: " 'tis the first time that
ever / I was forc'd to scold . . ." No wonder it feels that way to
him, considering what he has undergone from his mother, Volumnia:

There's no man in the world
More bound to his mother; yet here he lets me prate
Like one i' th' stocks.
(5.3. 158–60)

Bound by the umbilical cord, bound in swaddling clothes, bound
by unconscious sexuality, he is therefore bound to try to free
himself by imprisoning others: "here he lets me prate / Like one i'
th' stocks." Scold or not, Volumnia knows much about her boy
and about heroes. All this points as well to what is seductive about
the Christian myth and others like it: it is the myth of the unbound
hero, the hero truly father to himself, the hero whose desires have
been gratified even before being born and who is therefore born
free. And, coming back to Alexander, it is no surprise to find that
he was a devout son to his mother, Olympias. Even Samuel Clarke
recognized that and finished his biography with a tribute to
Alexander's filial piety: "His Mother *Olympias* was very severe
and morose in her carriage; and once *Antipater,* his *Vice-Roy* in
Europe, wrote large Letters of complaint to him against her; to
whom he returned this answer: *Knowest thou not that one little*

tear of my Mothers, will blot out a thousand of thy Letters of complaint. . . ."[25]

Dryden preserves, then, the outlines of heroic psychology in the manner of mock-heroic or (if his point is to satirize William III) in the manner of Pope's "Epistle to Augustus." As vanquished victor, Alexander, though a parodic hero, is not an impossible one. What counts about heroes is not so much that they are remarkably heroic, or even remarkably flawed, but that the mythology of heroism was a way of accommodating psychic strains—especially the strains of the boy grown into a man. The myth of the hero, that is, invested ordinary psychic reality with extraordinary value and was in its way more egalitarian than our egalitarian myth, which is always crumbling before observed fact. The myth of the hero held out the chance that at the center of experience heroism was *necessary.* Look around you, it seemed to say, and you will see heroes. Who would not, at least in some moods, want to live in such times? And in such moods who would not, like Dryden and Pope, want to preserve the heroic past even at the price of seeming to subvert what they most valued?

But "Alexander's Feast" is still far from over when the vanquished victor sinks on Thais's breast. He sleeps, perhaps to dream, but then there is waking up and, after the revels, history has to be attended to.[26] What follows in the poem anticipates in outline some of what follows the death of heroic myth and of the mock-heroic, which is the after-image of heroism. If the myth signifies integration, then the end of it signifies disintegration, dismemberment, schizophrenia. The hero becomes the orphan looking for his parent. He is tyrannical father figure or tormented child: Mr. Falkland or Caleb Williams.[27] He is colonizer or colonized: Robinson Crusoe or Friday. There are big people or there are little people; thinking up that idea *(pace* Samuel Johnson) was nothing less than to understand the new way of the world. And in the outcome of "Alexander's Feast" the little boy emperor wakes up and turns into Tamburlaine. The poem becomes a nightmare spectacle, such as history provides, of sound and furies and the firing of Persepolis:

> Revenge, Revenge, *Timotheus* cries,
>   See the Furies arise!

> See the Snakes that they rear,
> How they hiss in their Hair,
> And the Sparkles that flash from their Eyes!
> Behold a ghastly Band,
> Each a Torch in his Hand!
> Those are *Grecian* Ghosts, that in Battail were slayn,
> And unbury'd remain
> Inglorious on the Plain.
> Give the Vengeance due
> To the Valiant Crew.
> Behold how they toss their Torches on high,
> How they point to the *Persian* Abodes,
> And glitt'ring Temples of their Hostile Gods!
> The Princes applaud, with a furious Joy;
> And the King seyz'd a Flambeau, with Zeal to destroy;
> *Thais* led the Way,
> To light him to his Prey,
> And, like another *Hellen,* fir'd another *Troy.*

(Ll. 131–50)

In its lurid way it is wonderful stuff, and I have not resisted the impulse to quote it all; one needs to come to terms with the desire to join up.

To be sure, perhaps it is not only lurid. Even as the blooming Eastern bride turns into a malignant fury, there is a leftover touch of the mock-heroic about it. If Timotheus is father-figure in this Oedipal romance, Thais as bride, mistress, and mother plays Lady Macbeth or Volumnia to Alexander's Macbeth or Coriolanus. Alexander's will merges with hers, and we do not know for sure who is the principal agent of destruction:

> And the King seyz'd a Flambeau, with Zeal to destroy;
> *Thais* led the Way,
> To light him to his Prey,
> And, like another *Hellen,* fir'd another *Troy.*

Alexander seizes the torch but Thais leads and lights his way, and who is it then who fires another Troy? That almost looks like a heroic—or mock-heroic—question.

On the other hand, whatever the symbiotic possibilities in the relationships between Timotheus, Thais, and Alexander, the parallel between Thais and Helen is grim burlesque. The editor of a nineteenth-century school text asked his student-readers: "How far does this parallel between Thais and Hellen hold good?"[28] The answer is, not very far. This twisted simile puts an end to whatever is left of mock-heroism or psychic integration: the world of brute, literal fact—Alexander's and Thais's firing of Persepolis—supplants the world of moral values and responsibility. It is a moral question whether Helen's was the face that launched a thousand ships and burnt the topless towers of Ilium. It is only a factual question, in the long run, whether Thais or Alexander destroyed Persepolis. A remark of E. M. Cioran's will help make the point: "Mes Préférences: l'âge des Cavernes et le siècle des Lumières. Mais je n'oublie pas que les grottes ont débouché sur l'Histoire et les salons sur la Guillotine."[29] The destruction of Persepolis represents the emergence of history, of the guillotine, after a dream of reconciliation.

Understandably the last stanza has seemed an anticlimax. So it is, though not without interest. Suddenly Cecilia intrudes on the pagan scene: Alexander and Thais recede into the shadows to be replaced by officialdom. Maybe they were only Timotheus's creations anyway. Having made them, now he unmakes them—trying in the process to unmake history as well—and settles down to domesticity in the company of Cecilia, he playing on his flute and his lyre, she upon her organ, both comforting themselves with memories of what seems like glory:

> Let old *Timotheus* yield the Prize,
>   Or both divide the Crown;
> He rais'd a Mortal to the Skies;
>   She drew an Angel down.
>
>   (Ll. 167–70)

To say that Timotheus raised a mortal to the skies takes us back to the beginning ("A present Deity, they shout around: / A present Deity the vaulted Roofs rebound") but overlooks most of the facts. If anything, it is self-deification that Timotheus has had in mind. The deification of Alexander was a poetical fancy and only Timotheus survives his own drama: it is another case of the poet who in immortalizing another immortalizes himself. And if that is so, what about Cecilia? Perhaps she is her own angelic fancy: the scene threatens to self-destruct, leaving only domesticity and imaginary glories. Just for that reason it is likely to be an unstable duet. Someday, one suspects, Timotheus will want to call up the furies again and fire another Troy.

The strangeness of "Alexander's Feast" reveals itself best on a backward look. Its structure is preternaturally odd if one expects a logical progress, even of feeling. Granted the view that the ode, according to received opinion of Dryden's day, "should be rapturous, somewhat abrupt, and immethodical to a vulgar eye. That apparent order and connection which gives form and life to some compositions takes away the very soul of this."[30] But this received opinion (long since upended by classical scholarship) tells little about the actual way in which "Alexander's Feast" is put together, for the ode has the look of an upside-down tragedy, with a comic ending gratuitously attached. It parodies Aristotle's pattern of tragedy. The feelings come first, pride and pity and love. Then the holocaust. Then a kind of marriage. It is a drama of false, or missed, climaxes.

It might have been, for example, the tragedy of Darius—a possibility that Dryden seems to have imagined since he took the liberty of supposing Darius to have been slain before rather than after the destruction of Persepolis:

> He sung *Darius* Great and Good,
> By too severe a Fate,
> Fallen, fallen, fallen, fallen,
> Fallen from his high Estate
>   And weltring in his Blood:
> Deserted at his utmost Need,
> By those his former Bounty fed:
> On the bare Earth expos'd He lyes,
> With not a Friend to close his Eyes.
>
> (Ll. 75–83)

But the tragedy of Darius, Darius the Good as well as the Great, never becomes more than one occasion of feeling among the rest. The claim that it dominates the poem is wishful, not factual.[31]

Then there is a false climax as Alexander succumbs to love and wine and sleep. His stupefaction, engagingly infantile as it is, parodies cathartic experience: and calm of mind all passion spent. But in Alexander's world, unlike Samson's, all is not for the best because everything is topsy-turvy. Now that the drama of the passions seems over, it turns out that the action has not even begun. Timotheus has only been warming up, wringing the passions dry, making sure they will not change or impede the course of history. The unholy "Zeal" that animates Alexander and the "furious Joy" that drives his followers are only imitations of real feelings, motions of the mind evoked by actions of the body: "The Princes applaud, with a furious Joy; / And the King seyz'd a Flambeau, with Zeal to destroy." And we acquiesce (do we not?) in these behavioral motions. The sack of Persepolis, notwithstanding all the fireworks and flambeaux that shed a gaudy light on the scene, reenacts the instinctual groping for aspirin after a night's debauch and drinking. Burning great citadels is how great conquerors get over their nights before: the aim is not to create but to deaden feeling. But at least we think it is over, so decisive is the mood: "And, like another *Hellen,* fir'd another *Troy.*" Then it turns out, once again, not to be over.

"Sweet is Pleasure after Pain": in a sense the final "wedding" scene takes us back to the bacchanal of stanza 3, but how chaste and labored it seems. The ending recalls Tate's version of *Lear:* the forces of demonic energy are extinguished not in desolation but in poetic justice and reunion. The tragic integrations of the heroic give way to easy domesticity: Timotheus has not had to steer between Scylla and Charybdis. A thoroughgoing pessimism lurks as a possibility here. It is only three years from "Alexander's Feast" to Dryden's *Secular Masque,* which celebrated the close of the seventeenth century. Nor is it far when we measure the distance in terms of human feeling: "Thy Wars brought nothing about; / Thy Lovers were all untrue. / 'Tis well an Old Age is out, / And time to begin a New." In fact, the new age had already begun, and Dryden had helped to begin it in "Alexander's Feast," as well as elsewhere. The mode of the age is irony, the function of irony a blending of escape and preservation. But how unstable was the ironic balance. Hard on the heels of the escape into irony came the subsequent escape into sentiment and domesticity, the values of the hearth that Cowper celebrated in his postlapsarian venture at an epic: "Domestic happiness, thou only bliss / Of Paradise that has survived the fall!" *(The Task,* 2. 41–42). For all its immortal ragtime, in the phrase that Mark Van Doren indelibly but not quite wisely stamped on it, "Alexander's Feast" is a rich poem.[32] It *is* ironic. It tries to hold everything together in its double image of Alexander—an image that was to dissolve into moralistic singleness in the hands even of ironists like Swift and Fielding or, more dramatically, in the hands of a reformer like Godwin.[33] But the poem anticipates that dissolution, too, by recalling the brute facts of history and the devastation of Persepolis. In the actual childishness of its hero, it contributes fractionally to the incarnation of the child as hero—the process that begins in the picaresque, develops in a literature for and about children in the eighteenth century, and comes to a climax in Wordsworth. In its celebration of the artist's power, in its moments of self-reference, in its sequence of false climaxes with their almost Byronic orchestration, "Alexander's Feast" incorporates attitudes and tactics that the new age would claim as specifically its own. "Alexander's Feast" is not only rich but, in its way, is a prophetic poem.[34]

NOTES

1. Alethea Hayter, *Opium and the Romantic Imagination* (Berkeley and Los Angeles: University of California Press, 1968), p. 25, cites John Jones, *The Mysteries of Opium Reveal'd* (1700), as the source of these endearing trade names.

2. "Kubla Khan," l. 43.

3. *The Life of John Dryden,* ed. Bernard Kreissman (Lincoln: University of Nebraska Press, 1963), p. 345.

4. The poet had earlier complained in a letter to his sons (September 3, 1697) that the project was giving him trouble: "I am writeing a Song for St. Cecilia's feast, who you know is the Patroness of Musique. This is troublesome, & no way beneficiall." *The Letters of John Dryden,* ed. Charles E. Ward (Durham, N.C.: Duke University Press, 1942), p. 93.

5. Geoffrey H. Hartman's fine essay on "To Autumn" begins with a remark of Jonathan Wordsworth's: " 'Most English great poems have little or nothing to say.' " Says Hartman: "Few do that nothing so perfectly . . . as Keats's 'To Autumn.' " No doubt "To Autumn" does nothing more perfectly and more resolutely than "Alexander's Feast," but the comparison is of interest. Hartman's argument is "that 'To Autumn,' an ode that is hardly an ode, is best defined as an English or Hesperian model which overcomes not only the traditional type of sublime poem but the 'Eastern' or epiphanic consciousness that is essential to it." See "Poem and Ideology: A Study of Keats's 'To Autumn,' " *Literary Theory and Structure: Essays in Honor of William K. Wimsatt,* ed. Frank Brady, John Palmer, and Martin Price (New Haven, Conn.: Yale University Press, 1973), pp. 305, 307. If Dryden (as I argue here) sports with tradition, Keats transcends it.

6. Cf. John Hollander, *The Untuning of the Sky: Ideas of Music in English Poetry, 1500–1700* (Princeton, N.J.: Princeton University Press, 1961), pp. 411–22.

7. A useful survey of separate threads in the tradition is George Cary, *The Medieval Alexander* (Cambridge: At the University Press, 1956).

8. Paul Ramsey, *The Art of John Dryden* (Lexington, Ky: University of Kentucky Press, 1969), p. 126.

9. Earl Miner, *Dryden's Poetry* (Bloomington, Ind.: Indiana University Press, 1967), p. 268.

10. John Heath-Stubbs, "Dryden and the Heroic Ideal," in *Dryden's Mind and Art,* ed. Bruce King (Edinburgh: Oliver and Boyd, 1969), pp. 10, 22.

11. Bessie Proffitt, "Political Satire in Dryden's *Alexander's Feast,*" *TSLL* 11 (1969–70): 1307–16.

12. Cf. Miner, *Dryden's Poetry,* p. 273: "One wonders whether had it been Charles or James on the throne instead of William, Dryden would have written such a line as, 'The king seized a flambeau with zeal to destroy' "; and Miner's introduction to *Poems on the Reign of William III* (Los Angeles: Augustan Reprint Society, 1974), passim.

13. *The Life of Alexander the Great,* trans. by "several Gentlemen in the University of Cambridge" (1690), Sigs A7^r–A7^v. Tate's dedication to this translation of Quintus Curtius Rufus's life of Alexander is dedicated to Queen Mary.

14. Martin Price, *To the Palace of Wisdom: Studies in Order and Energy from Dryden to Blake* (Garden City, N.Y.: Doubleday, 1964), p. 372; Miner, *Dryden's Poetry,* p. 269.

15. Cf. Miner, *Dryden's Poetry,* p. 269: "Our condescension, and Dryden's, to Alexander is the source of our affection for him."

16. *Judgment on Alexander and Caesar; And also on Seneca, Plutarch, and Petronius* (1672), pp. 5, 29.

17. The text is that of the first edition (1697), reprinted by Geoffrey Tillotson, Paul Fussell, Jr., and Marshall Waingrow, eds., *Eighteenth-Century English Literature* (New York: Harcourt, Brace & World, 1969), pp. 169–71. Line numbers will be used throughout the essay.

18. Samuel Clarke, in *The Lives & Deaths of such Worthies Who by their Prudence, Policy, and Power have purchased, and procured to themselves the Surnames of Great* (1665). See *The Life & Death of Alexander the Great,* pp. 33–34.

19. Ibid., p. 34. Cf. Miner, *Dryden's Poetry,* p. 268: "The directive power of the simile reminds us that she is a courtesan. Not that we much mind."

20. Heath-Stubbs, "Dryden and the Heroic Ideal," p. 22.

21. Clarke, *The Life & Death of Alexander the Great,* p. 40. Clarke sets Alexander's affectation of divinity beside his reputation for drunkenness and cruelty.

22. Cary, *The Medieval Alexander,* pp. 98–99.

23. Christopher Anstey's parody of this scene heightens the fun:

> As when at the feast of the great ALEXANDER,
> TIMOTHEUS, the musical son of THERSANDER,
> Breath'd heavenly measures;
>   The prince was in pain,
>   And could not contain,
> While THAIS was sitting beside him;
>   But, before all his peers,
>   Was for shaking the Spheres,
> Such Goods the kind Gods did provide Him.
>   Grew bolder and bolder,
>   And cock'd up his Shoulder,

> Like the Son of great JUPITER AMMON,
> Till at length quite opprest,
> He sunk on her Breast,
> And lay there as dead as a Salmon.

New Bath Guide, 2d ed. (1766), Letter XIII, p. 100. There is more than a little truth to Horace Walpole's comment that after reading this there is no reading Dryden's version without laughing.

24. Cf. I. R. Browning, "*Coriolanus:* Boy of Tears," *EC* 5 (1955): 18–31. Eugeme M. Waith protests this view of Coriolanus in *The Herculean Hero in Marlowe, Shakespeare and Dryden* (New York: Columbia University Press, 1962), p. 143. For the text of *Coriolanus*, see *The Complete Plays and Poems of William Shakespeare,* ed. William Allan Neilson and Charles Jarvis Hill (Boston: Houghton Mifflin, 1942). Citations are from this edition.

25. Clarke, *The Life & Death of Alexander the Great*, p. 63. Cf. W. W. Tarn, *Alexander the Great* (Cambridge: At the University Press, 1948), 1:1: "Olympias was proud and terribly passionate, with an emotional side which made her a devotee of the orgiastic worships of Thrace; but she kept her son's love all his life, and though he inherited from Philip the solid qualities of capacity for affairs and military talent, his nature was largely hers, though not his mind."

26. In part a minor thievery from myself: see W. B. Carnochan, "Augustan Satire and the Gates of Dreams: A Utopian Essay," *SILI* 5 (1972): 1–18.

27. Mr. Falkland's self-identification with the "greatness" of Alexander produces one of the strangest and most vehement moments in Godwin's book: a dialogue between Falkland and Caleb in which Caleb wonders (as it were, naively) why Alexander should have been called "the Great" and Falkland rises wildly to the bait:

> Pray, sir, said I, one day as I was assisting Mr. Falkland in arranging some papers previously to their being transcribed into his collection how came Alexander of Macedon to be surnamed the Great?
> How came it? Did you never read his history?
> Yes, sir.
> Well, Williams, and could you find no reasons there?
> Why, I do not know, sir. I could find reasons why he should be famous; but every man that is talked of, is not admired. Judges differ about the merits of Alexander. Doctor Prideaux says in his Connections that he deserves only to be called the Great Cutthroat, and the author of Tom Jones has written a volume to prove that he and all other conquerors ought to be classed with Jonathan Wild.
> Mr. Falkland reddened at these citations.
> Accursed blasphemy! Did these authors think that by the coarseness of their ribaldry they could destroy his well-earned fame? Are learning, sensibility and taste no securities to exempt their possessor from this vulgar abuse? Did you ever read, Williams, of a man more gallant, generous and free? Was ever mortal so completely the reverse of every thing engrossing and selfish? He formed to himself a sublime image of excellence, and his only ambition was to realise it in his own story.

And so on for two more pages. See *Caleb Williams,* ed. David McCracken (Oxford: Oxford University Press, 1970), pp. 110–12.

28. J. W. Hales, ed., *"Alexander's Feast" and "MacFlecknoe"* (New York, 1887), p. 12.

29. E. M. Cioran, *Le Mauvais Démiurge* (Paris: Gallimard, 1969), p. 179.

30. Edward Young, "On Lyric Poetry," in Scott Elledge, ed., *Eighteenth-Century Critical Essays* (Ithaca, N.Y.: Cornell University Press, 1961), 1: 411. In the same essay Young calls "Alexander's Feast" "inferior to no composition of this kind" (1: 413).

31. Proffitt, "Political Satire in Dryden's *Alexander's Feast*," p. 1315. This reading, it is true, brings the ode into alignment with the "triumphal form" of Renaissance poetry and its "numerology of the centre." See Alistair Fowler, *Triumphal Forms: Structural Patterns in Elizabethan Poetry* (Cambridge: At the University Press, 1970), pp. 62–88. Perhaps the ode alludes to the numerology of the center by giving the reader, in Darius, not a monarch throned but a monarch five times "fallen." But in fact Alexander, as "joyless Victor" with "down-cast Looks," and Timotheus, as "Mighty Master," are nearer the precise center of the poem than is Darius.

32. Mark Van Doren, *The Poetry of John Dryden* (New York: Harcourt, Brace & Rowe, 1920), p. 258.

33. See n. 26. On Fielding's treatment of Jonathan Wild and Alexander, see especially C. J. Rawson, "Heroes, Clowns and Schoolboys: Mutations in Mock-heroic," in *Henry Fielding and the Augustan Ideal under Stress: "Nature's Dance of Death" and other Studies* (Boston: Routledge & Kegan Paul, 1972). Rawson set in motion my reflections on heroes and schoolboys. E.g., p. 186: "The Wild whom we encounter at such points is a kind of *alter ego* to the helpless clown. The mock-heroic reduction of hero to clown is reversed: the clown has become a hero again. And he is, in a sense, the hero as schoolboy."

34. In the beginning of this essay, I spoke of an "approach to a new consensus." Since those words were written, for an earlier version, at least three other readers have called Alexander's heroism into question. See John Dawson Carl Buck, "The Ascetic's Banquet: The Morality of *Alexander's Feast*," *TSLL* 17 (1975–76): 571–89; Ruth Smith, "The Argument and Contexts of Dryden's *Alexander's Feast*," *SEL* 18 (1978): 465–90; and Paul H. Fry, *The Poet's Calling in the English Ode* (New Haven, Conn.: Yale University Press, 1980), pp. 49–62. It seems as if something like a new consensus has been reached.

Concepts of the Hero in Comic Drama, 1660–1710

ROBERT D. HUME

Fujimura . . . makes . . . the fatal mistake of treating the "truewits" of the plays, whom other critics call their "heroes"—the Dorimants, Mirabels, Millamants, Horners, and Manleys—as more or less completely "sympathetic", non-laughter-provoking figures. . . . There are, properly speaking, no "heroes" or "heroines" in the best Restoration comedy, but only protagonists and antagonists.

Charles O. McDonald

Two vital factors . . . set the rake-hero apart from most of his devilish predecessors [vice-figures]. The first has to do with that more intellectual quality of his rebellion. . . . The second lies in the key word "hero". . . . Dorimant and Horner and Mirabell . . . do win. They create their own morality. . . . They make their spirit prevail.

Virginia Ogden Birdsall

THE crux in most critical disputes about late-seventeenth-century comedies boils down to a simple question: are the protagonists "heroes"? Obviously the answer depends on the definition. The term may be applied in a basic descriptive sense. First, the hero is the principal character. But the connotation of the term, from the late seventeenth century to the present, adds a very different and potentially confusing meaning. Second, the hero is a central personage taking an admirable part in the action; hence, a person regarded as a model. When we read the latter sense onto a comic

protagonist not conceived that way by his creator, we will emerge
with a decidedly peculiar reading of the play. The problem is to
determine reasonable assumptions and responses. Was Horner
presented to be admired? Was Mirabell? I argue that the role of the
protagonist varies drastically, that these plays are neither uni-
formly satiric (as McDonald would make them) nor Right-
Way/Wrong-Way dichotomies (as Fujimura and Holland suggest).
This essay demonstrates that most of the authors did not think of
the male leads in London-set comedies as heroes, and that to do so
seriously distorts the plays. When writers start to espouse this
Steelish view, we will find ourselves moving into exemplary
drama, which achieves dominance during the first decade of the
eighteenth century—essentially a new genre, and one beyond the
subject of this study.

1

Seventeenth-century disputes over comedy concern method. On
its function, the critics are agreed—it should teach while entertaining. How does it teach? Basically by positive or negative
example. Thus, John Wilson announces in 1663: "Comedy, either
is, or should be, the true Picture of Vertue, or Vice; yet so drawn
as to shew a man how to follow the one, and avoid the other."[1] A
third possibility, tending toward positive example, is the "reform"
of an erring protagonist who can then be rewarded.

The dominant comic theory in seventeenth-century criticism
rests on satire and negative example.[2] As Aristotle says, "Comedy
aims at representing men as worse, tragedy as better than in actual
life" and "comedy is . . . an imitation of characters of a lower
type; it does not, however, involve the full range of villains, but
only the ludicrous" (*Poetics*, 3.5). The comedy that sticks to the
letter of that prescription is in little danger of confusing its
audience. Ludicrous "low" characters will not elicit admiration.
When, however, the social level rises, and we follow a romance
plot, not a gulling action, confusion can ensue. In almost all
boy-gets-girl actions the audience is at least benevolently indifferent to the couple (as in Plautine comedy), and often seriously
sympathetic (as in Shakespearean romance). If such protagonists
are morally dubious specimens, what then? Depending on the

author's purposes (and our assumptions about them), there are several possibilities. First, we may be outraged at a deplorably attractive example. Second, we may hold that the example has no significant relevance to real life, and hence deny its moral applicability. Third, we may argue that the example, far from being made attractive, is actually the object of satire. And fourth, we may argue that the didactic effect has been misunderstood—that we are to admire the pledge of reform, not the behavior that necessitates it.

Outrage at "debauched" protagonists is easy to find, even without applying to Jeremy Collier. In the preface to his first play, *The Sullen Lovers* (1668), Shadwell laments that "in the *Playes* which have been wrote of late, there is no such thing as perfect Character, but the two chief persons are most commonly a Swearing, Drinking, Whoring, Ruffian for a Lover, and an impudent, ill-bred *tomrig* for a Mistress, and these are the fine People of the *Play*." In the preface to his next effort, *The Royal Shepherdess* (1669; an adaptation of Fountain's *The Rewards of Virtue*), Shadwell amplifies, touting his play:

> The Rules of Morality and good Manners are strictly observed in it: (Vertue being exalted and Vice depressed) and perhaps it might have been better received had neither been done in it: for I find, it pleases most to see Vice incouraged, by bringing the Characters of debauch'd People upon the Stage, and making them pass for fine Gentlemen.[3]

These opinions could be duplicated many times over in the next forty years. In a celebrated passage, for example, James Wright complains bitterly that "we seldom or never see a Character of True Worth, Integrity, and Honour, in any of these Comedies. . . . The Debauchee is always the fine Gentleman."[4]

Wright asks, explicitly, for exemplary protagonists. But one might argue that he and Shadwell are foolish in applying an elaborately artificial art form to life—such is the position made famous by Lamb and elaborated by John Palmer—cloud cuckooland. According to this hypothesis, no character could be considered a model, and hence the concept of "hero" is meaningless, save within the irrelevant confines of a meaningless fairy tale. This interpretation solves moral problems at the cost of making the drama meaningless.

Trying to rescue the plays from earlier critics' charges of triviality, Charles McDonald vigorously denies such "irrelevance," maintaining that the "debauched" protagonists were never meant to be exemplary models and are in fact actually attacked. He would contend simply that Shadwell and Wright misread, failing to observe satire. This theory is attractively simple. There are no heroes in "true" Restoration comedy; when a character is upheld as a model we have sentimental or proto-sentimental comedy. The resulting dichotomy can seem remarkably satisfying, but its accuracy is questionable at best. Are Horner and Dorimant the satiric butts this theory says they ought to be?

A less procrustean defense seems called for. Dryden's comments answering Shadwell and others in his preface to *An Evening's Love* (published 1671) are revealing.

> 'Tis charg'd upon me that I make debauch'd persons . . . my Protagonists, or the chief persons of the *Drama;* and that I make them happy in the conclusion of my Play; against the Law of Comedy, which is to reward virtue and punish vice. I answer first, that I know no such law to have been constantly observ'd in Comedy, either by the Ancient or Modern Poets. . . . The first end of Comedie is delight, and instruction only the second. . . . But, lest any man should think that I write this to make libertinism amiable . . . I must farther declare . . . that we make not vicious persons happy, but only as heaven makes sinners so: that is by reclaiming them first from vice. For so 'tis to be suppos'd they are, when they resolve to marry.[5]

Three observations are in order. First, Dryden was obviously smarting from complaints about his flawed protagonists—else why rebut them? Second, he argues that comedy is to divert and hence that exemplary poetic justice is not necessarily required. Third, backing away from a flat defense of imperfect characters, he maintains that we are to "suppose" a reformation in them. This is a backhanded claim to exemplary instruction. The comedy is said to imply a moral: reform and ye shall be rewarded.

The "reformation" argument is decidedly a complication. Reform may be treated very lightly indeed, as in *An Evening's Love*

(1668). Played seriously, it can be infused with dripping emotion, as in Cibber's *Love's Last Shift* (1696), or explicitly trumpeted as exemplary rectitude, as in Shadwell's *The Squire of Alsatia* (1688). There Belfond Jr. has a three-year-old bastard by a cast mistress, and in the course of the play seduces, abandons, and pays off a virtuous bourgeois girl. But when the wealthy object of his true affections inquires how she may "be secure you will not fall to your old courses agen?" he replies:

> I have been so sincere in my Confessions, you may trust me; but I call Heav'n to witness, I will hereafter be entirely yours. I look on Marriage as the most solemn Vow a Man can make; and 'tis by consequence, the basest Perjury to break it. (Shadwell, *Works*, 4:279)

And the audience is to take this seriously; Shadwell holds the young man up as a model. In short, "reform" can be a way of squaring flawed protagonists with demands for a "hero" in comedy.

We may fairly say that from the very outset of the period writers feel—and some resist—pressure to make the protagonist a hero. Thus in 1663 Cowley protests against criticism of Colonel Jolly in his *Cutter of Coleman-Street;* "I did not intend the Character of a *Hero,* one of exemplary virtue. . . . If I had designed here the celebration of the Virtues of our Friends [i.e., loyal cavaliers], I would have made the Scene nobler. . . . They should have stood in Odes, and Tragedies, and Epique poems."[6] Cowley denies the appropriateness of heroes to comedy. Other writers, desiring to "raise" comedy, wish to limn the virtues of gentlemen, and even the nobility. Corneille (in a discourse of 1660) had proposed the possibility of *comédie heroique,* and circa 1670 such writers as Dryden and Edward Howard experiment with the notion. The social refinement of *Marriage A-la-Mode* (dubbed simply "A Comedy" on the title page) is a clear proof of Dryden's attempt to get away from the "low comedy" for which he repeatedly expresses his "disgust." The dedication to Rochester makes much of class snob appeal and linguistic refinement, as does his dedication to Sedley of *The Assignation* the same year (1673).

The introduction of this kind of social snob appeal, like the presence of a major romance element, rapidly complicates the issue. Either one insists on the didactic clarity of a positive-negative example, or one does not. Those writers who do not so insist definitely fall outside the exemplary/satiric dichotomy constructed by McDonald. If one is not unduly upset by the presence in comedy of an "ordinary jovial Gentleman," as Cowley styles Colonel Jolly, the problem evaporates. For playwrights, the argument really comes down to whether a comedy *should* have a hero in the exemplary sense of the term. Or, from the affective point of view: does the audience necessarily take a successful protagonist in an exemplary way?

The dispute is neatly epitomized in the celebrated quarrel between Dennis and Steele over *The Man of Mode*. In *Spectator* No. 65 Steele decries the play's reputation as "the pattern of genteel comedy." "I will take for granted that a fine gentleman should be honest in his actions, and refined in his language. Instead of this, our *hero* [italics added] . . . is a direct knave in his designs, and a clown in his language." Steele goes on to demonstrate (accurately) that Dorimant's principles and actions are at variance with the ideal of the Christian Gentleman. He admits the play to be "nature, but it is nature in its utmost corruption and degeneracy." (To this McDonald could say—Wonderful! Quite right! It's a splendid *negative* example, and Steele himself proves it!) Obviously Steele's own moral standards play a large part in the vehemence of his denunciation; another critic might accept Dorimant's vices without such animus. But to view him as a *hero* in the sense of a pattern for imitation makes the play a treatise in favor of lying and fornication.

Dennis replies with his usual contentious gusto: "How little do they know of the Nature of true Comedy who believe that its proper Business is to set us Patterns for imitation. . . . 'Tis its proper Business to expose Persons to our View, whose Views we may shun, and whose Follies we may despise."[7] Thus Dennis touts negative example against Steele's call for positive example. Where, however, are we shown *in the play* that we should shun Dorimant's views and despise his follies? Dennis maintains that the Carolean audience would have known better than to take as a model "a young Courtier, haughty, vain, and prone to anger, amorous, false, and inconstant." Well, Steele certainly does *not* take him as an example, but he supposes Etherege to have thought him one. McDonald believes Dorimant to be debunked; I take him as an ironic but not hostile depiction of the way of the world.[8]

The problem is one of assumptions. Was the audience expected to supply an extrinsic moral standard, as McDonald hypothesizes? Evidence on the views of the playwrights is in short supply. We can quote Cowley and Dennis and Dryden to suggest that protagonists in comedy were not considered as examples; we can cite Shadwell, James Wright, and Steele to show that part of the audience may have taken them as such. Caught between the intentional fallacy and scant historical information, we may do best to consider the interpretive effects of variant assumptions on specific cases. Wycherley's last two plays, which have been the subject of much confusion and dispute, will serve as illustrations.

2

The Country Wife is a good epitome. First, if we assume that the comedy is one of negative example, we may conclude with Bonamy Dobrée that Horner is a "grim nightmare figure" in whom Wycherley presents the "utter vileness of his world." Anne Righter agrees, calling Horner a "wholly negative" "agent of destruction."[9] Second, if we assume Horner to be a hero in the exemplary sense, we may agree with Macaulay that Wycherley is a bestial fiend, or we may join Virginia Birdsall in seeing Horner as representing the "élan vital," "a wholly positive and creative comic hero . . . squarely on the side of health, of freedom, and . . . honesty."[10] Third, possibly the hero has been misidentified, and not Horner but Harcourt (with Alithea) shows the "Right-Way." Horner then becomes one of the "Wrong-Ways"—useful for showing up others, but debunked himself. Such an interpretation has been put forward by Holland, Zimbardo, Righter, and others.[11]

Of the first reading, we may ask how many people are all that upset by Horner. At the end of the play do we want him to be exposed, humiliated, and punished? Or are we pleased by his escape? What would *The Country Wife* be like with an *Alchemist* ending? Or with a *Volpone* ending? Is either really appealing? Of the second reading hypothesized above, we may inquire how many of us really find Horner all that glamorous, attractive, and suc-

cessful. To the reader who takes short stories in *Playboy* dead
seriously, perhaps he is. And of the third reading we may ask how
many theatergoers would take the vapid Harcourt and Alithea
seriously enough to make them an effective "satiric antithesis."

We are left to conclude that the play fails to present an effective
positive example—unless with Birdsall one enthusiastically en-
dorses Horner's sexual outlook. Nor is an effective negative example concocted. Horner succeeds in his designs and escapes the
consequences—a marvelous way of discouraging the audience
from following in his footsteps! If *The Country Wife* were meant
to be a crunching satire on "lust" (as Rose Zimbardo would have
it), why not let Horner catch the pox from Lady Fidget, become
impotent, and have his nose rot off? No—to make sense of the
play, the audience must abandon any desire to find it a simple
lecture. And in all the interpretive tangle, this is really the problem. Critics want to find a hero, or at least a satiric butt. If the play
happens not to be constituted that way, too bad for the play.
Critics look for a serious affirmation of values. *The Country Wife*,
I believe, presents instead a wry, farcical, often ugly caricature of
reality. To ask for positive or negative example requires the play to
be something it is not.

The Plain Dealer remains the subject of heated debate about
Manly. Dobrée suggests (as do many others) that Manly is
Wycherley, a noble figure railing against vileness. Alexander
Chorney argued (in 1950) that far from being an alter ego and
spokesman for Wycherley, Manly is a vigorously satirized
humours character and a comic butt.[12] Critical opinion has veered
back toward the earlier view in recent years, but Manly's violence,
irrationality, and especially his ineffectuality make him an unin-
spiring model. Birdsall suggests that we should pity Manly for his
inability to cope with a despicable society—and hence argues that
he is not satirized. The possibilities, then, seem to be these: Manly
is the noble hero; or, Manly is ineffectual, and hence either the
object of comic ridicule, or the recipient of sympathy. The latter
reading seems to make the play into a pathetic tragicomedy, with
distressed innocence finally given a sentimental reward. The
comic-butt reading is at odds with contemporary comment;[13] with
Wycherley's nickname; and with the character type associated with
Charles Hart, who created the role. A related possibility is that

Wycherley is deliberately creating satirical overtones around an ostensible "hero": Cynthia Matlack suggests outright that Manly is a sardonic parody of Almanzor.[14] This reading accounts tidily for both the heroic and the parodic elements. I cannot say that I respond to the play this way; I am more inclined to see an explanation of my mixed reactions in K. M. Rogers's hypothesis that there is a "fatal inconsistency" in Manly's serving both as comic misanthropist and as a serious satiric spokesman.[15]

In *The Plain Dealer* elements from foreign-set intrigue tragicomedy intersect with those of London-based social comedy. The peculiar status of Manly may be partly explicable as a function of this mixture. Genuine exemplary heroes are a commonplace in romantic tragicomedy from Tuke's *The Adventures of Five Hours* (1663) to Dryden's *Secret Love* (1667) and the top plot in *Marriage A-la-Mode* (1671). Spanish Romance (vastly popular in the 1660s) is full of them. In London comedies, however, the male lead is usually no better than the ordinary jovial gentleman—fairly good, but by no means an example, and often indeed the object of some satire. Wycherley's genuine satiric fervor, much of it communicated through Manly, lends the character a seriousness and heroic weight that ill accords with the half-role of comic misanthropist.

In *The Country Wife* we see dispute over the identity of the hero (if any); in *The Plain Dealer* we have an instance of disagreement over whether a protagonist is a hero or a gull. A subtler problem is presented by a character like Mellefont in *The Double-Dealer*. He is indisputably "good"; is he therefore the hero? Congreve says No, and vigorously protests against the audience tendency to find a hero in comedy.

> Another very wrong Objection has been made by some who have not taken leisure to distinguish the Characters. *The Hero of the Play* [italics added], as they are pleas'd to call him, (meaning *Mellefont)* is a Gull, and made a Fool and cheated. Is every Man a Gull and Fool that is deceiv'd? . . . I would have 'em again look into the Character of *Maskwell*, before they accuse any Body of weakness for being deceiv'd by him.[16]

As the title reveals, the focus of the play is on Maskwell, the villain. Mellefont exists in the play's design as a foil: ultimately he arrives at a happy ending, but the play is really a study of treachery, not a display of virtue rewarded. Evidently the audience felt that for a hero Mellefont is too obviously befooled. This is true: most of his part in the action, however blameless, cannot be found admirable—he is too ineffectual. In truth, there is no place in the design of *The Double-Dealer* for a hero-figure.

In light of disagreement over whether there is a hero, and who the hero is, and especially an author's flat denial that a virtuous protagonist should be styled the hero, we need to do some reconsidering. As a start, we must get away from the term and the assumptions it imposes in order to ask a simple and obvious question: what different sorts of protagonists *do* appear in the comic drama? Free of presuppositions, we will find a considerable spectrum.

3

I am going to propose, and shall try to demonstrate, that there are at least five basic categories of protagonist. Arranged according to the nature of the audience response, they elicit: (1) contempt or hatred; (2) tolerance; (3) sympathy; (4) respect; (5) admiration.

Accustomed to the polished Truewits in a few famous plays, the audience too readily forgets that the protagonist may be a scoundrel—and not just a rogue like Horner. Goodvile in Otway's *Friendship in Fashion* (1678) tries to palm off a cast mistress on a good friend for a wife, and attempts to debauch the intended wife of another friend—while that friend cuckolds him. Otway gives a savagely ugly picture of duplicity and sexual appetite in the fashionable London world. As in *The Country Wife* a smash is averted at the end: the "friendships" are patched up and the nasty farce goes on. But the tone is altogether bleaker. Horner is at least a disinterested friend to Harcourt; Goodvile is nothing but a vicious, selfish animal. His attractions are minimal: obviously Otway means to degrade the fine London society gentleman beyond any possibility of mistake.[17] Lee's Nemours is another such case, with further twists. *The Princess of Cleve* (1682) is a weird mélange of elements. Lee dubs it "Farce, Comedy, Tragedy or meer Play" in the dedication, adding that he has altered his source to disconcert the audience: "when they expected the most polish'd *Hero* in Nemours, I gave 'em a Ruffian reeking from Whetstone's Park" (a whores' hangout). Interestingly, Lee cites some other plays designed—at least in his opinion—to accomplish a similar exposure: "The fourth and Fifth Acts of The Chances . . . Marriage Alamode, where they are bare to the Waste; the Libertine, and Epsom-Wells, are but copies of his Villany."[18] Nemours is very much the Fine Gentleman—powerful, glamorous, brutal, treacherous, and unprincipled. The heroic love-death of the prince, his best friend, provides a startling juxtaposition of the Restoration heroic ethic against the rake. I believe that Summers is right in saying that Nemours is a mildly disguised picture of Rochester, recently deceased:[19] even the famous deathbed repentance is mockingly recollected in the final speech of the play—a startling and grossly unconvincing recantation. Dennis claims that Dorimant was a reflection of Rochester. Lee says in almost so many words: *this* is what your Dorimants are *really* like. Shadwell has nearly the same message in *The Libertine* (1675), his satirical tragedy. Here the Don Juan story becomes a biting satire on itself, the ethic and appetite exaggerated into a completely self-destructive burlesque. In their different ways, Lee, Otway, and Shadwell write vigorous protests against the attractiveness of the rake in comedy—or in life. They attack what they regard as false heroes.

To say that a character like Horner is attacked would be a considerable exaggeration. Horner is a rogue, but not a hateful rogue: he harms no one about whom we could feel any real concern. Hence we can tolerate him with amusement, and like Subtle, Face, and Dol Common, he can walk off unpunished, ready to pursue another such set of schemes. If we do not wish him a bad end, we can scarcely be imagined to think seriously ill of him. As a satiric vehicle he shows up others effectively. We may tolerate a rogue with amusement; in a related kind of response we may be benevolently indifferent to a stereotyped romantic lover or couple. The roistering cavalier bloods in Dryden's *An Evening's Love* or Behn's *1 Rover* elicit such a reaction. The audience is pleased to see their schemes (matrimonial or otherwise) succeed, but makes no serious identification with their interests: our concern for their success and well-being is strictly a pro forma granting of attention.

One step up, the audience becomes significantly sympathetic. (The difference may be illustrated with Hero from Shakespeare's *Much Ado* and Rosalind from *As You Like It:* to substitute Rosalind for Hero would be impossible—our outrage at Claudio's treatment of her would make their subsequent marriage violently unpalatable.) Valentine in Congreve's *Love for Love* (1695) elicits such a response. His folly has landed him in a mess; his trickery fails to get him out of it—until blatant lying and dissimulation by Angelica arrange a happy ending. But we like Valentine; he is engaging, amusing, and decent; we can rejoice in his happy ending with far more spirit than in the conventional romantic ending allowed Wildblood and Bellamy. Like them, he "repents," is taken to be reformed by the love of a good woman. He too has been a gay blade, but in him appears more serious emotion. To find his part in the action "admirable" would, however, be difficult. Farquhar's fortune-hunters in *The Beaux Stratagem* (1707) are similarly humanized and likeable—and when matters come to a head, Aimwell confesses all, upon which he is of course duly rewarded.[20] This rewarded conversion verges on the Cibberesque and is a sentimentalized form of the penitent rake story.[21]

A step above the sympathetic protagonist is the just plain good protagonist. His sins, if any, are venial, and he would be no bad model, though he is not explicitly presented as such. We do at least respect him. Farewel in Crowne's *Sir Courtly Nice* (1685) is an excellent example. The work's genre—lighthearted Spanish Romance—is perhaps a key to its chaste morals. Farewel and Leonora are no gay couple: The audience is to take the romantic purity of their discussion of elopement dead seriously. Farewel declares himself delighted to forfeit Leonora's dowry, since that proves that his love is not mercenary. This kind of declaration, common enough in romance plays from *The Committee* on, would sound odd indeed in Etherege, Southerne, or Congreve. Yet Congreve is decidedly capable of constructing a good character. Mirabell in *The Way of the World* is an instance. Smarting from Collier's criticisms, Congreve was more than careful to give us not a blameless but at least a good protagonist. His status can be exaggerated, however. Jean Gagen actually claims that Mirabell is not a rake; that his conduct is in no way reprehensible; that he never reforms because he does not need to.[22] Up to a point, this is correct: within the play his treatment of Mrs. Fainall is not criticized. Nor would a gentleman of Congreve's own circle have thought the episode discreditable. But does Congreve conceive his play as a showcase for his hero's virtues? If so, we have made a fascinating discovery—that Congreve and Steele have an identical theory of comedy, and differ only about the details of the morality that is to be held up as an example. This might accurately be said of Shadwell and Steele. Belfond Jr. in *The Squire of Alsatia* is loudly trumpeted as a moral example, though he is ten times the cad that Mirabell arguably may be.

Perfection is in the eye of the beholder. I have grouped these five sets of protagonists on the basis of my estimation of how the plays are designed to make them look. Whether we accept the presentation is quite a different matter. Belfond Jr. belongs, technically at least, in the final group—he is presented to be admired. "Exemplary comedy" is the name devised by John Harrington Smith for such a work. *The Conscious Lovers* (1722) is of course the famous example, though in a less complete and systematic way the method is anticipated in Shadwell's late plays and Steele's early ones.[23] Lord Hardy in *The Funeral* (1701) is more than just a good character: again and again we are invited by Steele to admire his nobility. By the fourth category (which chronologically speaking becomes important during the 1690s) the protagonist verges on the hero in the sense of a person regardable as a model; the fifth presents a person explicitly so designed.

4

"Restoration comedy" is far from being a monolith. The drastic variation in the status of the protagonist is a good index to its diversity. The nature, flavor, and tone of a comedy are—to say the least—greatly affected by the attitude evoked toward the central characters. *The Wives Excuse, Marriage A-la-Mode, The Recruiting Officer, The Double-Dealer,* and *Bury Fair* are all good comedies—and they are remarkably disparate in nature, ranging from harsh satire to sunny example. In various ways we could argue that all of them "teach," as contemporary theory insists they must, but they do so in varying ways. Positive and negative example exist—but also subtle, more interesting, more significant methods. At their best, these plays achieve a complex rendering of human experience. Some protagonists are designed to elicit a genuinely ambivalent response—as is Dorimant, for instance. He is not put down satirically; nor (in my opinion) is he presented as a model of the fine gentleman. The passion for making protagonists black or white seems remarkably perverse, especially among modern critics presumably without moral hangups. Seventeenth-century literary theory is simplistic in this respect, but the plays themselves are not, so why should we be?

If we look at the sorts of comedies produced in this half-century, we can see that the attitude adopted toward the principal characters tends to determine the nature of the resulting drama. At the extremes are exemplary drama and really harsh satire. In exemplary drama the hero (here the term is proper) is a good man presented not just uncritically but positively, as a moral exemplum. Serious satire is more complicated, and rather rare, Otway's three comedies being perhaps the best example. To flay obvious butts and fools, even with Wycherley's vehemence, does not make a serious satire. Wycherley ridicules grotesque exaggerations of the commonplace butts of Carolean comedy—the jealous husband, the lustful wives, the hypocritical villain, the country innocent. Society is presented as degraded and disgusting, but the criticisms are less than serious, for never is the audience shaken from a position of smug superiority. Despite the "presents you as you are" rhetoric in the prologue, the audience can feel safe.

Faced with the way of the world, the dramatists react variously. Steele finally sees that he wants to offer a better alternative. At the opposite pole Otway and Lee violently reject what they present. Wycherley comes close to doing so in *The Plain Dealer*. But usually the writers of comedy substantially accept the world they present—with dégagé amusement (Etherege); with a slightly sad sympathy (Congreve); with bitter amusement (Dryden); with resigned contempt (Southerne). In none of these writers will we find any real hope of change, nor any lasting outrage. Their plays can be wildly misread if we bring the wrong assumptions to them.

The female-swapping plot in *Marriage A-la-Mode*, for instance, is used for its titillative value, but Dryden is doing nothing so simplistic as either revelling in pornography or showing us a Wrong-Way. He very carefully brings the sex to naught, and produces a "Reformation"—admittedly one freighted with ironies. Probably the ironic complexities passed over much of the audience, which reacted on the basis of its own assumptions. Thus the Reverend Joseph Arrowsmith took the play for obnoxious and deliberate smut,[24] while an anonymous contemporary, defending Dryden's treatment of love and marriage, indignantly reports the audience's pleasure in the titillation.

> What is either wicked or silly in modish colours he has so well painted, as would divert any person that is owner of the least ingenuity, from both: more particularly this of shunning Marriage, and being entred perfidiously to break a vow so easy to be kept, in his Play of *Marriage a-la-Mode:* a more gentile Satyre against this sort of folly, no Pen can write, where he brings the very assignations that are commonly used about Town upon the stage; and to see both Boxes and Pitt so damnably crouded, in order to see themselves abused, and yet neither to be angry nor ashamed, argues such excess of stupidity, that this great Pen it self (if 'twere possible) would be put to a nonplus to express it.[25]

As this writer correctly asserts, Dryden is far from glamorizing his characters; he makes them "reform"—and very clearly implies that the reason they are willing to reform is simply that men are so vain and selfish that they will give up a sure sexual conquest for fear another man will poach on their present property in the interim. The comment on human nature is decidedly harsh—and Dryden is scarcely proposing to change human nature.

My point here is simply that where writers take so detached, sceptical, or ironical a view of their protagonists, the whole concept of the hero is misleading. The distinction toward which many recent critics have tended divides plays into good Restoration versus bad Sentimental, or satiric versus exemplary groups. Actually, hard satire on protagonists is a rarity, and one will not find satire lacking in the plays of Shadwell or Steele. To posit a theory of uniform response, whether positive (Birdsall)[26] or negative (McDonald) is procrustean: the plays vary, and plainly there is much middle ground.

As a means of facilitating a rough categorization, I would propose the following groupings. (1) *Destructive Satire*. Plainly we must distinguish between incidental attacks on minor characters

(Wycherley's honorable ladies) or good-humored ridicule of a harmless fop (Crowne's Sir Courtly Nice) from savage denunciation of a protagonist like Lee's Nemours. (2) *Hard Comedy.* Here the view of the subject is less harsh: it may be contemptuous, sardonic, bitter, or merely superiorly amused, but the ways of the world are at least accepted with resignation to their inevitability. Most so-called "Restoration comedy" is of this sort, whether cutting, cynical, and libertine *(The Country Wife, The Man of Mode)* or more engaged with or concerned for the subject *(Marriage A-la-Mode, The Wives Excuse, The Provok'd Wife).* (3) *Humane Comedy.* [27] Here the view of the subject matter becomes considerably more sympathetic. Faults are less harshly judged, and writers tend to feel that men can be pretty decent. Without going to the extreme of maintaining that uncorrupted human nature is intrinsically good, writers of humane comedy are able to acknowledge a basic goodness in individual men—as Vanbrugh does, so surprisingly, in *The Relapse* (1696), and Farquhar does in *The Beaux' Stratagem.* (4) *Exemplary Comedy.* In full-fledged form this is really a post-1710 development, but the inclination is developing by the later 1680s. [28]

Examining the status of the "hero" in these types, we can see that such a figure is central to exemplary comedy, and perhaps conceivable in humane comedy. Some recent critical disputes over Congreve are attributable to the way he—usually grouped with the hard comedy writers of the 1670s—tends to take a decidedly sympathetic view of a protagonist like Valentine (leading Zimbardo to call *Love for Love* "well on the way to sentimental comedy") or to present so relatively serious and moral a character as Mirabell. But to consider the protagonists in hard comedy as heroes in any sense weirdly distorts the nature of the plays—whose whole point lies in the author's sceptical, ironical view of his subject.

Historically speaking, we undoubtedly can see an overall shift from a preponderance of hard comedy in the Carolean court period toward humane and ultimately exemplary comedy in the post-1688 period. We should not ignore, however, the fact that plenty of heroes appear in the nonheroic drama from the very start of the period, though not in "London" comedies. What we see in the comedies of the 1680s and the 1690s is a domestication of the kind of protagonist popular in romantic tragicomedy and Spanish Romance. Returning to the original crux, we are left with a simple conclusion: protagonists in these comedies should not be considered heroes except in a small number of cases—the exemplary comedies. To assume the lead characters to be "heroes" is to impose Steelish assumptions on comedies not so designed.

NOTES

1. John Wilson, "The Author to the Reader," *The Cheats,* ed. Milton C. Nahm (Oxford: Basil Blackwell, 1935), p. 237.

2. I have treated the theoreticians' arguments more fully in "Theory of Comedy in the Restoration," *MP* 70 (1973): 302–18.

3. *The Complete Works of Thomas Shadwell,* ed. Montague Summers, 5 vols. (1927; reprint ed., New York: Blom, 1968), 1: 11, 100.

4. James Wright, *Country Conversations* (London: Bonwicke, 1694), p. 8.

5. *The Works of John Dryden,* ed. Maximillian E. Novak and George R. Guffey (Berkeley, Calif.: University of California Press, 1970), 10: 208–10.

6. *Cutter of Coleman-Street* (London: Herringman, 1663), Preface.

7. "A Defence of Sir Fopling Flutter," *The Critical Works of John Dennis,* ed. Edward Niles Hooker, 2 vols. (Baltimore, Md.: Johns Hopkins University Press, 1939, 1943), 2: 241–50.

8. I have analyzed the play at length in "Reading and Misreading *The Man of Mode,*" *Criticism* 14 (1972): 1–11. Charles O. McDonald, "Restoration Comedy as Drama of Satire: an Investigation into Seventeenth-Century Aesthetics," *SP* 61 (1964): 522–44.

9. Bonamy Dobrée, *Restoration Comedy* (London: Oxford University Press, 1924), ch. 6. Anne Righter, "William Wycherley," *Restoration Theatre,* ed. John Russell Brown and Bernard Harris (London: Edward Arnold, 1965), pp. 71–91.

10. Virginia Ogden Birdsall, *Wild Civility: The English Comic Spirit on the Restoration Stage* (Bloomington, Ind.: Indiana University Press, 1970), pp. 136, 156.

11. Norman N. Holland, *The First Modern Comedies* (1959; reprint ed. Bloomington, Ind.: Indiana University Press, 1967), ch. 8. Rose A. Zimbardo, *Wycherley's Drama* (New Haven, Conn.: Yale University Press, 1965).

12. Alexander H. Chorney, "Wycherley's Manly Reinterpreted," *Essays Critical and Historical Dedicated to Lily B. Campbell* (Berkeley, Calif.: University of California Press, 1950), pp. 161–69.

13. For example, see Dryden in "The Author's Apology for Heroic Poetry and Poetic License" (1677), *Of Dramatic Poesy and Other Critical Essays,* ed. George Watson, 2 vols. (London: J. M. Dent & Sons, 1962), 1: 199. Or Congreve's prologue for *Love for Love:* "Since the *Plain Dealers* Scenes of Manly Rage, / Not one has dar'd to lash this Crying Age."

14. Cynthia Matlack, "Parody and Burlesque of Heroic Ideals in Wycherley's Comedies: A Critical Reinterpretation of Contemporary Evidence," *PLL* 8 (1972): 273–86.

15. K. M. Rogers, "Fatal Inconsistency: Wycherley and *The Plain Dealer,*" *ELH* 28 (1961): 148–62.

16. *The Complete Plays of William Congreve,* ed. Herbert Davis (Chicago: University of Chicago Press, 1967), p. 120 (dedication).

17. See my "Otway and the Comic Muse," *SP* 73 (1976): 87–116.

18. *The Works of Nathaniel Lee,* ed. Thomas B. Stroup and Arthur L. Cooke, 2 vols. (1954–55; reprint ed., Metuchen, N.J.: Scarecrow Press, 1968), 2: 153. On this play see my "The Satiric Design of Nat. Lee's *The Princess of Cleve,*" *JEGP* 75 (1976): 117–38.

19. Montague Summers, *The Playhouse of Pepys* (1935; reprint ed., New York: Russell and Russell, 1964), p. 301.

20. [Aimwell] "Such Goodness who cou'd injure; I find my self unequal to the Task of Villain; she has gain'd my Soul, and made it honest like her own; ——I cannot, cannot hurt her. [Aside]

"Madam . . . I'm all a Lie, nor dare I give a Fiction to your Arms; I'm all Counterfeit except my Passion. . . . I am no Lord, but a poor needy Man, come with a mean, a scandalous Design to Prey upon your Fortune: —But the Beauties of your Mind and Person have so won me from my self, that like a trusty Servant, I prefer the Interest of my Mistress to my own." *The Complete Works of George Farquhar,* ed. Charles Stonehill, 2 vols. (1930; reprint ed., New York: Gordian, 1967), 2: 185.

21. See David S. Berkeley, "The Penitent Rake in Restoration Comedy," *MP* 49 (1952): 223–33. Of the numerous instances Berkeley finds before *Love's Last Shift* many occur in the plays of Behn, Durfey, and Shadwell. One wonders, if Mrs. Behn had lived a little longer, whether she might not have followed the others into proto-exemplary comedy.

22. Jean Gagen, "Congreve's Mirabell and the Ideal of the Gentleman," *PMLA* 79 (1964): 422–27. For a more sophisticated development of this position see Aubrey L. Williams, *An Approach to Congreve* (New Haven, Conn.: Yale University Press, 1979), ch. 10.

23. See Shirley Strum Kenny, "Richard Steele and the 'Pattern of Genteel Comedy,'" *MP* 70 (1972): 22–37.

24. See his satire on Dryden in a play called *The Reformation* (published 1673), a fascinating reply to *Marriage A-la-Mode* and a satire on Dryden's heroic work.

25. *Marriage Asserted* (London: Herringman, 1674), pp. 74–76, cited by Harold Brooks, "Some Notes on Dryden, Cowley, and Shadwell," *N&Q* (9 February 1935): 94–95.

26. See also Ben Ross Schneider, Jr., *The Ethos of Restoration Comedy* (Urbana, Ill.: University of Illinois Press, 1971), who finds the protagonists in all plays from *The Country Wife* to *The Conscious Lovers* exemplars of "generosity," a concept comprising liberality, plain-dealing, courage, and love. For a brief account of the eccentric methodology and fallacious conclusions in this study, see my review, *PQ* 51 (1972): 631–32.

27. For this term see Shirley Strum Kenny, "Humane Comedy," *MP* 75 (1977): 29–43, and my adaptation of it in "Marital Discord in English Comedy from Dryden to Fielding," *MP* 74 (1977): 248–72.

28. Most of John Harrington Smith's examples come quite late—for example, 1711, 1717, 1719, 1730, and 1744. Even so, the move toward the virtuous, exemplary protagonist is evident in such plays as Durfey's *The Virtuous Wife* (1679) and *The Banditti* (1686), Carlile's *The Fortune Hunters* (1689), Shadwell's *Bury Fair* (1689), and *The Scowrers* (1690), and Durfey's *Love for Money* (1691).

"I the Lofty Stile Decline":
Self-apology and the "Heroick Strain"
in Some of Swift's Poems

C. J. RAWSON

SWIFT disliked most forms of grand manner. He claimed, in a famous letter, never to have "written serious Couplets in my Life," although he insisted that he was not disclaiming seriousness of purpose, for he added: "yet never any without a moral View" (*Correspondence,* 4:52).[1] The denial of "serious Couplets" was partly, perhaps mainly, a matter of style. It seems to refer to his sparse use of the formal decasyllabic couplet, and to the fact that nearly all his poems contain signposted derision or parody of recognized "serious" genres: the inflated compliments of love-poetry, the grandiloquent Georgic *descriptio* of sunrise or storm, poems in praise of famous men, pastoral prettiness.

What is remarkable is that this most insistently parodic of satirists hardly ever attempted that favorite among contemporary poetic modes, the mock-*heroic* (in the strict sense, which implies mimicry of epic poems). There is, I think, no sustained example among his many poems, and the only example in his work as a whole is *The Battle of the Books.* The *Battle* is, in a sense, Swift's *Dunciad,* but its continuous epic reverberations, unlike the *Dunciad*'s, are flattened by another and competing parodic dimension, as well as by the humbler medium of prose. Between the Homeric or Virgilian mimicry and the modern fatuities of intellect which are played off against it in the *Battle,* an alternative and less majestic level of parody is interposed, that of mock-journalese. For the *Battle* is not only an inverted epic but also and simultaneously a newspaper report in prose: "A Full and True Account of the Battel Fought Last Friday. . . ."

This contributes to an impression that the epic parallels in the *Battle* derive their force from the ingenuity of Swift's misapplication of epic plot or of selected Homeric or Virgilian episodes, rather than from a sense of stylistic grandeurs deflated. In the *Dunciad*, by contrast, parallels of epic plot or incident are secondary objects of attention and are often loose or perfunctory, while the play of verbal majesty, of Virgilian or Miltonic resonance perverted to unworthy ends, is very strong. The dunces are not, like Swift's Moderns, allowed to find their natural mediocrity in the mimicry of Grub Street prose which Swift blends with the epic allusion. Or if they do, it is only in some of the notes that Pope added to the poem, and not in the original mock-epic structure. The mock-learning and the mock-epic are kept in separate compartments, whereas Swift's mock-epic and his mock-journalese are largely the same thing. There is also a continuous mock-learned thread in Swift's *Battle*, which purports to be both an epic and an edition of an epic, and this too is totally integrated into the primary text from the start, offering a further built-in buffer. In Pope's verse, on the other hand, nothing is interposed between epic grandiloquence and its grotesque application to the dunces, unless a constant reference away from verse to commentary permits the dunces to be seen, intermittently, in a more natural or quotidian absurdity. The epic formula is not in serious competition with any other level of parody within the poem, and the dunces, unlike Swift's Moderns, are allowed to mushroom out into a grotesque simulacrum of epic stature. Their lack of talent or grace, their venal depravity, their very insignificance swell into massive potency, acquiring a bloated magnitude from the epic majesty with which they are presented.

It is a truism that in the mock-heroic of Pope's *Dunciad*, the primary heroic grandeurs are disfigured rather than diminished in their duncic incarnation. At the same time a norm of rich epic eloquence is felt to survive the stylistic distortions, its residual majesties shining forth as a reminder of lost greatnesses and of an ideal of order and beauty longingly aspired to amid the disarray of the modern waste land. By an odd chemistry wholly foreign to Swift's manner, the world of the dunces is itself infected with these residual majesties: "Great Cibber's brazen, brainless brothers," "Slow rose a form, in majesty of Mud" (1. 32; 2. 326).

Swift never sought such effects. The risk of bringing them about may indeed have been one of the things that caused him normally to steer clear of mock-heroic. It is as though his avoidance of "lofty Stile" extended to whatever remnants of it might survive in the parody. Dryden had spoken in a well-known passage in the "Discourse Concerning Satire" of the grander forms of mock-heroic satire as "undoubtedly a species" of "heroic poetry itself" (Watson, 2: 149). The equivalence is one that Swift undoubtedly sensed and that could be expected to deter him. Dryden's praise of Boileau's Virgilian mock-heroic as "the most beautiful and most noble kind of satire," where "the majesty of the heroic" is "finely mixed" with satiric venom and raises what is "flat and vulgar, by the sublimity of the expression," would be enough by itself to turn Swift off, even if he had not already been temperamentally on his guard against "lofty Stiles." Dryden's description of Boileau's high mock-heroic occurs after a discussion of the lower and deliberately undignified satire called *burlesque,* which is identified with *Hudibras* and characterized by that octosyllabic "Doggrel Rhime" that Swift was soon to make his own (Watson 2: 147; *Poems,* 2: 631). Swift's despised "cousin" Dryden might almost have been laying down a scenario for Swift of what to go for and what to avoid.

Swift's avoidance of the high mock-heroic, with its echoes of Virgilian epic, derived mainly from a personal shyness of lofty postures. I suspect that there may also have been an instinctive recoil from situations in which his corrosive irony might risk accidentally subverting the revered epic originals, as his other parodies deliberately subverted the rhetoric of love-poetry or the solemn or falsifying routines of other genres. There is nothing in Swift's work quite like the *Dunciad's* Virgilian or Miltonic grandeurs, any more than of its other, nonepic, muddy majesties. He comes nearest to any kind of Dunciadic inflation in parts of a post-Dunciadic poem, "To Mr. Gay on his being Steward to the Duke of Queensberry" (1731; *Poems,* 2: 530 ff.), particularly in this portrait of a Minister (Walpole):

> A bloated M——r in all his Geer,
> With shameless Visage, and perfidious Leer,

Two Rows of Teeth arm each devouring Jaw;
And, *Ostrich*-like, his all-digesting Maw.
My Fancy drags this *Monster* to my View,
To show the World his chief Reverse in you.
Of loud un-meaning Sounds, a rapid Flood
Rolls from his Mouth in plenteous Streams of Mud;
With these, the Court and Senate-house he plies,
Made up of Noise, and Impudence, and Lies.

(Ll. 33–42)

But if this has a certain Dunciadic enormity, what it shares with the *Dunciad* is, appropriately, not so much the rolling heroic eloquence or the epic reminders, as the heaving grotesquerie. "Rolls from his Mouth in plenteous Streams of Mud" has something of Pope's large amplitudes of deformity, but little of the genuine stateliness with which, in Pope, the deformity is impregnated. In place of this stateliness are active energies of ugliness that are essentially Swiftian.

It is, however, even more characteristic of Swift to present these ugly energies in all their teeming unmitigated lowness, without any suggestion of grandeur. Pope's majestic evocation of "the large tribute of dead dogs" rolled by Fleet-ditch's "disemboguing streams" in *Dunciad*. 2. 271–72 is very different from the headlong chaotic animation of Swift's torrent of drowned puppies in "A Description of a City Shower":

Sweepings from Butchers Stalls, Dung, Guts, and Blood,
Drown'd Puppies, stinking Sprats, all drench'd in Mud,
Dead Cats and Turnip-Tops come tumbling down the Flood.
(Ll. 61–64; *Poems*, 1:139)

Pope allowed himself the risks of introducing large tributes of dead dogs in a work avowedly reminiscent of classical (notably Virgilian, but also Homeric and Miltonic) epic. His irony could take in the dunces without extending to their composite epic original, preserving some grandeurs of that original without insulting it. Swift both eschewed the grandeurs and guarded against the risk of insult, a risk to which his peculiarly destructive irony made him more vulnerable than Pope must have felt himself to be: it is significant that whereas both Dryden and Pope also produced "straight" heroic translations of the Homeric and Virgilian epics, Swift once attempted in 1692 to translate part of the *Aeneid* and found that it "sticks plaguily on my hands" (*Correspondence,* 1: 10). This was in the early period when Swift had not yet found his true voice and was, for the only time in his life, repeatedly attempting a sustained high style in his Pindaric odes. The broad Virgilian source of Swift's "City Shower" is Georgic, not epic, and the particular lines I have quoted interpose in addition a parody of Drydenian "triplets" between the notional evocation of Virgilian Georgic and the realities of a modern city shower, thus removing any element of literary mockery from a revered ancient to a despised modern. That "licentious Manner of modern Poets" made fashionable by "DRYDEN, and other Poets in the Reign of CHARLES II," to which Swift alerts us explicitly in a note of 1735, and which he mentions among some unflattering remarks about Dryden in a letter of the same year (*Poems,* 1:139–40n.; *Correspondence,* 4:321), does what the thread of mock-journalese had done in the *Battle.* It cushions the mimicked grandeurs of the ancients from the indignity of the modern duncehood to which they are applied: a modern stylistic buffer is provided whose own inflated pretensions can be mocked without risk of desecrating ancient altars.

It is pertinent to recall in this connection that Dryden appears in a humiliating encounter with Virgil himself in the *Battle.* His Virgilian pretensions express themselves in rusty armour and a helmet "nine times too large for the Head, which appeared Situate far in the hinder Part, . . . like a shrivled Beau from within the Pent-house of a modern Periwig" (*Works,* 1: 157–58). In the "City Shower," in a rare and subsidiary epic reminder alluding to Virgil's Trojan horse, the scene is likewise kept within the flattened confines of contemporary foppery, the "Bully *Greeks*" in Virgil's horse becoming modern beaux "Box'd in a Chair," who "Instead of paying Chair-men, run them thro" (ll. 43–52; *Poems,* 1: 139). Even this epic reminder avoids the normal mock-heroic procedure of setting up a grandiloquence for eventual puncturing. As in the *Battle* throughout, so in this more localized case the epic allusion is a matter of ingenious transposition rather than a parody of high style inappropriately applied. It evokes a Virgilian episode rather than the style in which that episode had been recounted. Its piquancy resides in the bizarre narrative parallel and not so much in the more usual form of upside-down mock-heroic rhetoric. As if to emphasize the point, the idiom of narration is flat, rather than impossibly high or outrageously low. Since Dryden, as we have seen, is deliberately derided within ten lines of this passage, it is more than probable that Dryden (who so conveniently translated Virgil's epic as well as his *Georgics*) was a notional presence in Swift's mind here also. The Virgil translation was famous, relatively recent, and undoubtedly under attack in *A Tale of a Tub* and the *Battle of the Books,* whose revised fifth edition appeared in the same year as "A Description of a City Shower" and probably within two months of it.[2] The verbal parallels with Dryden's translation of the episode of the wooden horse are not especially close, but the slightly ridiculous idea of him as the Mr. Virgil of his time was one which Swift would instinctively seek to exploit.[3] Swift's parody is not verbal, and no normal reader would rush to check the text. If Dryden's presence is sensed here in addition to being pointedly indicated in the triplet parody a few lines later, and in many other places throughout, then it acts by definition as a notional buffer between Swiftian parody and Virgilian original, letting Swift off any suspected anti-Virgilian hook or any unintended slur on epic dignity.

Swift's most explicit refusal of a "lofty Stile" occurs in *An Epistle to a Lady, Who Desired the Author to Make Verses on Her, in the Heroick Stile* (*Poems,* 2: 628–38). It contains an odd mixture of genial banter with some angry outbursts against Walpole and the Nation's Representers that sporadically strike a note of Juvenalian eloquence (the notion that Swift's poems, however, or his other works, are normally Juvenalian in manner is one of the oddities of Swift studies).[4] This Juvenalian element is not only sporadic and unstable in the *Epistle,* but is frequently mixed with and undercut by a variety of competing tones: some characteristically Swiftian touches of excremental slapstick, more informal gallantry of a Voiture-like mock-insulting sort to Lady Acheson, an appeal to Horatian lightness as a more effective satiric weapon than heavy denunciation. It is arguable that Swift is not much closer to Horace than to Juvenal, of course, though perhaps paradoxically nearer Horace's manner than was the high polished urbanity of Pope's Horatian *Imitations.*[5] The fact that Pope's Horatian poems often

had a Juvenalian flavor is nowadays well understood and com-
pounds the paradox, since this Juvenalian flavor makes itself felt
more frequently than in the supposedly Juvenalian Swift.

Horace, whom Swift "imitated" in a number of brisk flat and
mainly octosyllabic poems far removed in atmosphere from Pope's
majestic *Imitations* in English heroic meter, appealed to Swift not
because of his alleged urbanity, but because he too, as Dryden put
it, "refused . . . the loftiness of figures" and could be thought of as
often pitching his style rather "low" (Watson, 2: 144, 125 ff.).
Dryden's assertion that "Juvenal excels in the tragical satire, as
Horace does in the comical," and his frequent references to
Horace's tendency to "low style" by contrast with Juvenal's
"elevated . . . sonorous . . . noble . . . sublime and lofty" verse,
help us to understand how much likelier Swift might be to wish to
model himself on Horace than on Juvenal (Watson 2: 139–140,
130, 125–44). Again Dryden might almost be thought to have
provided a negative scenario for Swift, which is not of course to
say that Swift's tastes were determined by Dryden (any more than
it is to say that Swift disliked Juvenal's satire or the "serious"
grand style of the great classical epics, as distinct from not being
drawn to practice such styles himself).

The *Epistle to a Lady* is of particular interest here because it
contains a reasoned discussion of Swift's refusal of the "Heroick
Stile," and because this is presented as part of a portrait of his own
character. The *Epistle* is one of an important group of poetical
self-portraits, along with *Cadenus and Vanessa,* "The Author
upon Himself," and the *Verses on the Death,* which combine
perspicacious analysis with an element of self-mythologizing
apologia and place Swift in a rather public and exalted role. The
posture is "heroick," though in no strictly epic way, and Swift
undercuts it with some more or less embarrassed irony, as we shall
see. When the *Epistle* refuses a "Heroick Stile," it is at all events
only partly on grounds of literary theory, of notions about the
comparative force of Horatian and Juvenalian mockery, for
example. (On Swift's preference for the former, see also *Works,* 12:
33.) Nor is the "heroick" that Swift refuses here principally a matter
of epic, any more than the "heroick" postures he sometimes drifts
into are. It here embraces all poetic inflation, all grand gestures,
including especially those of compliments to women and those of

angry denunciation, though he flirts in this poem with the latter even as he pretends not to. There is in all this a guardedness that can be sensed implicitly in parodies of love-poetry (including those poems to Stella where stylistic undercutting coexists with undisguised personal tenderness), or in the self-deflating touches that accompany his flights of indignant asperity (however strongly intended, as in the attack on Walpole and the Nation's Representers in the *Epistle* itself, ll. 155 ff.). Swift's temperamental instinct to offer no high style without mocking it blends awkwardly with his self-exalting impulses, as well as helping to explain why he would not normally touch the epic forms of the "heroick," whether in parody or otherwise.

The *Epistle* is ostensibly concerned with the theory of satire and with the comparative effectiveness of different satiric methods. It describes, as I have argued elsewhere,[6] some special features of Swift's own highly individual and intimate form of aggression against his satiric victims. But what is especially interesting here is that the reasons he gives for refusing the "lofty Stile" (ll. 140, 210) are to a considerable extent autobiographical and introspective, even allowing for the element of lighthearted banter. It is not only that such a style is in some generalized way "against my nat'ral Vein" (l. 136):

> For your Sake, as well as mine,
> I the lofty Stile decline.
> I Shou'd make a Figure scurvy,
> And your Head turn Topsy-Turvy.
>
> (Ll. 217–20)

The last line is a genially finger-wagging throwaway, but the penultimate lets the light in on a temperamental truth, on that deep Swiftian guardedness against being caught in any posture of vulnerable solemnity, or any suspicion of that falsity that he was quick to attribute to most of the "high" styles practiced by his contemporaries. This guardedness, which goes beyond any mere sense of the ridiculousness of inflated rhetoric, is also, I believe, more personal than can be accounted for by canons of "classical restraint," which hardly restrained Swift in his more tearaway flights of comic fantasy, or by Horatian injunctions of *nil admirari*. Pope believed in and repeated such injunctions,[7] but they never get in the way of his effects of heroic or mock-heroic majesty, and are seldom used for the purpose of protective undercutting. Even the witty urbanities of Pope's Horatian poems are allowed their proud declamatory sweep, that confidently grandiloquent mastery exuded by Pope's use of the "serious Couplets" which Swift, as he tells us, almost never used. Swift's alternative choice of the octosyllabic "Doggrel Rhime" (l. 58, *Poems*, 2:631) as his normal verse-idiom proclaims among other things a need for self-undercutting that Pope seldom felt. The colloquial informality of Swift's imitations of Horace is a low-pitched thing, that of Pope's a proud and glowing urbanity. Pope is more "Augustan," though Swift, as I suggested, is perhaps closer to Horace. But the urge to self-deflation is largely Swift's own.

This "Doggrel Rhime" is the medium of most of the poems discussed in this paper: the *Epistle, On Poetry: A Rapsody, The Legion Club,* the *Verses on the Death*. It occurs, in other words, not only in outright parodies of poetic inflation that ostentatiously draw attention to the coarse vitality of our lower nature, as when the so-called scatological poems mock the routines of sentimental love-poetry or when "A Description of a City Shower" offers city squalor against descriptions of country scenes, but also in poems where Swift is concerned to project a self-image, and in which he seeks, with due show of reluctance and an embattled or embarrassed self-deflation, to fashion a "heroick" posture for himself.

I turn first to *On Poetry: A Rapsody* (1733; *Poems*, 2:639 ff.), a poem closely related in date and in matter to the *Epistle to a Lady*. It too, as the title indicates, bids to disengage itself, through signposted parody, from lofty styles, while quickening at times to intensities of denunciation whose manner is belied by the prevailing show of light-hearted badinage. Like the *Epistle, On Poetry* contains a political attack of some violence against Walpole's government, along with a somewhat different discussion of poetical matters. The anti-Walpole anger manifests itself less in intimacies of highly charged resentment than in a hard colloquial mimicry of the venal vulgarians of Walpole's world:

A Pamphlet in *Sir Rob's* Defense
Will never fail to bring in Pence;
Nor be concern'd about the Sale,
He pays his Workmen on the Nail.

(Ll. 187–90)

Walpole had no doubt of the violence of the satire and considered prosecuting Swift for this poem and the *Epistle*. It is not the first time in Swift that a display of punitive rage is flattened (not attenuated) by an eruption of harshly realistic impersonation. Much of the time, however, a loose, ostensibly genial lightness of Hudibrastic "Doggrel Rhime," and some notorious flights of mock-panegyric, complicate the tone. Queen Caroline was taken in by both the lightness and the irony, and had to be disabused of the notion that the poem was meant as a compliment.[8]

The poem has things in common with Pope's *Epistle to Augustus* (1737), a mock-panegyric whose irony was also missed, and which also deals with the difficulties met by living poets. (Swift was clearly thinking of Pope's Horatian original, *Epistle*, 2.1, where Augustus is addressed as a patron of the arts, and mentions it in a canceled passage: *Poems* 2. 658).[9] But although some of the outward tease is similar, there is about Pope's poem a polished externality that Swift lacks. This is not because Pope's ironic trickery is less complex:

> Besides, a fate attends on all I write,
> That when I aim at praise, they say I bite.
> *(Epistle to Augustus*, ll. 408–9)

The coils of this are beautifully ordered, and deserve the extra piquancy that they acquired when (as Pope must have anticipated) some people took for praise when he aimed to bite. But Pope's ironic effects, like the sharp finish of his verse, have a clarity of outline, a note of decorous authorial disengagement (we shall probably sense this whether we are "taken in" or not). And, whichever way one reads Pope's ironic scheme as a whole, it is clear which writers he is applauding (e.g., Swift, ll. 223 ff.) and which he is repudiating (e.g., Cibber, ll. 292–93).

Swift, on the other hand, writes in a fierce haze of ambiguity:

Not Beggar's Brat, on Bulk begot;
Nor Bastard of a Pedlar *Scot;*
Nor Boy brought up to cleaning Shoes,
The Spawn of *Bridewell,* or the Stews;
Nor Infants dropt, the spurious Pledges
Of *Gipsies* littering under Hedges,
Are so disqualified by Fate
To rise in *Church,* or *Law,* or *State,*
As he, whom *Phebus* in his Ire
Hath *blasted* with poetick Fire.

(Ll. 33–42)[10]

In one sense, Swift's posture is that of an enraged righteousness, the champion of poetry denouncing a vicious and philistine age, the true poet towering above Grub Street. The gesture of noble defiance is not sustained. But neither is it simply subverted by a formulaic drop from high to low. Swift does not subject it to the routine mechanical bathos that is the elementary staple of heroic burlesque. What might be called the high indignation of the Poet as Hero mingles instead with a more low-pitched note of irritated commiseration, with Swift hovering between the roles of embattled scourge and crushed victim, both poised against a poetry-scorning age. But there is also an ambiguous contempt for those who insist nevertheless on writing poems, the Grub Street poetasters as well as the true men, if any. Nora Jaffe has put it well: "every fool wants to write poetry, only a fool would want to be a poet."[11] The old paradoxes of folly and wisdom, no simple upside-down substitution of one for the other, but that unceasing reciprocal traffic which Erasmus taught Swift and to which Swift added new coils of ironic interpenetration in *A Tale of a Tub,* are actively in play here.

The testy commiseration and the dismissive contempt mingle with a kind of autobiographical self-involvement. The unlucky poet is part Swift, part Grub Street hack. The two are sometimes kept clearly separate, and sometimes not. I do not here refer to the supposed transition from an authorial speaker in the earlier part of the poem to the "old experienc'd Sinner, / Instructing thus a young Beginner" (ll. 75–76) who is sometimes said to take over from him.[12] This is no "new narrator," suddenly introduced to propound upside-down values, but the original authorial narrator inviting the poetic beginner in effect to "listen to an old hand." The critical inappropriateness of such tidy-minded searching for clearly separate personae is more than usually obvious here. The "old experienc'd Sinner" actually begins with some straight Swiftian good sense, soon admittedly to be undercut by a world-weary, cynical irony itself wholly characteristic of Swift (ll. 77 ff.). But more important still is the fact that this supposed "new narrator," unlike such speakers as Gulliver or the "author" of the *Tale,* is always fully conscious, when he utters his upside-down ironies, that he is himself being sarcastic, as distinct from being the innocent carrier of Swift's sarcasms: ("In modern Wit all printed Trash, is / Set off with num'rous *Breaks*————and *Dashes*————"; "Your Poem in its modish Dress, / Correctly fitted for the Press, / Convey by Penny-Post to *Lintot* . . ." ll. 93–94, 105–7).

But there are some more indefinite interpenetrations between Swift and the things he attacks that deserve notice here. Good poets and Grub Street hacks are to some extent in the same boat, and the hostility to poetry of a philistine age may in fact work against both in much the same way. Thus when a poet runs foul of malicious critics, and the Town marks him "for a Dunce," attributing to him "The vilest Doggrel *Grubstreet* sends . . . 'Till some fresh Blockhead takes your Place" (ll. 137–42), the context does not guarantee that the poor man is not, in fact, a dunce. But at the same time Swift's official animus is directed against the critics who abuse him, displaced "Blockhead" though he too might be, and Swift's own annoyance at misattribution to himself of Grub Street doggerel is also meant to be detected. A few lines earlier, Swift derisively advises poets not to own their poems, and to listen silently when these are discussed:

> Be sure at *Will*'s the following Day,
> Lie Snug, and hear what Criticks say.
> And if you find the general Vogue
> Pronounces you a stupid Rogue;
> Damns all your Thoughts as low and little,
> Sit still, and swallow down your Spittle.
>
> (Ll. 117–22)

If the poor poet gets his share of the satirist's contempt, he gets a rough commiseration too. It had happened to Swift. In 1710, he wrote to Stella: "I dined to-day at lady Lucy's, where they ran down my *Shower*; and said *Sid Hamet* was the silliest poem they ever read, and told Prior so, whom they thought to be the author of it."[13]

Elsewhere in the poem, Swift does not sympathize so openly with his Grub Street hacks. But even where they emerge as unequivocally bad, a queer unadmitted Swiftian participation enters into the account. The scurrying vitality with which Swift describes them actually mirrors their own busy, disorderly doings:

> Thro' ev'ry Alley to be found,
> In Garrets high, or under Ground:
> And when they join their *Pericranies*,
> Out skips a *Book of Miscellanies.*
>
> (Ll. 315–18)

We are nowadays used to the idea that Swift's writing often acquires exuberance when he is mimicking the unruly. But an uppish acerbity is quick to assert itself as he shows unruliness settling to a kind of unnatural "order":

> If, on *Parnassus'* Top you sit,
> You rarely bite, are always bit:
> Each Poet of inferior Size
> On you shall rail and criticize;
> And strive to tear you Limb from Limb,
> While others do as much for him.
>   The Vermin only teaze and pinch
> Their Foes superior by an Inch.
> So, Nat'ralists observe, a Flea
> Hath smaller Fleas that on him prey,
> And these have smaller Fleas to bite 'em,
> And so proceed *ad infinitum* . . .
>
> (Ll. 329–40)[14]

On this disorder, a pattern is, in a way, imposed. The flea-biting chain proceeds in regular gradation. But it is a regularity that not only stands "due Subordination" on its head, so that the lower eat the higher, but also proceeds, unchecked and uncheckable, ad infinitum. The disorders of Parnassus also occur in Pope. But Pope does not organize them into systems of "anti-order" so much as *containing* them in the true "order" of his witty eloquence and of his buoyant powers of summation:

> The Dog-star rages! nay 'tis past a doubt,
> All *Bedlam,* or *Parnassus,* is let out:
> Fire in each eye, and Papers in each hand,
> They rave, recite, and madden round the land.
> *(Epistle to Dr. Arbuthnot,* ll. 3–6)

The disorders seem almost created to display the control. Where Swift might be imagined sitting quizzically and self-mockingly on "*Parnassus*' Top," the high poet indistinguishable from any "Blockhead" who might take his place, Pope establishes himself overtly and without undercutting as the eminent poet, flatteringly besieged by mobs, openly enjoying his mock-annoyance as he craves protection from visitors ("Tye up the knocker, say I'm sick, I'm dead," l. 2) or protests at being blamed for the idleness of poetry-minded students and the elopement of wives (the fathers and husbands cursing "Wit, and Poetry, and *Pope*," ll. 23–26). When Pope's writing shows "due Subordination" formulaically reversed, as in the *Dunciad,* where bad poets become heroes, the reversal itself acquires a kind of positive grandeur, not only preserving some of the majesty against which the dunces are played off, but allowing this majesty to rub off on the dunces. Pope's dunces are raised to a queer heroic stature, meeting the poet's heroic speech at his level, if only as huge nuisances whose massiveness and urgency makes them worthy of high eloquence: Swift's dunces are allowed to be no more heroic than the poet himself, and Swift's irony more readily drops him to their level, than raises them to his.

The lofty poet on "*Parnassus*' Top," like the angry scourge of the early part of *On Poetry,* preserves something of his noble lineaments, complicated not by burlesque deflation but by a continuous unresolved skepticism about his own credentials, about the status of poetry (whoever the poet), and about the dignity of heroic postures. Such skepticism is not evident in Pope, even in the

Dunciad. And to the limited extent that Swift is prepared positively to indulge the heroic postures, they are never identified, as in
the *Dunciad*, with the epic. In the mock-panegyric on the king,
where celebration of martial conquest comes up for special disre-
pute, it is the historical Alexander the Great (a traditionally
accepted real-life example of evil tyranny) rather than any
"conqu'ring Hero" of ancient epic who is invoked:

> Confest the conqu'ring Hero stands.
> *Hydaspes, Indus,* and the *Ganges,*
> Dread from his Hand impending Changes.
>
> (Ll. 420–22)[15]

This is perhaps the nearest Swift comes in this poem to a more
traditional mock-heroic, and in it he notably sidesteps any
specifically *epic* allusion. The contempt for the heroic is unmixed,
both on stylistic and moral grounds, but the revered ancient epics
are untouched. Whether Swift was instinctively guarding against
an awkward and unacknowledged disrespect or merely displaying
his customary reluctance to lapse into "lofty Stile" even of a
reverse or Dunciadic sort, I am not sure. I suspect that both
elements were present in an obscure and subtle combination.

But of the oddly unresolved blend of lofty denunciation, proud
loyalty to *"Parnassus'* Top," instinctive deflation and self-
deflation, and self-implication in the low character and predica-
ment of the Grub Streeters, there is no doubt. It is a continuously
active ambivalence in the poem and a source of the poem's vital
strength. Swift's writings thrive on mixed feelings and unresolved
tensions: their urgency comes precisely from the unavailability of
comforting certainties. The poem's peculiar assurance comes partly
from its wholehearted mimicry of undignified types. Swift's own
superiority to them is easily implied. But its paradoxical coexis-
tence with a readiness to be identified with them at the same time
bears in its modest way the stamp of his major prose satires.

There is an aptness in the fact that Swift's exposure of a radical
and universal human folly in *A Tale of a Tub* or in *Gulliver's
Travels* should be felt in a sense to implicate him, since its radical
and universal character would by definition be questionable if it
did not. But a further sense of self-implication is felt in the sheer

inwardness with which Swift mimics the follies that he parodied. *A Tale of a Tub,* the first and greatest of Swift's major satires on Grub Street as *On Poetry: A Rapsody* is the last, is also the most striking example of the virtuosity and the high imaginative pressure with which Swift was able to imitate the authors he derided. All parody is impersonation, and it is arguable that its ubiquity in Swift's work springs from a certain temperamental reluctance to expose himself too openly in his own person, just as his frequent resort to the obliquities of irony protected him from the vulnerabilities and the simplifying commitments of plain statement. But the *Tale* is in particular a parody of authors who talk much about themselves, a practice that Swift both disliked in general and also himself (as I shall argue) indulged in. When he did so overtly, the results were usually awkward in proportion to the overtness. It is in that work, more than in any other, that Swift emerges in buoyant mastery of the chaos he exposes, but he achieves that mastery largely by an impersonation of the chaos. The satirist who displays this mastery is also vividly present, but the superiority that he earns both by his virtuosity and by his rightness and good sense is assumed, and not declared. The element of self-mockery is powerfully evident, but it is a self-mockery protected from self-inflation and unselfconsciously rendered because it is presented as mockery of others. It is absorbed in the universal satire without fuss. *On Poetry: A Rapsody* shares some of this power, though the poem is less brilliantly and less totally parodic than the *Tale.* The fact that it too is largely free from overt self-disclosure may be a reason for this power.

In the *Verses on the Death,* and perhaps even in the *Epistle to a Lady,* as in a self-justifying poem like *Cadenus and Vanessa,* Swift allows himself to be the subject of his own work in an explicit and prominent way, rather than in the manner which is merely implicit in *On Poetry: A Rapsody.* In these poems his determination not to "make a Figure scurvy" through the use of a "lofty Stile" sometimes comes into conflict with self-justifying purposes and the impulse to create a virtuous or impressive self-image. The irony implicit in the low-pitched chatter of the "Doggrel Rhime" and in a host of local self-undercutting devices turns into a simpering luxury of self-regard. Sterne has made us familiar with a self-mockery in which the author's very pretense of not taking himself seriously is in itself a way of taking himself seriously and of drawing attention to himself: to his wit, his perspicacity, his ability to laugh at himself. Swift saw into this particularly well. It is a trait which he mocked in *A Tale of a Tub* with such thorough and intimate understanding that Sterne later felt able to throw himself into the Tubbaean manner, mimicking Swift's mimicry and consciously outfacing Swift with the enhanced solipsistic luxury of an additional cherished coil of self-mockery. Tristram Shandy was pleased to think that his book would "swim down the gutter of Time" with Swift's *Tale*.[16]

Sterne had no inhibitions about displaying his self-regard, and was perfectly willing to cultivate "a Figure scurvy" if that advanced the opportunities for self-display. Swift lacked the same freedom. Swift's most spectacular self-displays reside in dazzling satiric tours de force of which he is not himself the subject, and the awkwardness that (as I suggested) often came over his writing when he came to talk about himself is especially evident when "lofty" or self-justifying claims needed making.

The *Verses on the Death* contain an attempt at presenting a noble image of himself (as incorruptible author, defender of freedom, national hero) that lacks the courage of its convictions. The poem is without that open readiness to eloquent self-apology which is traditionally permitted to and indeed expected of satirists, and which Pope shows in the *Epistle to Dr. Arbuthnot* and several other related Horatian poems. Swift hides behind the robes of his "impartial" commentator in a manner in no way analogous to his use of the "old experienc'd Sinner" of *On Poetry: A Rapsody*, who remains the authorial narrator and who as it happens does not have to praise or even talk much about himself. In the *Verses*, too, the "Doggrel Rhime" seems aimed unsuccessfully at toning down the glowing self-panegyric that most readers of the *Verses* take the commentator's speech to be. I sense in this a loss of nerve and even a certain falsity on Swift's part, to which I shall return and which is not on the whole evident in Sterne. Sterne is to this extent true to his ironic undercuttings that he genuinely does not seek to see himself in an *exalted* role, just as Pope, in the proud self-projections of the *Epistle to Dr. Arbuthnot*, genuinely *does*. Swift

clearly wished the credit both for meriting such a role and for
seeming not to claim it, and the result was a peculiarly transparent
half-heartedness on both fronts. (Similar embarrassments damage
Cadenus and Vanessa, a poem in which Swift is likewise bent on
setting up a righteous image of himself, though in the domain of
private relationships rather than of public (literary or political)
distinction. It is worth noting that, unlike Swift's, Sterne's irony is
usually free from earnest attempts at self-exculpation, just as it is
free of exalted pretensions to any kind of "heroic" achievement.
But *Cadenus and Vanessa* and other poems about Swift's personal
or private life are outside the scope of the present discussion).

The *Verses on the Death of Doctor Swift. Written by Himself:
Nov. 1731* (1739; *Poems,* 2: 551 ff.) begin, as is well known, with
La Rochefoucauld's maxim:

> "In all Distresses of our Friends
> We first consult our private Ends,
> While Nature kindly bent to ease us,
> Points out some Circumstance to please us."
>
> (Ll. 7–10)[17]

Swift goes on to exemplify this kind of envy, first generally (a
friend performs a heroic deed, but we want to crop his laurels
rather than to feel outdone, etc.), and then as it is found in himself.
A regrettable personal note is struck early. The lines in question
are favorites, and in a sense understandably:

> In POPE, I cannot read a Line,
> But with a Sigh, I wish it mine:
> When he can in one Couplet fix
> More Sense than I can do in Six . . .
>   Why must I be outdone by GAY,
> In my own hum'rous biting way?
>
> (Ll. 47 ff.)

We are fond of this form of coterie compliment, especially when
the members of the coteries are figures we admire. We respond, as
we are expected to respond, to this convivial solidarity among the

great, their aristocratic ease as they bow to a witty informality
while preserving an impressive eloquence amid the familiar and
colloquial talk. There is a long and distinguished tradition of such
poems, from the Renaissance to Yeats. But the example of Yeats
perhaps shows what is lacking here. Yeats could blend eloquence
of compliment with wit (and indeed with witty reservations) in a
way that gave full value to both and undercut neither:

> Lionel Johnson comes the first to mind,
> That loved his learning better than mankind,
> Though courteous to the worst; much falling he
> Brooded upon sanctity
> Till all his Greek and Latin learning seemed
> A long blast upon the horn that brought
> A little nearer to his thought
> A measureless consummation that he dreamed.[18]

Yeats is writing from a deep conviction that sublimity, or at least
high tributes, may coexist not only with the affectionate, but with
the ridiculous. Ezra Pound, recounting Mr. Verog's memories of
the same Lionel Johnson, also achieves such a blend, in a drier
idiom:

> For two hours he talked of Gallifet;
> Of Dowson; of the Rhymers' Club;
> Told me how Johnson (Lionel) died
> By falling from a high stool in a pub . . .[19]

These blends are outside Swift's range. His sensibility only allowed
the informal, or the ridiculous, to undermine, not reinforce, nor
interact on equal terms with, sublimity—or sublime pretension. In
Yeats, the bard and the joker, or clown, could unite in ways that
were temperamentally, and perhaps culturally, impossible for
Swift. Yeats, stalking on "through the terrible novelty of light,"
while the "great sea-horses bare their teeth and laugh at the dawn,"
has put on the guise of the mountebank: "Malachi Stilt-Jack am
I."[20] The clowns and mountebanks who rise above the crowd in
Swift's prose and verse, on the other hand, are always degraded
creatures, despite Swift's feeling at some level that they are instances of a radical folly that exists in him, as in all mankind. Or

perhaps *because* of this feeling, he felt the need to keep apart as much as possible the seriously cherished from the mockingly rejected in the "ridiculous tragedy" of life.

And so his mixture of high compliment and easy joke fails to hit the right note. The self-depreciation with which he involves himself in the universal charge that all men are envious turns *in fact* into a greater compliment to himself, than to Pope or Gay: for it shows, simperingly, that he is *not* envious of his friends, and generously recognizes their merit.[21]

The coterie-compliments go on to include other friends, and the compliment to Arbuthnot contains perhaps the most famous piece of self-assessment:

> ARBUTHNOT is no more my Friend,
> Who dares to Irony pretend;
> Which I was born to introduce,
> Refin'd it first, and shew'd its Use.
>
> (Ll. 55–58)

The poem then proceeds to apply La Rochefoucauld's saying by imagining, now that Swift is elderly, how people are forecasting his death, and how they will react when he dies. They talk of "his out-of-fashion'd Wit" (l. 92), his faded poetic talents (l. 99 ff.), his failing health—comforting themselves that "'it is not yet so bad with us'" (l. 116). When he dies, there will be barbed praise or open malice from both friends and foes:

> Some paragraph in ev'ry Paper,
> To *curse* the Dean, or *bless* the *Drapier*
>
> (Ll. 167–68);

and even "those I love" will take the news calmly:

> Poor POPE will grieve a Month; and GAY
> A Week; and ARBUTHNOTT a Day.
>
> (Ll. 207–8).

His "female Friends"

> Receive the News in *Doleful Dumps,*
> "The Dean is dead, *(and what is Trumps?)*"

and the detailed mimicry of their reaction elicits some characteristically amusing stylized reportage of trivial society talk (ll. 225 ff.). A year later, the Dean is half-forgotten, his books out of date, while Cibber, Duck, and Henley reign (ll. 245 ff.).

For over 200 lines, these praises and dispraises (often wittily and tellingly captured) carry on a pretense of wise lighthearted acknowledgment of the world's ways, while actually providing Swift with a context for talking about himself. It is not simply that an "excuse" is provided for self-apology (his services to Ireland, etc), or for satire of some favorite foes. It is that a formula of transparent but "saving" obliquity has been found for keeping the focus fondly trained on the person of the author, not only on what is said about him and by whom (with all the piquancies inherent in testing the comments against their source), but on the primary authorial self-consciousness that suffuses the very nature of the exercise. The result has the strange falsity to which I have referred. It is Shandean without the Shandean self-acceptance, claiming impersonal distance while indulging in a feast of self-regard.

Then, at ll. 299 ff., Swift moves in with a bid to set the record straight. "Suppose me dead," and then suppose a quite impartial commentator summing up "My Character," career, and achievement. The note of octosyllabic banter is maintained, often achieving a rather moving effect in its brisker, more low-pitched moments:

> "As for his Works in Verse and Prose,
> I own my self no Judge of those:
> Nor, can I tell what Criticks thought 'em;
> But, this I know, all People bought 'em."
>
> (Ll. 309–12)

But of course this pointed badinage has a new "speaker" and a new status. Some degree of witty disengagement is still presupposed, which actually permits some eloquent compliments to flower freely and claim an increased attention. The passage is famous for the many memorable epigrammatic formulations that have proved so seductive to critics, yielding their pithy quotability to feasts of affectionate allusion, or providing the titles of chapters and books:

> "Expos'd the Fool, and lash'd the Knave . . ."

"But what he writ was all his own . . ."

"Of no Man's Greatness was afraid . . ."

"Fair LIBERTY was all his Cry;
For her he stood prepar'd to die . . ."

Many of these claims were true. That is part of Swift's greatness, as a writer and as a man. That greatness does not, however, rest on his readiness to coin the luxuriously self-cherishing phrases, least of all to evade full responsibility for them by ascribing them to an impartial critic, preserving a Hudibrastic lightness, standing aside. On the themes of dedication to virtue, independence of the "great," or, for that matter, Irish patriotism, we may prefer the frankly heroic stances of Pope or of Yeats:

> Ask you what Provocation I have had?
> The strong Antipathy of Good to Bad.

> And who unknown defame me, let them be
> Scriblers or Peers, alike are *Mob* to me.[22]

> John Synge, I and Augusta Gregory, thought
> All that we did, all that we said or sang
> Must come from contact with the soil, from that
> Contact everything Antaeus-like grew strong.
> We three alone in modern times had brought
> Everything down to that sole test again,
> Dream of the noble and the beggar-man . . .

> . . . come to this hallowed place
> Where my friends' portraits hang and look thereon;
> Ireland's history in their lineaments trace;
> Think where man's glory most begins and ends,
> And say my glory was I had such friends.[23]

Swift dared not risk such things. This gives the praises of his impartial critic their awkwardness. They have a Yeatsian eloquence, but no Yeatsian commitment to it, and an unfocused self-humor gets in the way. Swift's most moving direct praise of himself and perhaps his only really Juvenalian utterance comes not in English verse, but in Latin prose, literally lapidary, distanced by the impersonal formality of an ancient language, and intended for posthumous reading—in his epitaph.[24] It was Yeats who translated this into memorable English lines:

> Swift has sailed into his rest;
> Savage indignation there
> Cannot lacerate his breast.
> Imitate him if you dare,
> World-besotted traveller; he
> Served human liberty.[25]

The last line recalls "Fair LIBERTY was all his Cry" in the discourse of Swift's impartial commentator (and, like it, has been used as the title of a book on Swift). But its strength is that it is not found in that discourse, and that Yeats, uninhibited in the utterance of such majesties, Englished it.

Neither Pope nor Yeats needed to pretend that they were not ennobling themselves. It is rightly accepted that their "masks" permitted this, that they were speaking in the robes of priests of the muses. We are often reminded that Swift was likewise adopting a "mask."[26] But the cases are different, and the reminders usually beg the question. Such personae are, of course, only tones of voice formalized into pseudo-fictions.[27] This fact does not diminish their importance. But it has become a fashion for critics to assume that "masks" can be divorced from authors, or that they absolve an author from responsibility for what he writes, including his adoption and his specific choice of "masks," and the use to which he puts them. If we must talk of "masks," we must consider the entire (and often intimate and awkward) relation of the "mask" to the poet and the poem. The majestic personae of Pope and of Yeats are frankly adopted in their own name and release some of these poets' finest energies, whereas those of Swift's *Verses on his Death* are coyly attributed to another and only succeed in turning Swift in on himself, confining and distorting his power.

I have assumed so far that the impartial commentator speaks only the truth, or truths that (granted a degree of defensive indirection on Swift's part) Swift wants us to take literally. This may not in all cases be so. Some readers like to see a mock-inflation and claim that some statements are meant to be recognized as teasingly untrue. Examples of this may occur in the early parts of the impartial commentator's speech (e.g., "'To steal a Hint was never known, / But all he writ was all his own'" [ll. 317–18], which, to the knowing reader, shows Swift doing exactly what he says he isn't in a manner that piquantly anticipates Tristram Shandy in the opening lines of the fifth volume of Sterne's novel).[28] And there is a note of poker-faced foolery near the end, beginning at l. 455: "'Perhaps I may allow, the Dean / Had too much Satyr in his Vein.'" In that section, it is claimed, for example, that "'Malice never was his Aim; / He lash'd the Vice but spar'd the Name'"; or that "'His Satyr points at no Defect, / But what all Mortals may correct.'" The claims are surprising for one who so often wrote *ad hominem,* and whose frequent pretense was that mankind was unmendable.[29] At least one critic has argued that such examples indicate a sustained undercutting of the entire panegyrick.[30] This seems very unlikely. It is almost more probable that, in claims that appear to us more literally untrue, Swift forgot himself so far as to think they were true, or at least (as in the two examples I quoted last) felt that they were proper claims for a satirist to make in a formal apologia.[31] But the passage beginning at ll. 455–56 does open with an avuncular concessiveness or mock-depreciation, and by the time we reach the end of the poem, a beautifully poised wry humor has unmistakably taken over:

> "He gave the little Wealth he had,
> To build a House for Fools and Mad:
> And shew'd by one satyric Touch,
> No Nation wanted it so much:
> That Kingdom he hath left his Debtor,
> I wish it soon may have a Better."

(Ll. 479–84)

The perfect modulation of this, its dry generosity and the sting in its tail, the final quick routine of macabre courtesy, laconically mock-modest yet just the sort of thing to say, are very impressive. They confirm that Swift has not been taking his own solemnity lying down and encourage our willingness to see more than the very generalized degree of humorous undercutting that we are aware of throughout. But the nature, degree, and direction of this undercutting remain uncertain and unclear. This uncertainty differs from those powerful bewilderments that Swift's great prose satires induce in the reader, in that it is here without point, a mere unclarity of focus not wholly in Swift's control, rather than a purposeful and unsettling satiric aggression. There is a relation between the two, which is to be found in that temperamental reluctance to put his emotional cards on the table which also led to the more formal devices of indirection and concealment in the poem's whole structure. In the *Tale, Gulliver,* the *Modest Proposal,* indirection and self-concealment were adapted to the purposes of a great satiric vision. Fiction gave release for the transformation of huge egocentric pressures into a deeply penetrating, and painfully self-implicating, imaginative vision of the human lot. Precisely the same pressures, recognized with whatever unconscious embarrassment, made him fail when the subject was, officially, himself.[32]

Swift came closest to the grand manner, as well as to direct self-revelation, in his late, angry poems on Irish affairs. A passage from the *Verses on the Death* is typical of this late style. Swift is looking back to the period after Queen Anne's death, when he felt himself to be exiled in Ireland,

> Pursu'd by base envenom'd Pens,
> Far to the Land of Slaves and Fens;
> A servile Race in Folly nurs'd,
> Who truckle most, when treated worst.
>
> (Ll. 395–98)

This looks back to the intensely painful exasperations of the Holyhead poems of 1727 (*Poems,* 2: 420 ff.), and forward to some somber, at times somewhat Brechtian, sarcasms like these, of 1736:

> Better we all were in our Graves
> Than live in Slavery to Slaves,
> Worse than the Anarchy at Sea,
> Where Fishes on each other prey;
> Where ev'ry Trout can make as high Rants
> O'er his Inferiors as our Tyrants;

And swagger while the Coast is clear:
But should a lordly Pike appear,
Away you see the Varlet scud,
Or hide his coward Snout in Mud.
Thus, if a Gudgeon meet a Roach
He dare not venture to approach;
Yet still has Impudence to rise,
And, like *Domitian*, leap at Flyes.

(Poems, 3: 824)

These angers differ from those of Swift's earlier political poems. They combine with an exceptional exposure of private feeling: the deep anxiety about Stella in the Holyhead verses, for example, and more generally the painful and highly personal blend of contempt and loyalty, dislike and affection, that he felt towards Ireland particularly in these late years. The result is not so much a more intense charge of feeling as such, but a more urgent warmth and directness of invective. The fierce flat astringency of such early political lampoons as "The Description of a Salamander" (1705; *Poems,* 1: 82 ff.) or "A Satirical Elegy on the Death of a Late Famous General" (1722; *Poems,* 1: 295 ff.) opens up, in the later poems, to a nakedness of indignation much less undercut by cool ironic indirections. The stylized elaboration of the animal formula in the "Salamander" gives way to the ritualized cataloguing directness of the animal imagery of "Better we all were in our Graves," and the polished sarcasms of both the "Salamander" and the "Late Famous General" turn into the headlong cursing of *Traulus* (1730; *Poems,* 3: 794 ff.):

Traulus of amphibious Breed,
Motly Fruit of Mungril Seed:
By the *Dam* from Lordlings sprung,
By the *Sire* exhal'd from Dung:
Think on ev'ry Vice in both,
Look on him and see their Growth. . . .

(Pt. 2. 1–6)

A list follows, full of splenetic hauteurs and a kind of cantankerous exuberance:

Let me now the Vices trace,
From his *Father*'s scoundrel Race,
Who cou'd give the Looby such Airs?
Were they Masons, were they Butchers?
Herald lend the Muse an answer;
From his *Atavus* and Grandsire;
This was dext'rous at his Trowel,
That was bred to kill a Cow well:
Hence the greazy clumsy Mien,
In his Dress and Figure seen. . . .

(Ll. 23–32)

But even here, where the hostility is entirely undisguised and the invective particularly direct, Swift does not allow us to feel that he is wholly abandoned to his indignation. He is playing, with a signposted and headlong exuberance, at the ancient satirist's game of the magical curse, of rituals aimed at rhyming rats or enemies to death. The primitive curse, from which satire has one of its deepest origins, was widely associated not only with the ancient Greeks, but (as Swift, along with many others, including Sidney, Spenser, Shakespeare, Jonson, and Sir William Temple, well knew) very commonly with the old Irish.[33] Indeed, some of the Irish examples (both of description and of imprecation) have the kind of brutal animal imagery Swift uses in *Traulus* and elsewhere.[34] A sense of the primitive fun of cursing comes through, and of the question-and-answer ritual that often goes with it, as well as the cheeky pleasures of clumsy rhyming, or of elegantly spiteful summations, which perhaps signal a more sophisticated poet playing with the primitive modes:

In him, tell me which prevail,
Female Vices most, or Male,
What produc'd them, can you tell?
Human Race, or *Imps* of *Hell*.

(Ll. 53–56)

We may compare this with Pope's portrait of Sporus (*Epistle to Dr. Arbuthnot*, 1734, ll. 305 ff.). The two passages, as it happens, share some memorable images, their victims being, each in his own way, "amphibious," and also noisomely (rather than grandly) Satanic, "familiar Toad" or "*Imp* of *Hell.*" Both lampoons combine the exacerbations of an intense hostility, with a certain manifest enjoyment of the act of satiric invective. But where Pope's passage purrs and crackles with loving exactitudes of spite, Swift's drums away with a crude ritual abandon. This is no mere undigested self-expression, however. Swift's apparent directness of imprecation is transformed, as it were, by its own own stylized exaggerations, into a semi-fictive domain of denunciation, with rules and pleasures peculiar to itself. The inventive automatism of accumulated insult leaves the poet slightly detached from the operation, most delicately ironic in effect when the verbal fabric is most crudely simple. This element of comic disengagement contrasts with Pope's extremely studied verbal precisions, and their suggestion of a very close and almost self-absorbed dedication to the attack. The fact affords no consolation to Lord Allen, Swift's victim, and hardly reduces Swift's hostility: but it does suggest that Swift (no less than Pope) is master of the invective, not its slave, and that hate can still be fun—not in self-enclosed luxuries of spite, but in an open, vigorous way.

The same is true of *The Legion Club* (1736; *Poems*, 3: 827 ff.), an attack on the Irish House of Commons, which wanted to deprive the Irish clergy of certain tithes. A series of personal curses on Irish M.P.s shows a ritual exuberance similar to that in *Traulus*. Sir Thomas Prendergast becomes

> . . . *Tom,* Halloo Boy,
> Worthy Offspring of a Shoeboy
> Footman, Traytor, vile Seducer,
> Perjur'd Rebel, Brib'd Accuser; . . . .
>
> (Ll. 67–70)

There is again a quality of primitive incantation about this, a high-spirited exercise (part mimicry, part angry indulgence) in the syncopated rhetoric of a magic chant. And the suggestion of magical ritual is increased by a question-and-answer routine, in which the poet asks the club's keeper to identify the various M.P.'s, or in which rhetorical questions call forth a stylized shower of excremental defilement—as here (on the subject of M.P.'s Harrison, Dilkes, and Clements):

> Such a Triplet could you tell
> Where to find on this Side Hell?
> *H*———, and *D*———, and *C*———,
> Souse them in their own Ex-crements.

(Ll. 183–86)

The hyphenation of the last word, if authorial, gives added signposting of the quality of delightedly rhythmic, ceremonial abuse.

This very strong and very angry poem would not have had its formidable power if Swift had been wholly and literally abandoned to the simple primary indignation that is at its core. A powerful stylization, a massive mechanization of hatred once again give to the apparent directness a saving hint of comic disengagement, a suggestion of authorial control and enjoyment.

The poem begins on an almost Audenesque note, with this picture of the frail individual against the background of a large impersonal government building:

> As I strole the City, oft I
> Spy a Building large and lofty . . .

But by the next two lines the speaker, instead of being overwhelmed by the monolithic institution, has taken its full measure:

> Not a Bow-shot from the College,
> Half the Globe from Sense and Knowledge.

By the end of the poem, it is the House and its inmates who have been annihilated by the poet's rich splendors of abusive performance. The stream of invective is framed or supported by a Swiftian mythology in which the Parliament becomes a Club, a madhouse, and Hell, and in which some of the most powerful satiric configurations of Swift's earlier writings reappear, for the last time. The Club's name comes from the unclean spirit in Mark 5:9 "My name is Legion: for we are many." Very rapidly it acquires overtones of

Yahoo-dom, with its busy dung-ridden quarrelsomeness, its "throwing" of "Ordure" (l. 19), its filthy besetting of the Gulliverian narrator ("By this odious Crew beset, / I began to rage and fret . . .," ll. 93–94). Very early, the image of the madhouse is established. It partakes of the Academy of Modern Bedlam (*Tale*, Sec. 9) and the School of Political Projectors (*Gulliver*, 3. 6.), the poet suggesting that the M.P.s be put

> Each within his proper Cell;
> With a Passage left to creep in,
> And a Hole above for peeping. . . .
>
> While they sit a picking Straws
> Let them rave of making Laws;
> While they never hold their Tongue,
> Let them dabble in their Dung. . . .
>   (Ll. 44–46, 49–52)

At the entrance is a world of Shadows, as though from the Cave of Spleen, with a customary mixture of allegorized abstractions, and "antic Shapes" gruesomely visualized:

> *Poverty,* and *Grief,* and *Care,*
> Causeless *Joy,* and true *Despair;*
> *Discord* periwigg'd with Snakes,. . .
>   (Ll. 89–91)

Throughout the entire poem run insistent evocations of Hell (Satanic and classical), and from l. 11 until the closing curse at l. 242, the members of the Legion Club are described as Demoniacs or Satanists: "May their God, the Devil confound 'em."

It is, oddly, in this most overtly low piece of neo-primitive invective, that Swift indulges in one of his most sustained flights of Virgilian allusion. Faulkner, cited by Harold Williams, identifies a series of evocations of *Aeneid*, 6. 264 ff., at ll. 83 ff. (*Poems*, 2: 832–33). It may be that the energy and exuberance released by the whole cursing explosion gave Swift a certain heady freedom. The sheer determined "lowness" of the enterprise carries a guarantee that no remnants of Virgilian "lofty Stile" would be allowed to rear their head, even where Swift was practicing a kind of indignant loftiness of his own, a loftiness based on the incandescences of anger (real or simulated or both) rather than on majesties of style or content. (Perhaps a rare Juvenalian element also enters, by the same token, into this ostensibly most unmajestic of poems.)

But the most important fact about the Virgilian allusion is that it is a rather special case, in which attention is drawn not to the more self-evidently "heroic" features of the epic original (to a hero's noble deeds, for example, or to the poet's high style), but to the Virgilian Hell. This provided Swift with a highly selective epic model, which could, unlike other Virgilian elements, be adapted by the satirist without necessarily being turned upside-down or too obviously reduced from high to low. The various epic Hells, including Milton's, served Pope in a similar way in the *Dunciad,* providing a grim universalizing resonance to the infernal regions of modern duncehood. The *Dunciad,* as it happens, preserved the epic grandeurs, too, but it is arguable that the exigencies of mock-heroic imitation, as distinct from the prevailing style of his own poem, did not compel him to this in the particular instance.

Swift's prevailing style entailed an opposite effect, and for once the epic model offered parallels that did not, in the normal way or to the usual extent, require routines of inflation and deflation that courted a Swiftian lapse into loftiness or risked insulting a lofty original. The gloomy regions of the Underworld lend themselves to the Satanic darkness of the modern madhouse as direct rather than upside-down parallels. The associated ideas of culpability that belong to a non-Pagan inferno accrete readily and without strain. Pope allowed this accretion to make itself felt through a massive evocation of Milton, interposed between the *Dunciad* and its classical models, and lending its own additional majesties. The Christian conception of Hell, which, unlike the classical Underworld, is exclusively associated with sin and damnation, is totally fused into the *Dunciad*'s system of epic allusion, creating an eschatological parallel for the modern hell on earth. Swift's poem also does this, but has little traffic with Milton. For him too, as for Pope, Hell is the place of damnation. But he makes Virgil serve his purpose not by grafting Miltonic associations onto the Virgilian ones, but by eliminating, as Peter Schakel has said, "those parts [of Virgil] which do not correspond to the Christian Hell."[35] Miltonic majesties, we might add, would (like most others) have embarrassed him here.

Familiarly, mad and bad are near of kin in *The Legion Club*. But the interesting thing on this occasion is that Swift has identified his satiric madhouse with the very place that he himself was proposing (on compassionate and philanthropic grounds) to bequeath to the Irish nation. He establishes the connection at the start:

> Yet should *Swift* endow the Schools
> For his Lunatics and Fools,
> With a Rood or two of Land,
> I allow the Pile may stand.
>
> (Ll. 35–38)

The wry joke at the end of the *Verses on the Death* loses some of its gruff affection in a deeper and more painful blurring of values. But this blurring also has a defiant exuberance, a teasing readiness to declare a certain complicity in the badness of the world, while standing cheekily outside the target area nonetheless. (So too the Yahoo parliamentarians are described as hurlers of ordure, even as Swift himself is showering excremental imprecations upon them.)

It is an eloquent confusion, profoundly true to Swift's satiric temperament and to his passionate but always ambiguous commitment to Irish affairs. Just as a dry joke on Irish folly concludes (and in my view helps to rescue from failure) the *Verses on the Death*, so, after passing through the dark chambers of *The Legion Club*, this folly became the subject of what is said to be Swift's last poem of all. On seeing a new building intended as a magazine for arms and powder, he wrote the following epigram in 1737:

> Behold! a proof of *Irish* sense!
> Here *Irish* wit is seen!
> When nothing's left, that's worth defence,
> We build a magazine.
>
> (*Poems*, 3: 843)

These late poems, then, might in a loose sense be said to belong to a new mode in which *saeva indignatio* appears more or less unadorned or unsubverted by ironies at the expense of its own "lofty Stile." Even here, I suspect, the indignations are not the "sublime and lofty" ones of Juvenal's "tragical satire" so much as those of a knowing and sophisticated replay of the low and primitive curse. For the strong raw feelings Swift wanted to express, he at last found an idiom that released high anger without committing him to the embarrassments of the more dignified high styles, even in their parodied form. His habit of undercutting took the form not so much of subverting his own rhetoric as of indicating that he was playing it for all it was worth. The knowing playfulness with which he signals his use of ritual imprecations reinforces (and perhaps even released) the exuberance of the exercise instead of qualifying or restraining it.

Play has replaced the old embarrassed coyness, while mimicry flowers without the self-disengagements of parody. The jokes about Irish folly, deserving of madhouses which Swift literally left money to build, or about *"Irish* sense" and *"Irish* wit" building magazines "When nothing's left, that's worth defence," do not serve to deflate the angry denunciations of Irish madness in the bedlam of *The Legion Club* or the larger madhouse of Hibernian life in that poem and elsewhere. They are a low-key counterpart, not a self-conscious ironic guard. Their control of modulated understatement and their witty sense of absurdity complement rather than undercut the massive expressions of indignation. They do not (even in the *Verses on the Death,* where the best-known of these jokes makes its appearance in the closing lines) constitute an oblique and defensively simpering display of self, although they may contain autobiographical disclosures like the one about Swift's legacy for the "House for Fools and Mad." A similar joke is absorbed into the angers of *The Legion Club* and is allowed to crackle testily among them without strain or incongruity (ll. 35 ff.), while the epigram about the "magazine" flowers on its own and keeps its cool. In both cases, the sense of comedy is free of the winking and nudging that, in much of the rest of the *Verses on the Death* and in some other autobiographical poems, show Swift eating his self-regarding cake and having it too. Whether low-key jokes are present or not, there is a dignity in those late "un-dignified" poems, in *Traulus* or *The Legion Club,* that is lacking in all Swift's poetic gestures, early and late, of witty self-awareness or knowing deflation.

NOTES

1. © Copyright C. J. Rawson. This essay is part of a larger study of Swift now in preparation. All quotations from Swift's prose works are from the edition of Herbert Davis and others, 14 vols. (Oxford:Basil Blackwell, 1939–68), unless otherwise noted. References to this edition are generally given by volume and page immediately after citation in the text or notes: sometimes, to avoid a local ambiguity, the title is given in abbreviated form as *Works*. *Correspondence* and *Poems* refer to the editions by Harold Williams, 5 vols. (Oxford: Clarendon Press, 1963–65) and 3 vols., 2d ed. (Oxford: Clarendon Press, 1958), respectively. "Watson" refers to Dryden, *Of Dramatic Poesy and Other Critical Essays*, 2 vols. (London: J. M. Dent & Sons, 1962).

2. The poem appeared in *Tatler*, No. 238, 14–17 October 1710. The revised fifth edition of the *Tale* was published late in the same year.

3. The passages from Dryden's translation of the *Aeneid* that are pertinent to Swift's account of the Trojan horse are at 2. 17ff., 52–69, 306 ff. It would be misleading to assert that these particular lines of Dryden's were being followed in any close verbal detail, but for an undoubted and larger context of Drydenian and other allusion in Swift's poem, see Irvin Ehrenpreis, *Swift: The Man, His Works and the Age*, vol. 2, *Dr. Swift* (Cambridge, Mass.: Harvard University Press, 1969), p. 385n.

For other allusions to Virgil in Swift's poems, see the index to *Poems*. The only significant Homeric allusion among the few recorded in the index and appearing in a poem is to the special case of Thersites, who is also the subject of an extended allusion in the *Battle of the Books (Poems*, 3: 775; *Works*, 1: 160–61). The peculiar character of the allusions to Thersites are discussed more fully in a separate study now in progress. It is sufficient to note here that the episode from *Iliad*, 2. 211 ff. was often regarded as aberrant and beneath heroic dignity.

4. The thinness of any real resemblance between Juvenal and Swift comes through in the survey of the question by R.I.W. Westgate and P. L. MacKendrick, "Juvenal and Swift," *Classical Journal* 37 (1942): 468–82. Felicity Nussbaum surveys the relationship of Juvenal's sixth satire to the tradition of satires on women in "Juvenal, Swift, and *The Folly of Love*," *ECS* 9 (1976): 540–52, but makes it clear that in Swift's case she is "not arguing for a direct influence or even for a rich allusive texture . . . but rather for a context of commonplaces and set scenes which increase our understanding of Swift's boudoir poems" (p. 541).

5. For some remarks on Horace and Swift see my essay, "The Nightmares of Strephon: Nymphs of the City in the Poems of Swift, Baudelaire, Eliot," in *English Literature in the Age of Disguise*, ed. Maximillian E. Novak (Berkeley, and Los Angeles, Calif.: University of California Press, 1977), pp. 83, 98 n.51.

6. See Rawson, "Nightmares of Strephon," pp. 79–84; *Gulliver and the Gentle Reader* (Boston: Routledge & Kegan Paul, 1973), pp. 11–14, 158 n.64.

7. See Alexander Pope, *The Sixth Epistle of the First Book of Horace Imitated*. ll. 1 ff. and Twickenham edition commentary.

8. See Williams in *Poems*, 2:640, and George P. Mayhew, *Rage or Raillery* (San Marino, Calif.: The Huntington Library, 1967), pp. 95, 112–13. The mock-praise of the King and Queen occurs at ll. 411 ff. See also John Irwin Fischer, *On Swift's Poetry*, (Gainesville, Fla.: University Presses of Florida, 1978), pp. 177–82, who sees the poem as parodying Edward Young and his praise of the same royal personages and of Walpole. On the background to Swift's mock-panegyrics see James L. Tyne, "Swift's Mock Panegyrics in 'On Poetry: A Rapsody,'" *PLL* 10 (1974): 279–86.

9. On canceled passages, see also Mayhew, *Rage and Raillery*, pp. 97–100.

10. The opening lines of this passage may have been borrowed from John Gay, *Trivia, Poems*, 2. 140–42. See Clive T. Probyn, "Swift's Borrowing from Gay," *Notes and Queries* 214 (1969):184.

11. Nora Crow Jaffe, *The Poet Swift* (Hanover, N.H.: University Presses of New England, 1977), p. 45.

12. See Fischer, *Swift's Poetry*, p. 187.

13. *Journal to Stella*, ed. Harold Williams (Oxford: Clarendon Press, 1948), 1:90. Swift went through some amusing embarrassments of a related sort over *A Tale of a Tub*, whose authorship he did not wish to claim openly, but which he was mortified to see attributed in part to his cousin Thomas Swift. The question of Thomas Swift's possible part-authorship has been reopened in recent years, although it is outside the scope of the present discussion; but for Jonathan Swift's concern at contemporary gossip about the authorship, see *Correspondence*, 1: 165–67; *Journal to Stella*, 1. 279–80 and n. The whole subject has wider connections with Swift's habit of keeping up an ostentatious and often humorous mystification about the authorship of his anonymous and pseudonymous works, even within the works themselves, as in both the *Tale* and *Gulliver's Travels.*

14. The passage has similarities with Gay's "The Elephant and the Bookseller" (Fable 10, 1727), whose theme is that authors are worse than other animals at preying on each other. Compare not only the present passage from Swift's poem, but also ll. 383 ff., beginning: "In Bulk there are not more Degrees, / From *Elephants* to *Mites* in Cheese, / Than what a curious Eye may trace / In Creatures of the rhiming Race. . . ."

15. The "conqu'ring Hero" is clearly Alexander, as the rivers in the second line make clear. The blowsy cadences invite suspicions of yet another mocking Drydenian allusion, this time to "Alexander's Feast." By an odd coincidence, the famous lines by Morell in Handel's *Judas Maccabeus* (1747) and *Joshua* (1748)—"See, the conquering hero comes! / Sound the trumpets, beat the drums!"—which are later than Swift, repeat one of Dryden's lines—"Sound the Trumpets; beat the Drums"—in "Alexander's Feast," l. 50. For the appearances of "See, the conquering hero" in Handel's two oratorios, see Winton Dean, *Handel's Dramatic Oratorios and Masques* (New York: Oxford University Press, 1959), pp. 460–81, 498–510, esp. 470, 475–77, 480, 505–8. According to *Stevenson's Book of Quotations*, ed. Burton Stevenson, 10th ed. (London: Cassell, 1967), p. 297, no. 11, Morell's lines were "introduced into the later stage versions of Nathaniel Lee's *The Rival Queens* Act ii, sc. 1." Lee's play, 1677, is also about Alexander and I assume that the lines got into a version posthumous to both Lee and Swift. I have not been able to trace a pre-Swiftian "conq'ring Hero," though I suspect the phrase occurs in some place well known to Swift and his readers.

The corresponding section of Horace's *Epistle to Augustus* (*Ep.* 2.1. 232–70, esp. 245 ff.), of which Swift's poem is to some extent an "imitation," is concerned with a comparison between Alexander and Augustus. In Pope's version of the *Epistle to Augustus* (1737), ll. 390–91, which is later than Swift's poem, the parallel phrase to Swift's is "conqu'ring Chief."

Historical conquerors like Alexander and Caesar were common or convenient targets for anti-heroic attitudes that sought to bypass mockery of epic poems by avoiding or attenuating slurs on Homeric or Virgilian heroes. See the discussion in my *Henry Fielding and the Augustan Ideal under Stress* (Boston: Routledge & Kegan Paul, 1972), chs. 4–6, esp. ch. 5, "Epic *vs.* History: *Jonathan Wild* and Augustan Mock-Heroic," and see W. B. Carnochan, "Dryden's Alexander," in this volume.

A few lines later in his poem (ll. 429 ff.), Swift identifies the Prince of Wales as "our eldest Hope, divine *Iülus.*" Iülus is the alternative name of Virgil's Ascanius, son of Aeneas, in his role as ancestor of the Julian race, from which Julius Caesar was descended, as well as Augustus by adoption. The Virgilian allusion is here also rapidly deflected to historical rather than epic figures. A note in the Faulkner edition of Swift's *Works* (1735), 2:453, cites part of the famous passage in *Aeneid*, 6. 789 ff., prophesying the conquests of Caesar and Augustus, and all the line of Iülus. Another 1735 note identifies an allusion to Horace,

Epistles 1.12. 27–28, which refers to historical Roman conquests. And see the allusions to Virgil and Horace in the "canceled lines" at *Poems*, 2: 658–59, also concerned with the historical Augustus.

16. *Tristram Shandy*, 9.8.

17. The most comprehensive and distinguished study of this poem is an article by Arthur H. Scouten and Robert D. Hume, "Pope and Swift: Text and Interpretation of Swift's Verses on His Death," *Philological Quarterly* 52 (1973): 205–31. Its information on the poem's complex publication history, and on its relation to less authentic versions and to Swift's related autobiographical poem, *The Life and Genuine Character of Doctor Swift*, is of the first importance. The critical discussion of the poem's controversial passages of self-praise is an authoritatively sensible and subtle appraisal. I differ from the authors on some details of the poem's tone and in my valuation of the *Verses*, which is lower than theirs. But like all subsequent students of this awkward poem, I am in their debt.

Many discussions of this poem have appeared in recent years. They are most fully listed in James Woolley, "Friends and Enemies in *Verses on the Death of Dr. Swift*," *Studies in Eighteenth-Century Culture* 8 (1979): 225–26.

18. Yeats, "In Memory of Major Robert Gregory," *Collected Poems* (London: Macmillan & Co., 1952) pp. 148–49.

19. Pound, *Hugh Selwyn Mauberley, Selected Poems*, ed. T. S. Eliot (London: Faber and Faber, 1948), p. 177.

20. Yeats, "High Talk," *Collected Poems*, p. 386.

21. For a very charming compliment to Pope that is free of this self-regarding element, see "Advice to the Grub-street Verse-Writers" (1726; *Poems*, 2: 394–5). Other examples, where Swift does indulge in genial self-depreciation, but less heavily and more attractively than in the *Verses on the Death*, are "Dr. Sw—— to Mr. P——e, While he was Writing the *Dunciad*" (1727, *Poems*, 2: 405–06), and "A Pastoral Dialogue between Richmond-Lodge and Marble-Hill" (1727; *Poems*, 2: 407 ff). I do not wish to suggest that all Swift's coterie poems are marred by the uncomfortable kind of personal intrusiveness that is found in the *Verses*. There are many charming poems involving his literary and other friends (Delany, Sheridan, Ford and many others).

22. Pope, *One Thousand Seven Hundred and Thirty Eight* ("Epilogue to the Satires"), 2. 197–98; *The First Satire of the Second Book of Horace Imitated*, ll. 139–40.

23. Yeats, "The Municipal Gallery Revisited," *Collected Poems*, pp. 369–70.

24. On "Juvenal's language" in Swift's epitaph, see Westgate and MacKendrick, "Juvenal and Swift," p. 482.

25. Yeats, "Swift's Epitaph," *Collected Poems*, p. 277.

26. A short section is devoted to this poem, for example, in W. B. Ewald, Jr., *The Masks of Jonathan Swift* (Oxford: Basil Blackwell, 1954), pp. 182–83. In the two most recent books on Swift's poems there are interesting attempts to see the impartial commentator as a persona or even a separate character, who intermittently and in varying degrees expresses more or less Swiftian positions, but who is separate and subject to undercutting from Swift's irony: see Fischer, *Swift's Poetry*, pp. 169 ff., and Peter J. Schakel, *The Poetry of Jonathan Swift* (Madison, Wisc.: University of Wisconsin Press, 1978), pp. 143–46.

27. For a reading of the poem as a play of several Swiftian selves, see David M. Vieth, "The Mystery of Personal Identity: Swift's Verses on His Own Death," in *The Author in His Work: Essays on a Problem in Criticism*, eds. Louis L. Martz and Aubrey Williams (New Haven, Conn.: Yale University Press, 1978), pp. 245–62.

28. The second line of this couplet repeats or parodies a line in Denham's elegy "On Mr. Abraham Cowley," l. 30. See the similar trick in *Tristram Shandy*, 5.1, ed. James A. Work (New York: The Odyssey Press, 1940), p. 342n. On Swift's lines, see Barry Slepian, "The

Ironic Intention of Swift's Verses on his Own Death," *RES*, n.s., vol. 14 (1963); 255, citing G. Birkbeck Hill's note in Johnson's *Lives of the English Poets* (Oxford: Clarendon Press, 1905), 3:66 n.

29. Slepian, "Ironic Intention of Swift's Verses," pp. 254–56. Swift certainly wanted satire to name names. See for example his letter of July–August 1732 to Charles Wogan *(Correspondence,* 4:53). William King, Pope and others who were much involved with the publication of the London edition of the poem felt at the time that the claim was "not, strictly speaking, a just part of his character; because several persons have been lashed by name . . ." *(Correspondence,* 5: 139–40; see Scouten and Hume, "Pope and Swift," pp. 216–17).

30. Slepian, "Ironic Intention of Swift's Verses," pp. 249–56, esp. 254–56. Scouten and Hume, "Pope and Swift," p. 228, say well of Slepian's argument as a whole that it "seems to explain the technique but not the point."

31. See, on this, Marshall Waingrow, *"Verses on the Death of Dr. Swift," SEL* 5 (1965): 516–17. Waingrow offers a good corrective to Slepian, but in my view overrates the poem.

32. Critics sometimes feel, with Harold Williams, that "we are closer to Swift in his verse, and in his letters, than in his prose-writings" *(Poems,* 1: xlvi). This is true of the poems in some obvious senses: they more frequently deal with Swift and his friends, and they often have a light, informal manner. Whether the poems bring us as closely as the great prose fictions to Swift's deeper and most urgent feelings is more questionable. On Swift's letters, which require separate discussion, see Oliver W. Ferguson, "'Nature and Friendship': The Personal Letters of Jonathan Swift," in *The Familiar Letter in the Eighteenth Century,* ed. Howard Anderson, Philip B. Daghlian, and Irvin Ehrenpreis (Lawrence, Kans.: University of Kansas, Press, 1968), pp. 14–33; John Holloway, "Dean of St. Patrick's: A View from the Letters," in *The World of Jonathan Swift,* ed. Brian Vickers (Oxford: Basil Blackwell, 1968), pp. 258–68; Irvin Ehrenpreis, "Swift's Letters," in *Focus: Swift,* ed. C. J. Rawson, London: Sphere Books, 1971), pp. 197–215.

33. See Robert C. Elliott, *The Power of Satire: Magic, Ritual, Art* (Princeton, N.J.: Princeton University Press, 1960), pp. 3 ff., 18–48, 277, 285–92.

34. E.g., Elliott, *Power of Satire,* pp. 22, 42 ff.

35. Schakel, *Poetry of Swift,* p. 172. I am skeptical of some of Mr. Schakel's additional discoveries of Virgilian allusion, although he offers a useful listing, pp. 170–77.

Fielding and the Disappearance of Heroes

J. PAUL HUNTER

THACKERAY'S subtitle for *Vanity Fair*—"A novel without a hero"—implies many things about Victorian culture, the English national character, relationships between men and women, and the proper way of making novels, but practically none of its resonance, perhaps not even the subtitle itself, would exist without *Tom Jones*. Thackeray was not a good reader of Fielding; his own youthful habits, his later renunciation of them, and his crippling habit of casting himself as both the chief character and creator of other people's novels left him hopelessly at his own mercy as a reader of novelists as healthy and spirited as Fielding. But he was a close reader, and his later objections to Fielding—after his early intemperate praise—suggest not only a century-after diagnosis of Fielding's limits but the context that Fielding was up against in his own time because of readers whose expectations were definitively formed and morally rigid. Much of that context involved ideas of the hero and heroism, and Thackeray's comments in *English Humourists of the Eighteenth Century*—misguided as they are—articulate the persistent assumptions that Fielding was in fact addressing when he created "our Heroe" Tom Jones:

> I can't say that I think Mr. Jones a virtuous character; I can't say but that I think Fielding's evident liking and admiration for Mr. Jones shows that the great humourist's moral sense was blunted by his life, and that here, in Art and Ethics, there is a great error. If it is right to have a hero whom we may admire, let us at least take care that he is admirable. . . . But a hero with a flawed reputation; a hero spunging for a guinea; a hero who can't pay his landlady, and is obliged to let his honour out to hire, is absurd, and his claim to heroic rank untenable. I protest against

116

Mr. Thomas Jones holding such rank at all. I protest even against his being considered a more than ordinary young fellow, ruddy-cheeked, broad-shouldered, and fond of wine and pleasure. He would not rob a church, but that is all. . . .[1]

Unflawed heroes are hard to find, and heroes of any sort seem to be getting scarcer. Many ages have, of course, thought themselves especially beggared when they have taken a census of their contemporary heroes, but in true poverty of heroism there are some ages that have undeniably just claims—including our own. The idea of heroism, we may say, the *very* idea. Gone are the days when thundering hoofbeats could come out of the past and escort us to heroic days of yesteryear, or to exotic places like Persia, or Siam, or the moon. Their names have changed now, and future generations will find, even in space—that celebrated "last frontier"—our flags and our garbage, the start of a junkyard and city dump where our dreams once soared. No doubt much of the aura of heroes and heroines involves safe distance and bad memory. Facts are perhaps an enemy of heroism, and reality may be destined to produce few real heroes when observers have their eyes open. But what of our closed eyes, what of our dreams, the lands where heroes are made? Do we not measure ourselves by the heroes we can imagine? Are we not, like other ages, defined both by what we want to believe and what we can?

The literary part of a cultural crisis over heroes has always involved the contexts of credibility, for in times unheroic it is difficult for writers to write persuasively about a viable hero. History seems to suggest that ages that respect themselves—the Elizabethan age, for example—produce not only the grandest artistic visions but the most heroic populace for them, and lesser ages struggle to imagine beyond the clouds of a present moment. Imaginative navigation with such low ceilings is an especially crucial psychological problem, for the laws of supply and demand take a strange twist when applied to ideas. The more flawed the age the more unflawed must its heroes be, for ages abnormally debased feel desperately a messianic need for ideals left unstained and models still uncorrupted. What Thackeray knew reflected his age, ours, and the one in which Fielding grew up, for it anchors a recurrent historical pattern. What Fielding did provokes such a woodenly obtuse response because he refused to honor the code of absolutes. It may be that the cycle is endless, but it is at least clear that for every Thackeray there had better be a Fielding to provide a paradigm for mortal compromise.

1

In comparing Horace and Juvenal, Dryden once noted that Horace's Augustan context was "better for the man, but worse for the satirist" than the declining years of imperial culture chronicled by Juvenal: times bad for the man are good for the satirist. Times good for the satirist are also notoriously difficult for readers of any other kind of literature, whatever its tone and intention, for the most persuasive of panegyrical and heroic literature seems hopelessly incredible in times good for the satirist. "Too good to be true" is a phrase from a satirist's mouth—usually plaintive, often hopeful, but firmly convinced that Truth and Nature seldom give us anything very heroic.

Fielding was born into an age good for the satirist, bad for the man, and his formative years were those dominated in English letters by the greatest satirists in the tradition. *Gulliver's Travels* appeared when Fielding was nineteen years old, Pope's first version of the *Dunciad* when Fielding was twenty-one. Fielding's early literary efforts are almost embarrassingly fawning and dependent upon the lead of the reigning wits, and often one feels that his satire on the time in his early plays is merely a mouthing of conventional carpings about manners and railings upon human nature. Fielding is often loud in his denunciations, sometimes scathing in his judgments, but he projects a comedic confidence that vitiates much of the criticism. In his best-known play, for example, written when he was twenty-three, Fielding portrays a pint-sized hero come to rescue King Arthur's kingdom from the giants who threaten it. The play is called, in its early versions, *The Life of Tom Thumb the Great, a Tragedy*, and the tragic hero, Tom, does in fact come to a bad end at last. Before that, though, he vaunts and blusters about, doing all the things that great men are supposed to do in saving kingdoms from distress, comporting himself with all the majesty of Golbasto Momaren Evlame Gurdilo Shefin Mully Ully Gue, Emperor of Lilliput. Normal-sized women fall in love with him—including Arthur's queen and also his daughter—and so does a giantess, amidst much hilarity about sex and sizes. A hero named Tom Thumb in a series of love scenes is not exactly a drawing-room joke, and Fielding knows where the laughs come from. Often the play reminds us, in its physical mismatches, of Gulliver's clumsy, protesting-too-much attempt to defend his honor in the matter of Flimnap's Lilliputian wife, except that in Fielding's version it is the hero who is dwarfed—and no one, including his lovers, seems to notice.

Tom Thumb depends in fact very much upon Swift in other ways, too. The whole matter of size—rendering the modern hero as Lilliputian but fit for the latter-day descendants of King Arthur—owes much to formulations in *Gulliver's Travels,* even though the metaphor of pygmies and giants for moderns and ancients is a very old one, dating back at least six centuries, and Swift is merely Fielding's vehicle. For it is Swift's version of the metaphor that had gained popular currency so that Fielding could assume it and exploit it.

In his later published version of the play as *The Tragedy of Tragedies,* Fielding is similarly dependent upon expectations created by Pope. He took over almost bodily the notion of absurd "learned" notes from Pope's elaborate Variorum version of *The Dunciad,* and he is also heavily dependent on a context established by another Scriblerian, John Gay. It is *The Beggar's Opera* (1728) that provides the political thrust of Fielding's play, not because Gay invented the term *great man* for Walpole but because he gave it widespread popular currency. After 1728, no one could mention a "great man" or even speak of "greatness" without triggering the image of the prime minister, and Fielding was far from the only contemporary figure to exploit the term and its accreted associations of inflated pride, smallness in high places, and false grandeur. As Tom Thumb the Great, little Tom's struttings and posturings must have seemed hysterical to the political Opposition, and courtiers named Noodle, Doodle, and Foodle add little to the dignity of the court, nor does Queen Dollalolla, nor the aggressive Princess Huncamunca. And yet the swath is wider than Walpole and the court of the moment, for Foodle is a courtier out of place, and the king as Arthur reminds us how many reigns have come and gone without a fundamental difference except for a general shrinkage of possibility.

What Fielding derives from Swift, Pope, and Gay does not constitute a literary debt in the usual senses, for although he uses their phrasing, structural devices, and conceptions, his dependence on them involves the effects they have already wrought in eighteenth-century audiences. He is dependent on expectations they have set up, and the sparkling surface and the feeling of comfortable joy in the play sometimes works at cross purposes with the darker Augustan vision. What is illustrated in the conflicting commitments of *Tom Thumb* is Fielding's difference from the major Augustans even when he is most dependent on them. Temperamentally, he is unable to feel as bleak as he thinks he ought to, and the bad end to which he brings his hero is more farcical than tragic, not only in its absurdist trappings, but in its implications. Poor little Tom is eaten by a cow "of larger than the usual size"—off stage, fortunately—and in their grief everyone else goes mad and kills each other. Seven deaths occur in eight lines; it breaks the record. Tom's demise testifies absurdly to a bovine scheme of order, and the play provides a demonstration that modern heroes are destined for something other than dignity. But the whole ending is so ludicrous and its ostensible meanings so simple that it hardly jars us into any profound recognition.

It is interesting and perhaps instructive to compare two other absurdist endings that derive from real Augustan visions. The end of Gulliver may be thought of in two ways, appropriate to his two statuses as character and as putative satirist. In the book itself the reader last sees Gulliver at home, nostalgic about his days among the Houyhnhnms. He would like us to think of him there at table, with his wife and clinging children quietly at one end trying not to smell human, while way at the other end is Gulliver, neighing to himself and attended by a groom from the stable whose smell will perhaps cheer up Gulliver—if any smell at all gets through a nose stuffed with lavender, tobacco leaves, and rue, those sensory barriers Gulliver uses to divorce himself completely from any reminder of his human mortality. It is a ludicrous picture, absurd. Yet its meanings are depressingly clear in the midst of the comedy; in fact the meanings flow from the comedy: man in isolation, man alone, man ashamed beyond redemption, man spending his life learning lessons on how to live among others and then at last tragically, comically, absurdly, setting up his private hermitage instead of a family home, unable "during the first Year . . . [to] endure my Wife or Children in my Presence, the very Smell of them was intolerable; much less could I suffer them to eat in the same Room." And in the next sentence one hears the tones of the Anglican priest behind the voice of Gulliver. "To this Hour," Gulliver reports flatly, "they dare not presume to touch my Bread, or drink out of the same Cup; neither was I ever able to let one of them take me by the Hand." Whatever one's view of the Houyhnhnms themselves, Gulliver's devotion to horses at the end is absurd and pathetic. He is not at all like the priest, poet, prophet, and public man Jonathan Swift, who fought public nuisances all his life—even when they ruled his country—rather than stopping his nose with tobacco and lavender and rue.

The other last look at Gulliver is as the letter-writer to Cousin Sympson, in the letter prefaced to later editions of the *Travels*. Here he is the satirist and recounter of his adventures—bitterly lamenting that his book has done no good:

I do in the next Place complain of my own great Want of Judgment, in being prevailed upon by the Intreaties and false Reasonings of you and some others, very much against mine own Opinion, to suffer my Travels to be published. Pray bring to your Mind how often I desired you to consider, when you insisted on the Motive of *publick Good;* that the *Yahoos* were a species of Animals utterly incapable of Amendment by Precepts or Examples: and so it hath proved; for instead of seeing a full Stop put to all Abuses and Corruptions, at least in this little Island, as I had Reason to expect: Behold, after above six Months Warning, I cannot learn that my Book hath produced one single Effect according to mine Intentions: I desired you would let me know by a Letter, when Party and Faction were extinguished; Judges learned and upright; Pleaders honest and modest, with some Tincture of common Sense; and *Smithfield* blazing with Pyraminds of Law-Books; the young Nobility's Education entirely changed; the Physicians banished; the female *Yahoos* abounding in Virtue, Honour, Truth and good Sense: Courts and Levees of great Ministers thoroughly weeded and swept; Wit, Merit and learning rewarded; all Disgracers of the Press in Prose and Verse, condemned to eat nothing but their own Cotten, and quench their Thirst with their own Ink. These, and a Thousand other Reformations, I firmly counted upon by your Encouragement; as indeed they were plainly deducible from the Precepts delivered in Time to correct every Vice and Folly to which *Yahoos* are subject; if their Natures had been capable of the least Disposition to Virtue or Wisdom. . . .[2]

Absurdist again, but the comedy bites home as Fielding's genial cow does not.

Conclusions nearly as grim lie behind the so-called comic ending of *The Beggar's Opera*. Macheath is about to be hanged for his many crimes in an enactment of poetic justice—not the kind of event that would set audiences to overthrowing the judicial system—when lo and behold, the beggar whose opera it is reappears, bows to contemporary taste for happy endings, and reprieves the scoundrel "hero." The point of the play is not that thieves are as good as prime ministers, although some productions have played it that way, but that prime ministers are as bad as thieves, and a society that depends on, admires, and reprieves Macheath cannot be altogether healthy. The grand, absurd festivity has a grim point, turned emphatically outward from the play's world to that of the audience.

I am not arguing that Fielding was less talented than his older contemporaries, that *Tom Thumb* is a flawed play, or even that at twenty-three Fielding still had much to learn about keeping his effects under control. My point is that his exuberance was of a different sort from the exuberance of Swift or Gay. The Augustans had a satiric exuberance nearly unique in literary history, earned by their terrible heroism of struggle within a philosophical frame that promised them certain defeat. They celebrate human spirit up against the wall, and they celebrate the wall; no later generation would ever find the resources and burdens of the humanist heritage and modern change in such tenuous balance.

Fielding's attraction to Augustan visions and Augustan metaphors was balanced by his temperamental distrust and distaste. Even while he was writing their kind of play in *Tom Thumb* he was also writing, it has recently been discovered, a mock-epic attack on the Augustan satirists, using of course the mode and the techniques perfected by those he was attacking.[3] At various levels of consciousness he was thus perceiving his reservations about the Augustans and his temperamental difference from them. This difference determined a very different route to literary success for him, and it meant that as he worked out his own temperamental needs he had to work against the established contexts of those writers who had early been his inspiration and his model.

Fielding never quite accepted the inevitability of Dulness the way the Augustans did, and their source of strength was thus not available to him. He could never, for example, participate in modern madness with dazzling vicariousness, as Swift did:

> One of [Nature's] Laws . . . is, to put her best Furniture forward. And therefore, in order to save the Charges of all such expensive Anatomy for the Time to come; I do here think fit to inform the Reader, that in such Conclusions as these, Reason is certainly in the Right; and that in most Corporeal Beings, which have fallen under my Cognizance, the *Outside* hath been infinitely preferable to the *In:* Whereof I have been farther convinced from some late Experiments. Last Week I saw a Woman *flay'd,* and you will hardly believe, how much it altered her Person for the worse. Yesterday I ordered the Carcass of a *Beau* to be stript in my Presence; when we were all amazed to find so many unsuspected Faults under one Suit of Cloaths: Then I laid open his *Brain,* his *Heart,* and his *Spleen;* But, I plainly perceived at every Operation, that the farther we proceeded, we found the Defects encreased upon us in Number and Bulk: from all which, I justly formed this Conclusion to my self; That whatever Philosopher or Projector can find out an Art to sodder and patch up the Flaws and Imperfections of Nature, will deserve much better of Mankind, and teach us a more useful Science, than that so much in present Esteem, of widening and exposing them (like him who held *Anatomy* to be the ultimate End of *Physick*). . . .
> But to return to *Madness.*[4]

The energy of this passage derives not only from Swift's disgust but equally from his sense that striking out against the inevitable meant participatory parody, a purging of one's own self-hatred and urge toward destruction and inanity by channeling it into a travesty that uses the rage within to strike out against the rage within.

Fielding could not quite do that. He lacked both the certainties of the humanist heritage and the certainty that the chaos within would grow, expand, and become universal. Ultimately it is the times that made Fielding different, and in a world without clocks it would be profitable to speculate about the limits of apocalypse, about the unstable mix of uncertainty, sentimentality, and dogmatism that lie in the wake of apocalypses when men outlive them, about what happens when crises are culturally strung out so that they never really get solved and never really go away, but are just tediously survived. But whether the determinants were in the times or in the man, Henry Fielding—forty years younger than Swift— always felt the modern threats differently. The enemy for him was so near a neighbor to his heroic self that when he travestied someone else he was rejecting a possible self, not just indulging an undercurrent and purging a self clearly defined. All his parodic targets are men he might well have been but feared becoming. The more prominent rejected selves were all satiric targets: Samuel Richardson, Sir Robert Walpole, Colley Cibber, George Whitefield, John Rich, Conyers Middleton. Fielding's relationship with them all—like that with another of his ambiguous models, Don Quixote—was a complex blend of attraction and repulsion. His first poem was called *The Masquerade* and his first play *Love in Several Masques;* he never gave up masking as a procedure, and he used it mercilessly in his attempt to find out who he was.[5]

2

Tom Jones is a long way from *Tom Thumb,* and I have dwelt so long on Fielding's relation to the older generation of eighteenth-century writers because his mature work is an attempt to grapple—very nearly a systematic attempt to grapple—with the literary world they introduced him to. That world was entirely without viable heroes, a world where protagonists were malignant in one or more of several ways. In each, their hopeless singularity stands paradoxically for the derangement of society. Each is a sort of Everymadman whose mind and morality is a morass of distinctionless mush. A very brief census of some of these early eighteenth-century heroes may help us to consider the career of Tom Jones in its proper historical setting. It is in poetry where the demise of the heroic tradition is the clearest because reminders of its earlier grandeur are continually present, and it is Pope who best exemplifies the heroic contexts, for it was he who set the standard for others and whose concerns thus became dominant for the age's lesser poets.

A poem like Pope's *Rape of the Lock* may not at first glance seem to consider the issue of human heroism at all because it is so concerned with the everyday, so full of loving attention to elegant filigree and china teacups and the courtly etiquette of London's beautiful people. Clearly it satirizes the ways of early eighteenth-century society, but clearly too Pope feels the appeal of its fragile and decadent beauty, and his objections are not so violent to his society in 1714, when he is twenty-five, as they are a decade later when he anatomizes the body of English society and finds it rotten to the soul. Still, the indictment of *The Rape of the Lock* is a strong one, in spite of its caressing touches. The society's values are nothing less than perverted versions of traditional classical and Christian values, and the seductive appeal results from a parodic closeness to respected and still relevant standards. Preening in front of her mirror, Belinda reenacts a perversion of the mass, and over and over, in a hundred ways, we are introduced to modern debasements, inappropriate comparisons, things unsorted, and things not wisely sorted but too well:

> Here Files of Pins extend their shining Rows,
> Puffs, Powders, Patches, Bibles, Billet-doux.[6]
>
> (1. 137–38)

The chaos of values, and the potential of their destructiveness, is repeatedly underscored by allusions to familiar biblical events and phrases and to *Paradise Lost.* Here, for example, is a passage where we are asked to think of the supposed model for Belinda's virginity and conception of herself. It is one of those perverted mani-festations of Supernature, a sylph, who, lisping and slithering,

> Seem'd to her Ear his winning Lips to lay,
> And thus in Whispers said, or seem'd to say.

And he proceeds with the Annunciation:

> Fairest of Mortals, thou distinguish'd Care
> Of thousand bright Inhabitants of Air!

If e'er one Vision touch'd thy infant Thought,
Of all the Nurse and all the Priest have taught,
Of airy Elves by Moonlight Shadows seen,
The silver Token, and the circled Green,
Of Virgins visited by Angel-Pow'rs,
With Golden Crowns and Wreaths of heav'nly Flow'rs,
Hear and believe! thy own Importance know,
Nor bound thy narrow Views to Things below.

(1. 25–36)[7]

How absurd such self-conception and self-importance is becomes
clear only later in Belinda's absurdist actions as she turns a game of
love into a real battle of the sexes understood literally. Perhaps the
height of her absurdity comes when she insists that her antagonist
(for so he has become) *restore* the lock that he has cut off. It is at
this point in the proceedings that we hear the only male dialogue,
for Belinda appeals to Sir Plume, whose values justly represent the
world of Hampton Court and whose empty dignity indexes his
capability as an upholder of social order:

(*Sir Plume*, of *Amber Snuff-box* justly vain,
And the nice Conduct of a *clouded Cane*)
With earnest Eyes, and round unthinking Face,
He first the Snuff-box open'd, then the Case,
And thus broke out—'My Lord, why, what the Devil?
Z——ds! damn the Lock! 'fore Gad, you must be civil!
Plague on't! 'tis past a Jest—nay prithee, Pox!
Give her the Hair'—he spoke, and rapp'd his Box.[8]

(4. 123–30)

Captured and preserved in the amber of his accessories, Sir Plume
is a better snuffer than casuist. Like Gulliver he is dedicated to
preserving familiar forms and makes sights and smells support his
isolation. But opening and rapping are his talents, not dis-
criminating and articulating, and the substance as well as the style
of Late Queen Anne heroism is very nearly summarized in the
empty oaths that punctuate his faltering attempt to complete a
single sentence.

Because its emphasis on the reversal of sexual roles is so great,
The Rape of the Lock could be called a poem without a hero just as

accurately as *Vanity Fair* can be called a novel without one. And because it is about so many other things (the manners of the age, the preoccupation with surfaces, mistaken self-conception, the refusal to accept the limits of mortality), it is easy to ignore the demise of heroism that Pope signals in *The Rape of the Lock*. But there is no mistaking his proclamation of the void in *The Dunciad*. By 1728, after a decade with Homer, Pope was sure that the only heroic poem fit for his society was an anti-epic, even though he always longed for the contextual power that could grant him a traditional epic after all. And thus his careful imitation of Vergil's career through its proper qualifying stages—what has come to be called the "Vergilian progression" from pastoral to georgic to epic poems—arrived at its zenith in a blaze of bathos. Like *The Rape of the Lock, The Dunciad* is easy to undervalue as a cultural statement—it is so comic and its precise historical references are so easy to translate into simple spleen and personal vindictiveness— but whatever its tones and origins it stands as one of the most devastating cultural indictments of all time. Not only does it so shrewdly point to historical changes in reader perception and the modes of artistic possibility that Marshall McLuhan can regard it as a landmark in Western consciousness, but its rhetoric makes Pope's charges stick with dazzling ease. The encroaching mindlessness that Pope sees as a modern imitation of the original void before the first creative Word, rolls like a fog through the poem, cutting off clarities of vision, blurring distinctions, magnifying matters close at hand so that they seem to be all there is. The mindlessness is collective, and Pope populates the world of Dulness persuasively with the most meager of his contemporaries. Their attempt to glut the sensory world during the noise contest in the "high heroic games" leads finally to "an universal hum," and their names as well as their works seem to demand their destiny among the damned who rule such an empire by mass without distinction:

> Now thousand tongues are heard in one loud din:
> The Monkey-mimicks rush discordant in.
> 'Twas chatt'ring, grinning, mouthing, jabb'ring all,
> And Noise, and Norton, Brangling, and Breval,
> Dennis and Dissonance; and captious Art,
> And Snip-snap short, and Interruption smart.

"Hold (cry'd the Queen) A Catcall each shall win,
Equal your merits! equal is your din!"

(2. 227–34)[9]

Presiding over all of the minor functionaries is the King-Elect, the
rightful heir of his high place not because he is worse than all the
rest but because he is typical in many different ways at the same
time. Lewis Theobald earned his heroic status in the first *Dunciad*
as a hack writer, editor, and promiser. His "promised" translation
of Aeschylus, for which he received advance payment, was years
overdue, and through all his procrastination and failures as a playwright he continued to strut pompously and make loud claims of
brilliance and originality. As an editor and emender of Shakespeare
he is now justly remembered, but in 1728 that world was still
before him. He had only announced his Shakespearean intention,
as he had announced his intention regarding Aeschylus, except that
in announcing Shakespeare he had first published a whole book
attacking Pope's edition, 194 pages of points, quibbles, and vitup-
eration, a performance that was, at the least, graceless and ill-
timed.

Theobald's significance as a hero is twofold: he is, first of all, a
real person made fictional: he is actual, recognizable, distorted
only to underscore salient characteristics. He may never have
literally sat curled on the lap of a Goddess Dulness in a grotesque
travesty of the Madonna and child, but figuratively he was often
comforted by the muse of imagined imagination and the forces of
Anti-Life. Theobald's second significance involves his averageness.
The "hero" of Augustan poetry does not stand out in a crowd; he
is the crowd.

Pope's 1743 reworking of the *Dunciad* crowned a new monarch,
the poet laureate Colley Cibber. As an anti-hero Cibber was an
improvement over Theobald because his official position specified
him as a leader in the arts even though by his own admission he
was no poet. By 1743 Cibber had been for thirteen years dutifully
turning out his two odes a year, although his real talents lay in
prose, theatrical flair, and impersonation. As a patentee of the
Royal Theatre and a playwright for nearly a half century, Cibber
had a long record as taste-*maker* as well as taster of the modern
consciousness. As actor he had played many parts, both on stage

and off, and when he wrote his autobiography in 1740, *An Apology for the Life of Colley Cibber, Comedian,* he defended the indiscretions of his life this way:

> And now you will say, the World will find me, under my own Hand, a weaker Man than perhaps I may have pass'd for, even among my enemies. . . . [The pleasures of] Follies, without the Reproach of Guilt upon them, are not inconsistent with Happiness. —But why make my Follies publick? Why not?[10]

Such are the major heroes of Pope, an inarticulate fop, a playwright who—failing to write like Shakespeare—hoped to emend him, and an actor-playwright-producer who wrote prosaic lyrics to celebrate prosaic kings, queens, and ministers of state. Both of the latter figures are capable of a defense, but they are so perfect as symbols of the modern proliferation of ephemeral print and democratization of taste that they seem appropriate and convincing as demonstrations of the "heroic" in the first half of the eighteenth century. All of them derive from persons in real life, but all of them take the power of their anti-heroic status from the fact that they fictionally stand for averageness and mediocrity raised to a prominent place.

I have already glanced at two major heroes of Jonathan Swift who, as the leading prose writer of the first half of the century, is an equally valid index to literary heroism of the time. Both the teller of *A Tale of a Tub* and Lemuel Gulliver are, like Pope's protganoists, "modern" heroes, and both claim to be typical of the age. Neither is, strictly speaking, based on a real person, but each is a composite of qualities and characteristics that Swift saw in his contemporaries; each has a kind of cumulative or acquisitive consciousness consisting of pride, naiveté, concern with the petty and trivial, and individualism slipped into total solipsism. Of similar character are the narrators of two of Swift's best-known short satires, the *Argument against Abolishing Christianity* and *A Modest Proposal.* Like the longer works, these pamphlets rely heavily upon local parody and specific satiric targets, but their ultimate focus is upon a kind of corporate modern consciousness. In slightly different circumstances, the Tale teller could propose such a modest proposal, or Gulliver could construct such an

argument in favor of nominal Christianity. Swift and Pope dis-
agreed about whether satire should name names, but both were
ultimately up to much the same thing, an isolation of shared
characteristics that defined the generality of modern man—a con-
glomerate of consciousness, an anti-hero who epitomized and
contained the literary and moral values that had come to dominate
London and redefine England in the reign of the early Hano-
verians.

One might argue that Pope and Swift are hardly the "typical"
writers of the early eighteenth century and that to isolate the idea
of the hero in their time one ought to turn to lesser figures who
more justly reflected popular taste. There is, of course, a sense in
which lesser figures do better express the temper of the age, but I
have concentrated on Pope and Swift for several reasons. One
reason involves the modern perspective: theirs is the artistic vision
of the times that has over the years prevailed and, rightly or
wrongly, we are most likely to be concerned with what good artists
thought than what lesser ones did. But two other reasons are
historically more important. First, Fielding was demonstrably
responding to their vision when he created his heroes, from Tom
Thumb to Tom Jones; it was their world and their vision that he
felt obliged to respond to. Second, it is the vision of Pope and Swift
that dominated literary practice through most of the first half of
the century, for the Pope circle set the tone for the rest, and even
those who attacked Pope most violently and were themselves most
vigorously attacked allowed him to dictate the terms of the battle.
Pope was the reigning talent, and even those who disputed his taste
paid their respect to it in their own grudging imitative and parodic
ways.

But there were attempts to go against the prevailing temper and
there are some genuine heroes, and I must speak briefly about the
few successful and the many failed ones because both categories
show what Fielding was up against. Among the more successful is
Robinson Crusoe, a hero who is instructive in two ways, first
because he is not altogether exemplary and second because his
heroism occurs in what one may safely describe as a nonsocial
setting. His nonexemplary status is shown in many ways, not only
as he flees from his station and calling early in the book but as he
makes do on the island. He once spends "three or four weeks"

trying to tug and roll a beached boat to shore; almost immediately thereafter he begins to build a "canoe," spending more than five months on the project but forgetting to consider that he is a hundred yards *downhill* from the water. And the canoe is so large he cannot even "stir" it, despite a canal he digs and many other labor-creating strategies. Over and over he takes the long way round in his projects, proving perhaps the ingenuity of Englishmen in primitive circumstances, but earning low marks for remembering tools he has already rescued from the ship and stored up in what must have been enormous unsorted piles. Crusoe may be able to *do* almost anything if he stays at it long enough—and twenty-eight years give him ample time for his projects—but he apparently cannot find anything. As an observer, he comforts us in our own blind thick-headedness, and as a Christian everyman he is equally comforting spiritually, too proud of his own halting steps forward, too smug as he thinks himself monarch of the island that is his world, and literally frightened into a cave of total privacy and isolation when he sees the first sign of human confrontation. That famous solitary footprint lingers in our minds as a memento of what may be out there waiting for us, of what drives us into ourselves, of the combination of anticipation and terror that is the challenge of any human contact to our loneliness within. Crusoe, with all of his limits and terrible trials, is as close as we get in the early eighteenth century to a character with whom we can identify. And it is worth noting that Defoe has to take him a long way from England to raise Crusoe as high as he does. Later he does reintegrate Crusoe, of course, with his social surroundings, returning him to Spain and ultimately across the Pyrenees and home. But readers have always found these the least satisfying of Crusoe's adventures, even though the events in this part, involving the judgments and interactions of other people, clearly make Crusoe's difficulties greater here than in his solitude. Defoe is here employing a very old device—exportation—to make a hero. It was the standard way in the heroic drama of the Restoration to treat heroism—find a remote and exotic place where heroism might perhaps be plausible—and romances of the eighteenth century continued to try to exploit it. How Defoe brought it off, just once, is an amazing story, taking us into matters of myth, metaphor, and various substrata of the cultural consciousness.

Defoe's other heroes did not succeed this way, even though Defoe frantically sent them to further and wilder places, and the failed heroes of other novels, romances, and epics met similar incredulousness or lack of interest in their audiences. For there were other would-be heroes, many of them; stubborn minor talents continued to assert and fabricate long after their betters had tested the age's limits. Sir Richard Blackmore, for example, physician to Queen Anne and quite a sane and sensible man when at his rightful trade, kept his left hand busy with epics, writing one after another in quest of a hero his age could believe. And he failed time after time, despite choosing the grand figures of British mythology, of classical antiquity, and of Biblical history as his subjects. For writer after writer, in book after book, the qualities of King Arthur, or Julius Caesar, or David and Abraham and Joseph could not be made believable to the age. It was not only that the age did not grow heroes but also that it could not conceive them in other ages and places—that is, it could only imagine them in Homer's world or Vergil's and could not find modern language or project a modern world view that could plausibly sponsor them.

Defoe's signal success points in a curious way to Henry Fielding, for both of them tackled the problem of a modern hero rather than trying to get some ancient grandeur by on its past reputation. But their ways were wholly different, even if both of them draw upon Milton's attempt to define a Christian hero, for Defoe simply strikes out for his target, straightforwardly and with the direct use of the metaphors born into his bones as they were into Milton's. Fielding, on the other hand, sneaks up on his subject, fully conscious of the debasement of his age and knowing he had to subvert before he could circumvent. Defoe was one with Sir Richard Steele and George Lillo in thinking he could postulate a Christian hero as a modern alternative to Augustan versions of anti-hero; he was early and not intimidated.[11] Fielding saw and felt the forces of doubt, cynicism, and despair over the fulfillment of history, and he used irony against itself. My point is neither to disparage an instinctive Defoe and praise an ingenious Fielding, nor is it to praise the genius of Defoe and decry Fielding's artifice. Each artist was who he was as a man, and each did what his character and times permitted in facing a particular historical circumstance. What Fielding thought of their differences may perhaps be surmised by the episode in *Tom Jones* involving the misanthropic hermit, the Man of the Hill, who (besides being Bunyanesque) is clad in skins and suspiciously resembles Crusoe's descriptions of himself.[12]

3

We have returned again to Henry Fielding, and I want to take only one more short excursion before rejoining Tom Jones and Sophia Western at the gates of Paradise Hall. That turn is merely to fill in briefly Fielding's career between the creation of Tom Thumb and Tom Jones. From 1731 to 1737 Fielding continued to write facetious, political, quasi-Augustan plays creating modern hero after modern hero—corrupt lawyers and judges, quack doctors, hack artists, "modern" husbands, and politicians in all walks of life. Some of the heroes are easily identifiable as real figures— Lewis Theobald, Colley Cibber and his even lesser son Theophilus, Orator Henley, the auctioneer Christopher Cock, the Prince of Wales, Sir Robert Walpole—even though the names they bear are Don Tragedio, Sir Farcical Comic, Marplays Sr. and Jr., Dr. Orator, Mr. Hen, Sir Owen Apshinken, and First Politician. Again in 1743 he published a prose satire in the same mold, *Jonathan Wild*, although it was probably written earlier. There, as in *The Beggar's Opera*, the "great man" is both a famous under-world figure and Sir Robert, prime minister until 1742. Such a great man is posited as a typical hero, not only of modern times but of other times as well, and the shadow expands so widely as to include Greek greats like Alexander and many of the standard Romans. Fielding also presents a foil to the great man, a "good man" named Heartfree, but few readers have found him a viable alternative and, if he were Fielding's only answer to the satiric vision, history would remember the horns of Fielding's dilemma rather than the compromises he worked out for his age.

But Fielding had already done better by the time *Jonathan Wild* was published, and he had accomplished it in responding to what seemed to him the misguided efforts of Samuel Richardson to make goodness attractive. Richardson's 1740 celebration of Pamela's simple and dogged virtues became, in Fielding's parodic version, an exposure of prudential scheming in its most seductive form:

how Pamela won souls by her shining example became how Shamela parlayed her "vartue" into a fortune by hoarding supply and manipulating demand. Fielding's 1741 "realistic" version of what modern heroines are like still pays its respects to the premises of Augustan travesty, but whether he knew it or not, his laughing rhetoric was already on its way toward rejecting the claims of impossible ideals and redeeming among the imperfect a viable sense of the possible.

Pamela was on Fielding's mind again when he wrote *Joseph Andrews* (1742), and he exploits the contexts of expectation. He seems very much up to his old parodic tricks when he identifies Joseph as Pamela's brother and insists that Joseph is a spotless instance of male chastity because he is inspired by his sister's irresistible example. Joseph's heritage and model-consciousness make him, at the beginning, anything but an exemplary and admirable hero, not because Fielding conceives him inadequately but because the effects Fielding is after involve the redemption of audience values as much as they involve the maturation of Joseph. Early on, Fielding leeringly compares Joseph's duties around the Booby estate to the functions of Priapus, protector of gardens and obscene god of fertility, and as Joseph grows older he soon faces tests that, in their farcical tone and allusive weight, manipulate readers conditioned to believe that common sense and idealism are mutually exclusive, that goodness is incredible, and that heroes are viable only as buffoons. Lady Booby grieves for six days over the death of her husband, but then concludes that her virtue has earned a sabbath, and she sets her sights on Joseph in a celebrated bedroom farce:

> "What would you think, *Joseph*, if I admitted you to kiss me?" *Joseph* reply'd, "he would sooner die than have any such Thought." "And yet, *Joseph*," returned she, "Ladies have admitted their Footmen to such Familiarities; and Footmen, I confess to you, much less deserving them; Fellows without half your Charms: for such might almost excuse the Crime. Tell me, therefore, *Joseph*, if I should admit you to such Freedom, what would you think of me?—tell me freely." "Madam," said *Joseph*, "I should think your Ladyship condescended a great deal below yourself." "Pugh!" said she, "that I am to answer to myself: but would not you insist on more? Would you be

contented with a Kiss? Would not your Inclinations be all on fire
rather by such a Favour?" "Madam," said Joseph, "if they were,
I hope I should be able to controll them, without suffering them
to get the better of my Virtue."—You have heard, Reader, Poets
talk of the *Statue of Surprize;* you have heard likewise, or else
you have heard very little, how Surprize made one of the Sons of
Croesus speak tho' he was dumb. . . . Not from the inimitable
Pencil of my Friend *Hogarth,* could you receive such an Idea of
Surprize, as would have entered in at your Eyes, had they beheld
the Lady *Booby,* when those last Words issued out from the Lips
of *Joseph.*—"Your Virtue! (said the lady recovering after a
silence of two Minutes) I shall never survive it. Your Virtue!
Intolerable Confidence! Have you the Assurance to pretend,
that when a Lady demeans herself to throw aside the Rules of
Decency, in order to honour you with the highest Favour in her
Power, your Virtue should resist her Inclination? That when she
had conquer'd her own Virtue, she should find an Obstruction
in yours?" "Madam," said *Joseph,* "I can't see why her having
no Virtue should be Reason against my having any. Or why,
because I am a Man, or because I am poor, my Virtue must be
subservient to her Pleasures." "I am out of patience," cries the
lady: "Did ever Mortal hear of a Man's Virtue! Did ever the
greatest, or the gravest Men pretend to any of this Kind! Will
Magistrates who punish Lewdness, or Parsons, who preach
against it, make any scruple of committing it? And can a Boy, a
Stripling, have the Confidence to talk of his Virtue?" "Madam,"
says *Joseph,* "that Boy is the Brother of *Pamela,* and would be
ashamed that the Chastity of his Family, which is preserved in
her, should be stained in him.[13]

There is not much wrong with the ideas Joseph expresses here (he
asserts a single sexual standard for different sexes and different
social classes), but his timing is terrible, and no one would, I think,
predict much of a future for him as servant, lecturer, or hero. But
Fielding brings it off, in spite of Parson Adams's prelapsarian
guidance through a postlapsarian world—and despite farcical
forays that keep Pamela's haughty purity in view while introducing
a whole family of Boobies and even a heroine named Fanny. *How*
Fielding manages such a triumph of rhetoric, tone, and expanded
vision is a story too complex to be told here, but I do wish to
record that he accomplishes it, transforming Joseph at last into an

admirable instance of charity worthy of his Biblical namesake. Joseph may not be a very interesting hero, but he is a viable one, and Fielding achieves his credibility by first seducing the reader into thinking he is doing something entirely, almost diametrically, different.

In *Tom Jones* the techniques of seduction are far more sophisticated, and Fielding fathers a far superior hero. Again he begins belittlingly, and when he repeatedly speaks of "our Heroe" he seems downright patronizing. He does not promise pruriently as he had done in *Joseph Andrews*, but he flashily demonstrates how he can manipulate us at will:

> As we determined, when we first sat down to write this History, to flatter no Man; but to guide our Pen throughout by the Directions of Truth, we are obliged to bring our Heroe on the Stage in a much more disadvantageous Manner than we could wish; and to declare honestly, even at his first Appearance, that it was the universal Opinion of all Mr. *Allworthy*'s Family that he was certainly born to be hanged.
>
> Indeed, I am sorry to say, there was too much Reason for this Conjecture. The Lad having, from his earliest Years, discovered a Propensity to many Vices, and especially to one, which hath as direct a Tendency as any other to that Fate, which we have just now observed to have been prophetically denounced against him. He had been already convicted of three Robberies, *viz.* of robbing an Orchard, of stealing a Duck out of a Farmer's Yard, and of picking Master *Blifil*'s Pocket of a Ball.
>
> The Vices of this young Man were, moreover, heightened by the disadvantageous Light in which they appeared, when opposed to the Virtues of Master *Blifil*, his companion: A Youth of so different a Cast from little *Jones*, that not only the Family, but all the Neighbourhood, resounded his Praises. . . .
>
> *Tom Jones*, . . . bad as he is, must serve for the Heroe of this History.[14]

The continual teasing that Tom seems to have been "born to be hanged" is not just a vague rhetorical threat; an alert reader of 1749 must have thought he knew what to expect, and the more knowledgeable the reader the more he is misled. The year before *Tom Jones* appeared, London was the scene of an especially brutal rape and murder, and one Thomas Jones was arrested and sentenced to be hanged. Those with good memories must have been reminded of one of London's more notorious trials of a generation before when another "Tom Jones" went on trial in a sensational case involving his alleged affair with the wife of a prominent public figure. Like Joseph Andrews, that Tom Jones was the footboy of his "Mistress," and published pamphlets describing the trial offer evidence suggesting a scene rather like that which a reader anticipates from the early Joseph and Lady Booby scenes.[15]

Fielding used, it seems clear, such expectations again in *Tom Jones* to suggest to disappointed readers of *Joseph Andrews* that in this new "History of Tom Jones" they would find a sequel with rather different focal events based upon "history" and "truth." Fielding further teases the expectations of knowledgable readers in the Man of the Hill episode to which I have already referred. The Man occupies a place in the novel similar to that of Mr. Wilson in *Joseph Andrews,* and like Wilson he tells the story of his life, a rather dreary, humorless account that parodies contemporary spiritual autobiographies. Joseph sleeps through part of Wilson's story, conveniently and understandably, and he thus misses the account of Wilson's son having been stolen by gypsies and also misses Wilson's account of the famous strawberry birthmark that he, of course, bears. That convenient nap delays the discovery of Joseph's true parentage and enables the second half of the novel to exist. The structure of episodes involving the Man of the Hill is so deliberately similar that it clearly preys upon our expectations and misleads us badly about Tom's possible parents, just as the apparent facts about Jenny Jones mislead us earlier and those about the identity of Mrs. Waters mislead us later to think that Tom has slept with his own mother. The more attentive the reader and the more knowledgeable he is about historical events, contemporary literature, and Fielding's earlier work, the more fully he is misled. Fielding's training in parody and travesty made him a master of self-allusion, and at his best he can create readers in a way that not only anticipates Sterne but surpasses him.[16] Reading *Tom Jones* is, in fact, a lesson in humility, and a good deal of Fielding's point involves just that stripping and re-education of the reader that Augustan satire aspired to but often only half accomplished.

Those rhetorical stunts are crucial to his creation of a hero, too, for he is responding to the anti-heroic context I have described. In the middle of the eighteenth century, one cannot begin *ex nihilo*, building as if all one had to do was develop a basically probable human being in a world clamoring for, or at least willing to accept, a hero. Rather, Fielding's contemporaries every new day found a London increasingly crowded, stinking, polluted, and crime-ridden, a dilated version of Gin Lane, and it was governed by men who, many thought, made the old Walpole years seem like a Golden Age. The country had just survived "the '45," a rebellion that came very close to changing, yet once more, English "constitutional monarchy." Some readers might rush to weep for Clarissa and worship her coffin, but most sophisticated people at mid-century were still cynics and skeptics about human nature, and they did not weep when they were asked or admire when they were told to. Fielding wrote for such tough-minded readers, and he gave them value for their money. Not all of his strategy of making heroes involves outsmarting smart-aleck readers, but much of it begins there, for the first task is not to make the reader laugh at you and the second is to get his or her responses under control. Once that happens, and once some imaginative sympathy begins to develop for a major character, the making of a hero is well on its way, although the crucial questions of what may constitute heroism in a particular context, and in a particular society, may as yet be unaddressed.

Tom Jones is a hero, and if he is not great or grand enough for every reader he is yet an example of what a person may be at a particular moment in history. The time in history is very important to Fielding's intention and accomplishment, for Fielding's claims to have written a "comic epic in prose" or a "heroic, historical, prosaic poem" rest upon a conviction that such a work must reflect a national spirit and record the realities, hopes, and ideals of a specific cultural moment. It is no accident that in the middle six books of the novel the Jacobite rebellion of '45 has such a prominent place. Tom meets and briefly joins, before being wounded, a regiment marching against the Pretender, Sophia is mistaken at an inn for the Pretender's mistress Jenny Cameron, and several people discuss their political views ad nauseam, most notably Squire Western and his sister and the old Man of the Hill. What is not so emphatic, although equally important, is that the events in London take place at precisely the moment of England's greatest danger, in November and December of '45, when the Pretender was marching on London and when thoughtful observers genuinely feared that the government would fall. One of those thoughtful observers was Henry Fielding, who in the periodical he was then editing (ironically titled *The Jacobite's Journal)* wrote vehemently of the present danger. Yet the London beau monde in *Tom Jones* seems to know nothing of it and pays no mind, secure in daily rounds of intrigue and ennui. Fielding's silence about their responses, after he has been so careful to set up the time of action, is the strongest comment he could make on the smugness and apathy of London life, fully as unpleasant as the aggressive barbarity of the Westerns when they translate the national crisis into a domestic one.

It is against this backdrop of English life at a critical moment that Fielding defines the heroism of a Tom Jones. Tom is not a military hero, a great warrior who can save the nation singlehandedly at a moment of crisis. Neither is he a national leader who can stir crowds and spur lesser men to the active pursuit of the nation's goals. Fielding is writing for 1749, for moments after the "the '45," not for the crisis of the '45 itself, and he makes Tom the new man of mid-century English society, a citizen, altogether unsure of his identity for a long time but ultimately sure of a rightful place as heir and proprietor of a large, and resonant, estate. Like princes of the past, he must be prepared for his high responsibility by education and experience—and so must the citizen-reader, through Fielding's Thomapaedia.

The resonant overtones of Tom's estate and of our relationship to him are built into the novel from the beginning in some rather complex ways. Tom's role as proprietary outcast suggests his mythic human function from nearly the first, even before he is expelled from Paradise Hall and condemned to wander in search of his identity. As he begins the wandering in the middle third of the novel, Fielding takes the trouble to tell us, Miltonically, that "the world . . . lay all before him." Fielding builds the mythic dimensions carefully according to standard readings of the Judeo-Christian myth, but he mutes them carefully so that a simple allegorical explication will not take over and simplify his designs, which are particular and historical as well as grand and universal. He does not, for example, mention the name of Paradise Hall until the story is well begun, and he does not jar us with repeated underscorings. And he modifies myth, too, to his own needs, disinheriting the Satanic Blifil only at the end when he has, Luciferlike, proved unworthy of his legally rightful place. It is only when Blifil has, by action, forfeited that right that a fallible mortal can assume his place as heir and earn the right to a future life in Paradise Hall, taking up residence meanwhile in the adjoining Western estate.

Fielding draws on other myths as well, allowing Tom often to echo the familiar archetype of wanderers, Ulysses, who acquires wisdom through experience, as Tom acquires Sophia only after he has circuitously moved through the English countryside and the preparatory experiences of Molly Seagrim, Mrs. Waters, and Lady Bellaston—in the country, on the road, and in the city. Tom echoes, too, Ulysses' lesser son, Telemachus, who finally finds his father and in so doing finds himself. But Fielding is most careful to domesticate the metaphor of travel as experience. Tom's is a journey, a quest, a pilgrimage; the standard metaphors of move-ment through space as the acquisition of self is carefully Englished so that Tom does not need to go beyond the borders of his beloved homeland to become what he can become. The models Tom echoes thus suggest ideals of classical antiquity and the Christian ideal, but the version he achieves is modern, mortal, thoroughly English, and specifically eighteenth century.

Fielding claims no absolutes as possible, and it is significant that the historical setting involves a defense of constitutional monarchy, not an absolutist position at all but one that had been hammered out on the anvil of English history, heated by the fires of civil war and tempered by human grief and uncertainty. It is a compromise position admitting human error and insisting that the fabric of public life must finally depend on the responsibility of its citizens. Fielding's psychological and moral point is the same, for he is dealing with a fallen paradise where solutions and rights must be worked out in the light of covenants broken and the rights of birth forfeited. The maturation of Tom Jones has not always seemed persuasive to readers, and there are many who (with Thackeray) remember his pranks better than his repentance, who find his high spirits more impressive than his chastened judgment, and who prefer his ranging and jaunty courtships to the narrowed marital gates of his sure estate. Such doubts and preferences are defensible and may even suggest the historical limits of Fielding's rhetoric, but they need to be examined within the contexts of history and ideas of a hero that Augustan satire normalized. For Fielding told his contemporaries—and at least partly showed them—that a fairly ordinary mortal would do as a hero, if good nature was modified and restrained by practical wisdom, and if one didn't expect too much.

It is a long way from *Tom Thumb* to *Tom Jones,* and in the latter Fielding finds a hero more to his own temperamental needs and the needs of his contemporaries starved for a hero yet skeptical of claims of superhuman perfection. In one of his poems, Dryden caustically describes two earlier Toms who had succeeded him as poet-laureate and historiographer-royal:

> But now, not I, but poetry is curst
> For Tom the second reigns like Tom the First.

Pope picked up the line in *The Dunciad,* modifying it to his needs, new kings, and their cosmic extension:

Now Dunce the Second reigns like Dunce the First.

Fielding, on the other hand, describes a changed mood and a changed world. Tom Jones is no Ulysses, certainly no second Adam, but he will do. A new reign of possibility has come, rescued from the human farce of contemporary history and the crippling limits it placed on man's ability to believe in better times and better people. Thackeray's quarrel is less with Fielding's morality than with his own imperfect world; he had come of age in the reign of Wordsworth and Shelley, Scott and Keats, and even if his Georges were no better than those who ruled Fielding's England, his literary fathers could not only make literary utopias but could actually plot them for reality. "Hero-worship" is almost unimaginable in Fielding's world, and if the fact of Tom testifies to human growth, the presence of Blifil shouts the human depravity that Fielding thought mortals were up against. Tom is no object for worship nor even a model for imitation, but he is a proof that human values can survive falls and pratfalls, assertions of possibility in the contexts of doubt. One might argue that Thackeray and Gulliver dream loftier dreams, but Fielding is the artist of the possible, and his contemporaries would hardly want a greater hero, nor could they imagine a grander one.

NOTES

1. William Makepeace Thackeray, *The English Humourists of the Eighteenth Century* (London: Smith, Elder, & Co., 1869), p. 320.

2. Jonathan Swift, *The Prose Writings of Jonathan Swift*, vol. 11, *Gulliver's Travels*, ed. Herbert Davis (Oxford: Basil Blackwell, 1959), pp. 6–7.

3. See Isobel Grundy, "New Verse by Henry Fielding," *PMLA* 87 (1972): 213–45.

4. Swift, *Writings of Swift*, vol. 1, *A Tale of a Tub and Other Early Works, 1696–1707*, ed. Davis, pp. 109–10.

5. I have treated this matter—and several others mentioned passingly in this essay—in more detail in *Occasional Form: Henry Fielding and the Chains of Circumstance* (Baltimore, Md.: Johns Hopkins University Press, 1975).

6. Alexander Pope, *The Poems of Alexander Pope*, Twickenham ed., vol. 2, *The Rape of the Lock and Other Poems*, ed. Geoffrey Tillotson (London: Methuen & Co., 1966), p. 156.

7. Ibid., pp. 147–48.

8. Ibid., p. 194.

9. Pope, *Poems*, vol. 5, *The Dunciad*, ed. James Sutherland (London: Methuen & Co., 1965), pp. 128–29.

10. 2d. ed. (London, 1740), p. 2.

11. Lillo's play, *The Christian Hero* (1735), is of course about Scanderbeg, not a contemporary figure, but Lillo's rhetoric makes it clear that he means to present a relevant modern model. On the earlier tradition of the "Christian Hero," see especially John M. Steadman, *Milton and the Renaissance Hero* (Oxford: Clarendon Press, 1967), and Michael West, "Dryden and the Disintegration of Renaissance Heroic Ideals," *Costerus* 7 (1973): 193–222.

12. I am indebted for this point to Paul Alkon.

13. Henry Fielding, *The Works of Henry Fielding*, Wesleyan ed., vol. 1, *Joseph Andrews*, ed. Martin C. Battestin (Middletown, Conn.: Wesleyan University Press, 1967), pp. 40–41.

14. Fielding, *Works*, vol. 3, *Tom Jones*, ed. Martin C. Battestin (Middletown, Conn.: Wesleyan University Press, 1975), 1: 118–19.

15. For a brief account of one such pamphlet, see Ian P. Watt, "The Naming of Characters in Defoe, Richardson and Fielding," *RES* 25 (1949): 322–38. Watt draws, however, rather different conclusions.

16. See John Preston, *The Created Self: The Reader's Role in Eighteenth-Century Fiction* (London: Heinemann, 1970), esp. p. 113, and Ronald Paulson, *Satire and the Novel in Eighteenth-Century England* (New Haven, Conn.: Yale University Press, 1967), esp. pp. 145–50.

Johnson's Heroes

ROBERT FOLKENFLIK

SAMUEL Johnson has been amply discussed as hero. Boswell's *Life* begins by likening him to Ulysses, presents him as a Monarch of Literature throughout, and ends on a note of reverence. (Indeed, as Marshall Waingrow has pointed out, "reverence" is the last word in the book.) In the following century Carlyle was quick to see, even if his contemporaries were not, that Johnson's heroism was a main theme of Boswell's biography, and he enthroned Johnson as his own prime example of the hero as Man of Letters in *On Heroes and Hero-Worship*. And in this century Bertrand Bronson has written memorably of "Johnson Agonistes." Yet there has been almost nothing said of Johnson's own conception of heroism, the anti-heroic element in his thought, and the embodiment of his ideas in the heroes of his works, especially those of his biographies.

Johnson was no admirer of the conventional hero of history. The literature of the century was redefining the concept of the hero, and a distinctly anti-heroic strain runs through much of his thinking. It is Johnson, after all, who praises England's greatest dramatist by saying "Shakespeare has no heroes: his scenes are occupied only by men." In an *Adventurer* essay on the dangers of judging actions "by the event" he stops to make his purpose clear:

I am far from intending to vindicate the sanguinary projects of heroes and conquerors, and would wish rather to diminish the reputation of their success, than the infamy of their miscarriages: for I cannot conceive why he that has burnt cities, and wasted

143

nations, and filled the world with horror and desolation, should be more kindly regarded by mankind, than he that died in the rudiments of wickedness; why he that accomplished mischief should be glorious, and he that only endeavoured it should be criminal: I would wish Caesar and Catiline, Xerxes and Alexander, Charles and Peter, huddled together in obscurity or detestation.[1]

There is, of course, nothing contradictory about Johnson's attack on conventional heroes and his own conception of human heroism. Even those most interested in a heroic ethic in this period attempt to redefine heroism partly through attacks on received notions. At the end of the seventeenth century in his "Dedication to *Fables*" Dryden breaks into invective to describe an important example of the heroes he dislikes: "Science distinguishes a man of honour from one of those athletic brutes whom, undeservedly, we call heroes. Cursed be the poet, who first honoured with that name a mere Ajax, a man-killing idiot." And just after the end of the eighteenth century Blake can speak of "the silly Greek & Latin slaves of the Sword."

Johnson's attitude is apparent very early in his career. In the beginning of "Upon the Feast of St. Simon and St. Jude" (1726?), a religious poem that has not yet received the praise it deserves, Johnson opposes the heroism of the saints he celebrates to that of the warrior and king:

> Of fields with dead bestrew'd around
> And cities smoking on the ground
>   Let vulgar poets sing;
> Let them prolong their turgid lays
> With some victorious heroe's praise
>   Or weep some falling king,
>
> While I to nobler themes aspire.[2]

In his opposition of saints and martyrs to these figures and his trenchantly anti-heroic thought, Johnson had some important predecessors. Milton's reorientation of epic tradition included battles enough, and yet in *Paradise Lost* the attack on traditional heroism is powerful:

> To overcome in Battel, and subdue
> Nations, and bring home spoils with infinite
> Man-slaughter, shall be held the highest pitch
> Of human Glorie, and for Glorie done
> Of triumph, to be stil'd great Conquerors,
> Patrons of Mankind, Gods and Sons of Gods,
> Destroyers rightlier calld and Plagues of men."
>
> (Ll. 691–97)

Milton would instead speak "of Patience and Heroic Martyrdom" (9. 32). Johnson, in his great essay on Biography, *Rambler* No. 60, says that the biographer should pay little attention to "vulgar greatness," but instead focus on that part of life in which "men excel each other only by prudence and by virtue." Behind Milton and Johnson lies a Christian tradition that owes much to such Renaissance humanists as Colet, Erasmus, and More.[3] And in general we can say that for Johnson the Christian ethic always controls or places limits on the heroic.

The seventeenth-century moralists of France, such as La Rochefoucauld and Pascal, whom Johnson admired, certainly also did a good deal to undermine the heroic ethic. As Paul Bénichou notes, for example, in his chapter on the "démolition du héros" in *Morales du Grand Siècle,* "La Rochefoucauld's enumeration of the disguises of *amour-propre* is identical with the list of chivalric virtues."[4]

When Johnson reaches a point in his own work where he must in some way come to terms with traditional notions of heroism, the result is his weakest major production, *Irene* (1749). The title promised something perhaps along the lines of Nicholas Rowe's she-tragedies, and Johnson's intention to write a Christian tragedy that would contain an implicit critique of the tragedies of the last age is at least plausible: *Clarissa* appeared the year before.[5] Johnson implores his audience to attend to *Irene* even

> If no wild draught depart from reason's rules,
> Nor gods his heroes, nor his lovers fools.

The "mighty moral" he promises is close to what *The Vanity of Human Wishes* would teach:

Learn here how Heav'n supports the virtuous mind,
Daring, tho' calm; and vigorous, tho' resign'd.[6]

In the context of the play these lines describe the conduct of
Aspasia in contrast to the guilty and ironically though deservedly
defeated Irene. Yet they have a wider range of reference as well.

The "Prologue to *Irene*" tells the most important facts about
Johnson's relation to the heroic tradition received from tragedy: he
was rejecting the conception of the heroes, as he perceived them, of
Restoration tragedy. This is stated most explicitly in Johnson's
"Dedication" to Charlotte Lennox's *Shakespear Illustrated* (1753),
the forerunner of his more famous comment in his own "Preface
to *Shakespeare*":

> Among his other excellencies it ought to be remarked, because it
> has hitherto been unnoticed, that his *heroes are men,* that the
> love and hatred, the hopes and fears of his chief personages are
> such as are common to other human beings, and not like those
> which later times have exhibited, peculiar to phantoms that strut
> upon the stage.[7]

The critics who read Johnson's "Shakespeare has no heroes: his
scenes are occupied only by men," and, when they catch their
breaths, retort that Shakespeare has heroes indeed, have evidently
not read this passage with attention nor seen the historical context
of Johnson's remarks. Many of Johnson's comments on the hero
in drama, especially in his Shakespeare criticism, are best seen as a
reaction to the extravagant heroes of Restoration tragedy (and to
the vogue of the "fairy way of writing"—Johnson clearly prefers
Propero to Ariel and Caliban, Hamlet to Hamlet's ghost).

What Johnson says of *The Conquest of Grenada* is typical (and,
incidentally, if the pejorative phraseology is removed, a very good
description of the intentions of Dryden's tragedy):

> The two parts of *The Conquest of Grenada* are written with a
> seeming determination to glut the publick with dramatick won-
> ders; to exhibit in its highest elevation a theatrical meteor of
> incredible love and impossible valor, and to leave no room for a
> wilder flight to the extravagance of posterity. All the rays of
> romantick heat, whether amorous or warlike, glow in Almanzor

by a kind of concentration. He is above all laws; he is exempt from all restraints; he ranges the world at will, and governs wherever he appears. He fights without enquiring the cause, and loves in spite of the obligations of justice, of rejection by his mistress, and of prohibition from the dead. Yet the scenes are, for the most part, delightful; they exhibit a kind of illustrious depravity and majestick madness: such as, if it is sometimes despised, is often reverenced, and in which the ridiculous is mingled with the astonishing.[8]

Johnson does not love a wonder, but it is to his credit that he recognizes the hold that Dryden's extravagant hero has upon the imagination. In Johnson's own work such a figure appears not in his tragedy, but in *The Vanity of Human Wishes.*

Charles XII is infrequently the subject in Johnson's writings or talk, but he is present often enough to be taken as the type for Johnson of the hero as warrior. It may well be that Johnson intended to write a tragedy about him. *Adventurer* No. 99 displays him as "the last of the royal projectors with whom the world has been troubled." Usually when the portrait of Charles XII in *The Vanity of Human Wishes* is examined, it is compared, naturally enough, with the original, Juvenal's portrait of Hannibal. Yet here it is perhaps more revealing to compare it with its most probable historical source, Voltaire's *Histoire de Charles XII.* Even if Johnson was not working from Voltaire, the attitude is similar and the historical information is almost point by point what Johnson had to go on.

That Johnson admired this biography, as a friend of his claimed, is easy to credit despite some of Johnson's astringent remarks about Voltaire elsewhere. Voltaire's ironic "Discourse on the History of Charles XII," which prefaces his book, begins: "Few are the Princes whose actions merit a particular history. In vain have most of them been the objects of slander or flattery: small is their number whose memory is preserved, and would be yet smaller, were the good only remembered."[9] He goes on to defend his own undertaking in words that could serve as a headnote to Johnson's portrait of Charles:

Must not any King who reads the story of *Charles* the twelfth, be immediately cured of the vanity [*folie*] of being a conqueror.

Where is the Prince who can say, I have greater courage, more virtues, more resolution, more strength of body, greater skill in war, or better troops than *Charles* the twelfth. If with all this assistance, and after so many victories, he was so unfortunate; what may other Princes expect, who shall have as great ambition, with less capacity and fewer advantages?[10]

Voltaire states his challenge in terms of the traditional justification of history as a school for princes; Johnson would probably defend it in terms of the more general justification of tragedy: if such a man fell, it should cure anyone's vanity.

We should not permit the difference between Johnson's and Dryden's translations of Juvenal X to obscure the closeness of Johnson to Dryden's usual satiric technique. Johnson's portraits are far closer to Dryden's in *Absalom and Achitophel* than to those of Pope or to the debasing images of Swift, whose works he so resolutely underestimated. This is why Ian Jack's adaptation of Dryden's phrase "tragical satire" to describe *The Vanity of Human Wishes* is so just. Yet Johnson's figures have more dignity than Dryden's. Voltaire calls Charles "a man the most extraordinary, perhaps, that ever appeared in the world. All the great qualities of his ancestors were united in him; nor had he any other fault or misfortune, but that he carried them beyond all bounds."[11] Johnson's Charles is the embodiment of heroic evil. There is no room in Johnson's portraits for Juvenal's *pelves* ("pisspots" in Dryden's translation). Swift can present his satiric targets as nasty triflers, but Johnson is superior to Charles before his fall only in the knowing narrative voice that presents him.

The portrait of Charles has been justly admired (T. S. Eliot set the tone for the twentieth century in this respect, as in so many others), but if we look at Voltaire we can see how much biographical knowledge is registered in Johnson's complex lines:

> A frame of adamant, a soul of fire,
> No dangers fright him, and no labours tire;
> O'er love, o'er fear, extends his wide domain,
> Unconquer'd lord of pleasure and of pain;
> No joys to him pacific scepters yield,
> War sounds the trump, he rushes to the field.[12]

Behind this lies Voltaire's account of the king who, having just sloughed off the regency of his mother, prepares for his first battle:

> From the moment he prepared for the war, he entered upon a new course of life, from which he never after departed in one single particular. . . . He no more admired magnificence, sports, and recreations; he reduced his table to the utmost frugality. He had been fond of gaiety and dress, but was ever after clad like a common soldier. [His counsellors] had suspected him of having entertained a passion for a lady of his court; but whether the suspicion was just or no, 'tis certain he renounced all conversation with the women for ever after, not only through fear of becoming a slave to them, but to give his soldiers an example of his resolution to restrain himself to the severest discipline; or it may be, through the vanity of being the sole Prince who knew how to suppress an inclination so difficult to be conquered.[13]

In short, this "unconquer'd lord of pleasure and of pain" has become inhuman in order to be superhuman.

A knowledge of the historical background also makes yet more biting the exquisite ironies of Charles in his fall

> Condemn'd a needy supplicant to wait,
> While ladies interpose, and slaves debate.

The tripping rhythms of the first half of the latter line make their own commentary, as do the heavier, more earnest rhythms of the second. Charles, who was all action, is forced into anguished passivity while the frivolous and the powerless speak in his favor (though he is far from being the only "supplicant" in the poem). On the one hand is the suggestion of an aid that will accomplish its ends by vaguely sexual means, and on the other a puppet parliament. As Voltaire makes clear, not only had Charles renounced the sex, but the very act that made him king overthrew his mother, the queen-regent, on the grounds that it was not fit for him or his soldiers to "'receive orders from a woman.'"[14] The historical events behind this couplet reveal that the "ladies" were probably one woman, the mother of the sultan, who attempted to take the part of Charles while he spent months cooling his heels in Constantinople.[15] The slaves are even more interesting, for they can only be Baltagi Mahomet, "a slave brought up in idleness and the silence of a Seraglio, made a Visir by interest and a General against his inclinations" and the janissaries, "for," according to Voltaire, "the rapacity of the Grand Signior is scare ever felt by any but the Officers of the empire, who, whatever they are else, are domestick slaves of the Sultan."[16] Baltagi Mahomet had served, as his very name signifies, as a slave who cut wood for the princes in the seraglio. Johnson purposely avoids saying that the attempts to help or hinder Charles were carried out by royalty and rulers so that he can more pointedly show the depth of Charles's fall. Charles considered himself destiny's master, and his seemingly miraculous escapes convinced him that he was invulnerable.

The final ironies come when Charles at last attempts to break out of his Turkish captivity—in which he was maintained royally, if tiresomely, by the sultan—and instead of meeting Peter the Great in a cataclysmic battle,

> His fall was destin'd to a barren strand,
> A petty fortress, and a dubious hand.

It would seem difficult to improve on this couplet, with its casual urbanity of tone and chillingly precise adjectives for its reduction of Charles in his own terms. Charles would not understand a Swiftian critique of his heroism; this is his own shame. Yet Johnson moves in summary from the event to its meaning in a concluding couplet which is even better:

> He left the name, at which the world grew pale,
> To point a moral, or adorn a tale.

The first line works up to three heavy accents in a phrase that clearly represents what Charles wanted, but the immediate deflation, as we see how little this "achievement" amounts to, allows no appeal. When Johnson speaks of the hero's "empty splendor" elsewhere, the phrase itself may seem empty; here he has earned the right to his own moral.[17]

Johnson's *The Vanity of Human Wishes* takes in all conditions, but it is at its extremities a critique of Faustian man. He distrusts human wishes, not only because "Fate wings with every wish the Afflictive dart," but also because wishes in themselves tend toward aggrandizement and the quest toward infinite experience. Johnson considers that there are some experiences man cannot have if he is to remain a human being. He always tries to pull down vanity.

Johnson's only biography of a king, Charles Frederick of Prussia, strews antimonarchical jibes along the way. (It is suggestive that he wrote it at the height of his disgust for the Seven Years' War and his dissatisfaction with the policies of George II.) The conclusion is, I believe, meant to be taken ironically:

> The lives of princes, like the histories of nations, have their periods. We shall here suspend our narrative of the king of Prussia, who was now at the height of human greatness, giving laws to his enemies, and courted by all the powers of Europe.[18]

Although the word *suspend* would seem to point to an intention to continue the narrative at a later time, it is rather meant to be seen in the context of the first sentence. Johnson's paragraph is addressed to those who are aware of the vanity of human wishes. They will realize that, unlike a narrative, life, which exists in continuous time, cannot be suspended and that the picture of Frederick "at the height of human greatness" is therefore a false one. We leave the king to his successes with the knowledge that soon he, like Charles XII, will merely point a moral or adorn a tale. So much for the man whom others were to call Frederick the Great.

At least one reason for the attitude toward kings in Johnson's narratives is the nature of his audience. In Johnson's only well-known work of fiction, one character says to another:

> "Let us cease to consider what, perhaps, may never happen, and what, when it shall happen, will laugh at human speculation. We will not endeavour to modify the motions of the elements, or to fix the destiny of kingdoms. It is our business to consider what beings like us may perform, each labouring for his own happiness by promoting within his circle, however narrow, the happiness of others."[19]

One would hardly guess that these remarks from a continuation of "A Disquisition on Greatness" are spoken by a prince to a princess. It is noteworthy that fixing the destiny of kingdoms, an action to which Rasselas could easily have aspired, is put on the same level as attempting to control the weather, the madness to which the astronomer later succumbs. The audience for this work is middle-class. Thomas Rymer and others could take tragedy as a school for princes, and history could be conceived of generally as philosophy teaching by examples, those that a ruling elite should learn (one source of Johnson's dissatisfaction with history as a mode of knowledge); but now the consumers of literature had changed. How fitting, therefore, that Johnson's hero is a prince who abdicates precisely those responsibilities that sixteenth- and seventeenth-century moral treatises such as Machiavelli's *The Prince*, Elyot's *The Gouernour*, and Erasmus's *The Education of a Christian Prince*, taught in their very different ways.

In order to examine a wide enough variety of men to enable us to discern Johnson's heroes and villains with some clarity we will have to return to his biographies. Yet it is a delicate task, for he conceives of biography in a distinctly anti-heroic spirit. In one of his two most impressive statements about biography Johnson warns that "he that recounts the life of another, commonly dwells most upon conspicuous events, lessens the familiarity of his tale to increase its dignity, shews his favourite at a distance decorated and magnified like the ancient actors in their tragic dress, and endeavours to hide the man that he may produce a hero."[20] Johnson would retreat from this extremity and try to focus on the similarity between men so that "those whom fortune or nature places at the greatest distance may afford instruction to each other." Thus Johnson, though no democrat, contributes to the development of the democratic hero. His comparison of the prince to a farmer in his essay is sardonic enough to be placed alongside some of Swift's remarks in *A Tale of a Tub*: "The prince feels the same pain when an invader seizes a province, as the farmer when a thief drives away his cow." Johnson had been anticipated here by Dryden, who recognizes that by biography's emphasis on the private over the public, "the pageantry of life is taken away; you see the poor reasonable animal, as naked as ever nature made him; and are made acquainted with his passions and his follies, and find the Demy-God a man."[21]

We might begin with Johnson's attitude towards activity in the world. Although his biographies are permeated with his religious values and the vanity of human wishes is one of his constant themes, Johnson does not believe that human accomplishment necessarily is vain. What these biographies help to define is the range of human possibilities and the proper sphere of achievement. In one of his sermons he says,

> There are two circumstances which, either single or united, make any attainments estimable among men. The first is the usefulness of it to society. The other is the capacity or application necessary for acquiring it.[22]

The first criterion explains his great respect for ministers, doctors, inventors, and certain men of letters. In the "Life of Boerhaave" he treats the career of one who was kept from becoming a minister because he was unjustly accused of subscribing to the views of Spinoza. Instead, Boerhaave became a physician, "a profession, not, indeed, of equal dignity or importance, but which must, undoubtedly, claim the second place among those which are of the greatest benefit to mankind."[23] The "Life of Boerhaave" was Johnson's second biography; his first was that of a priest, Father Paul Sarpi. Among his early subjects were such medical men as Sydenham, Morin, and Browne. His short biographies for James's *Medicinal Dictionary* (1743) must have been congenial work. It is highly appropriate that his most memorable nonsatiric poem should be an elegy for a doctor, Robert Levet. Of the four men whose works were added to the *Lives of the Poets* by Johnson's request, three were ministers and the fourth was a doctor.[24]

The second criterion provides much of the force behind Johnsonian biography. His staunch belief in the exemplary function of narratives of human excellence—and Johnson the biographer is more interested in excellence than Johnson the biographical theorist—is underscored by the value he puts on even the bizarre or ludicrous action, provided it takes capacity or application:

> Every thing that enlarges the sphere of human powers, that

shows man he can do what he thought he could not do, is valuable. The first man who balanced a straw upon his nose; Johnson, who rode upon three horses at a time; in short all such men deserve the applause of mankind, not on account of the use of what they did, but of the dexterity which they displayed.[25]

There is no topic that he more readily discusses than the necessity of striving, of diligence, and persistence in the pursuit of an impossible perfection.[26] Anyone blinded by the eighteenth-century ideal of prudent mediocrity or focusing only on Johnson's religious dicta will be apt to miss this important facet of his thought.

Although an anti-heroic strain runs throughout Johnson's thinking on history and biography, it applies chiefly to social matters. Intellectually, Johnson believes in ambition. In *Adventurer* No. 81 he makes the distinction clear and offers a biographical sketch of the Admirable Crichton by way of illustration. If we should overrate our own abilities with respect to others, there is a danger that we will arrogate things to ourselves that we do not deserve and consequently contribute to the destruction of order, "but to rate our powers high in proportion to things, and imagine ourselves equal to great undertakings, while we leave others in possession of the same abilities, cannot with equal justice provoke censure."[27] He is aware that self-love may distort our estimate, but here no harm is done.

This plea for a reach that may exceed one's grasp, which he represents as a break with common prescriptions, is evident in many of Johnson's essays. The fantastic life of Crichton, poet, swordsman, musician, painter, athlete, etc., is intended as an example of what a man may possibly accomplish if he dares to set his sights high. Not surprisingly, polymaths play an important role in the biographies written by a man who believed in freedom of the will and who maintained that genius was "a mind of large general powers, accidentally determined to some particular direction" (*Lives*, 1: 2). Crichton, however, is so clearly a figure of wish-fulfillment that only Johnson's interest in making his point could overcome his usual skepticism when faced by marvelous feats.

There are also more believable polymaths to be found in Johnson's pages. The modest, humble Herman Boerhaave, the subject of one of Johnson's best early biographies, served successively as professor of physics, botany, and chemistry, finally becoming chief physician at Saint Augustin's Hospital and governor of the University of Leyden. His books won him a European reputation, and he was elected to the Académie Française and the Royal Society. Johnson's admiration for Isaac Watts is also immediately apparent; along with Boerhaave, Watts is the most saintly of any of his subjects.[28] In Watts's character piety predominates, but what clearly impresses Johnson is the combination of Christian piety with varied intellectual attainments. Johnson admits that Watts does not achieve greatness in any single area of literary endeavor, but commends his scope—poet, philosopher, divine, and writer of "a catechism for children in their fourth year" (*Lives*, 3: 308). His praise of Watts for "combating Locke" *and* making a child's catechism reminds us of his praise of Milton for writing the *Accidence commenced Grammar,* "a little book which has nothing remarkable, but that its author, who had been lately defending the supreme powers of his country and was then writing *Paradise Lost,* could descend from his elevation to rescue children from the perplexity of grammatical confusion" (*Lives*, 1: 132). His respect for broad accomplishment explains why he asserted that the greatest man among the Queen Anne wits was Dr. Arbuthnot.[29] And he also was reported to have said that the only man he would rather have been other than himself was Hugo Grotius, diplomat, poet, historian and defender of religion.[30] A phrase in his epitaph for Goldsmith, not the famous line but the one before it, *"Qui nullum fere scribendi genus Non tetigit"* ("Who almost none of the kinds of writing did not touch"), praises his friend's breadth of achievement in words that might well stand on his own tombstone. It is the "comprehensive" mind that deserves the most praise. The epic is the highest of genres because "it requires an assemblage of all the powers which are singly sufficient for other compositions" (*Lives*, 1: 170).

These men who do not limit themselves to specialties share another important characteristic of the Johnsonian hero: they recognize their own abilities. "Self-confidence," he says in the *Life of Pope*, "is the first requisite to great undertakings" (*Lives*, 3:89). And in the lives of the greatest poets whose biographies he writes, he is certain to discuss this theme. The *Life of Milton* provides the best example of the value and dangers of self-confidence. Although he scourges Milton's egoism in writing in favor of divorce, his sympathetic account of Milton's literary intentions, as revealed in *The Reason of Church Government,* deals with the same quality of mind in another context:

> In this book he discovers, not with ostentatious exultation, but with calm confidence, his high opinion of his own powers; and promises to undertake something, he yet knows not what, that may be of use and honour to his country. (*Lives,* 1:102)

This paragraph, thoroughly Johnsonian in its approbation, should prepare the reader for his praise of *Paradise Lost.* Similar praise of self-confidence can be found in his biographies of Dryden, Addison, and Savage (*Lives,* 1:396; 2:120, 403).

Without self-confidence one cannot expect to find genius, which is described in a famous passage from the *Life of Pope* as

> a mind active, ambitious, and adventurous, always investigating, always aspiring; in its wider searches still longing to go forward, in its highest flights still wishing to be higher; always imagining something greater than it knows, always endeavouring more than it can do. (*Lives,* 3:217)

As he puts it in *Rambler* No. 137, "It is the proper ambition of the heroes in literature to enlarge the boundaries of knowledge by discovering and conquering new regions of the intellectual world."[31]

The failure to strive for greatness leads to mediocre accomplishments. The dull-witted Blackmore had written a series of epic poems, but Johnson thinks it unlikely that he "had ever elevated his views to that ideal perfection which every genius born to excel is condemned always to pursue, and never overtake" (*Lives,* 2:253). Of a piece with these views are some of his comments on the metaphysical poets. The transition from his asperities to a more sympathetic judgment is accomplished through his recognition of the essentially ambitious nature of their poetry (*Lives,* 1:21).

A related characteristic that clearly interests him but obtains his approbation only when combined with other qualities that he desires is the rise of "worth by poverty depressed." He had intended to write the life of Cromwell, "saying, that he thought it must be highly curious to trace his extraordinary rise to the supreme power."[32] This, we can be almost certain, is not the central impression that a *Life of Cromwell* by Samuel Johnson would have made, but the Horatio Alger interest is hardly accidental. In praising Walton's *Lives*, he found it "wonderful that Walton who was in a very low situation in life, should have been familiarly received by so many great men, and that at a time when the ranks of society were kept more separate than they are now."[33] Though Johnson is jealous for the prerogatives of station and has nothing but contempt for those who, like Swift, attempt to behave too familiarly with their superiors, he heartily approves of the self-made man.

His interest is strikingly manifested in a little-known discussion of two great lawyers as possible subjects for biography. Weighing the claims of Lord Mansfield, he says:

> Born of a noble family, reared with a costly education, and entering the world with all Scotland at his heels, what is there to wonder at in his elevation? If his nurse had foretold it, you wouldn't have taken her for a witch. No, sir. If I were to write the life of an English lawyer it should be the life of Lord Hardwicke, a son of the earth, with no education but what he gave himself, no friends but of his own making, who still lived to preside in the highest Court of the Kingdom with more authority, in the Cabinet with more weight, and in the Senate with more dignity, than any man who had gone before him. His was indeed an elevation to be wondered at. If his nurse had dared to foretell of him that he would rise to such a height, sir, she'd have swum for it.[34]

In the "Life of Cave" Johnson discusses a man who has "risen to eminence." And he emphasizes what Cave, who as a boy at Rugby was blamed for the pranks committed by those "who were far above him in rank and expectations," accomplishes through diligence and literary abilities.[35] He also has a grudging respect for that shrewd literary businessman, Alexander Pope, who built a personal fortune from his brilliant poems. One of the less prominent but persistent themes of his biographies is keynoted by references, as in the *Life of Prior,* to "those that have burst out from an obscure original" (*Lives,* 2:180).

In Johnson's treatment of his subjects there is another important element, as his reference to the "heroes in literature" as discoverers and conquerors suggests, that is not apparent in his biographical theory. This is his tendency to draw on heroic imagery in describing his intellectual heroes. "Those who cannot strike with force, can, however, poison their weapon, and, weak as they are, give mortal wounds, and bring a hero to the grave." Had Johnson said this about what happens in *Hamlet,* we would take his comment as a truism, but applied to the calumnious report that Boerhaave had become a disciple of Spinoza, it gives a metaphorical power to his description.[36] If Johnson was wary of the biographer who "endeavours to hide the man that he may produce a hero," he nevertheless frequently enough dignified and elevated his subjects by comparing them to traditional heroes. Johnson's brilliant adaptation of Suetonius's praise of Augustus as builder of Rome (*"lateritiam invenit, marmoream reliquit,"* "he found it brick, and he left it marble") describes Dryden's gift to English poetry (*Lives,* 1: 469). And early in the *Life of Milton* Johnson claims, in words that find their echo in his definition of genius in the *Life of Pope,* that "Milton's delight was to sport in the wide regions of possibility; reality was a scene too narrow for his mind. He sent his faculties out upon discovery, into worlds where only imagination can travel" (*Lives,* 1: 177–78). Johnson seems to be conscious of the heroic analogy in his biographies. In referring to Dryden's criticism of Shakespeare as "a perpetual model of encomiastick criticism," he says, "The praise lavished by Longinus, on the attestation of the heroes of Marathon by Demosthenes, fades away before it" (*Lives,* 1: 412).

The heroic analogy is not always employed for purposes of elevating the subject, however. Johnson's attitude towards traditional heroes was too ambiguous for that. In the early *Life of Savage* the irony of his comparison clearly cuts both ways: "The Heroes of literary as well as civil History have been very often no less remarkable for what they have suffered, than for what they have achieved."[37] And having said that he would not "wish that Milton had been a rhymer," despite his opinion of blank verse,

Johnson adds, "yet like other heroes, he is to be admired rather than imitated" (*Lives*, 1: 194). Indeed, the description of the death of Pope is, as Paul Fussell has noted, distinctly mock-heroic in its overtones:

> The death of great men is not always proportioned to the lustre of their lives. Hannibal, says Juvenal, did not perish by a javelin or a sword; the slaughters of Cannae were revenged by a ring. The death of Pope was imputed by some of his friends to a silver saucepan, in which it was his delight to heat potted lampreys. (*Lives*, 3: 200)

It is worth noting also that this heroic analogue itself is drawn from a satire, in fact from the very portrait on which Johnson's character of Charles XII is modeled.

The excellence of which I have been speaking, however socially useful, is not equivalent to virtue, which always elicits higher praise. Paradoxically, those qualities that gain a man the fame that makes him an interesting subject for biography are not valued most highly in Johnsonian biography. Herman Boerhaave's "knowledge, however uncommon, holds, in his character, but the second place; his virtue was yet more uncommon than his learning."[38] Sydenham's "skill in physick was not his highest excellence; . . . his whole character was amiable; . . . his chief view was the benefit of mankind, and the chief motive of his actions, the will of God."[39] The virtues that Johnson praises may be conveniently divided into social and individual virtues; both types are, in Johnson's works, preeminently Christian. Among the social virtues explicitly singled out for approval in Johnson's biographies are charity and compassion, turning one's cheek and forgiving one's enemy. Richard Savage had many bad traits, but Johnson thought that "compassion" was his "distinguishing quality." Savage's gift of half of his only guinea to the woman who had testified against him at his murder trial was

> an action which in some Ages would have made a Saint, and perhaps in others a Hero, and which, without any hyperbolical Encomiums, must be allowed to be an Instance of uncommon Generosity, an Act of complicated Virtue; by which he at once relieved the Poor, corrected the Vicious, and forgave an Enemy;

by which he at once remitted the strongest Provocations, and exercised the most ardent Charity.[40]

His act is at once rational and passionate; he overcomes the base emotion of revenge but there is warmth in his charity. Unlike the Stoics, with whom he has, as we shall see, certain affinities, Johnson does not wish to extinguish human passions—a task at once impossible and dehumanizing; he wants to regulate and encourage those that concur with virtue.

Charity he looked upon as one of the foremost virtues, and he will often mention specific acts of charity and even name the sums involved. Pope helped Dodsley open shop and was the principal donor of Savage's subscription. Having detailed these acts in short scope, Johnson adds, "he was accused of loving money, but his love was eagerness to gain, not solicitude to keep it" (*Lives*, 3: 214). Swift's charity, on the other hand, was faulty, for although he offered the poor loans without interest, he insisted that they be paid punctually and took those who were tardy to court. This charity with "no provision of patience or pity" can hardly, in Johnson's eyes, be considered charity at all, for it ignores the facts of human frailty. And he finds Congreve culpable for squandering a legacy upon Henrietta, duchess of Marlborough, who had no need for money, while a branch of his own family was penurious. A large part of the short *Life of Garth* is devoted to the background of the *Dispensary* and praises the charitableness of Garth and of physicians in general for attempting to set up a system to treat the poor without pay.

Yoked to Johnson's insistence on active virtue is an equal insistence on the importance of what he called in the eighteenth-century sense of the word *modesty*. This term includes our current meaning, but it also means "self-distrust." And self-distrust is the basic attitude towards life that Johnson recommends. Watts, for example, was resentful by nature, "but by his established and habitual practice he was gentle, modest and inoffensive" (*Lives*, 3: 307).[41] And his distinction as a writer seems to reside in bringing this cast of mind to his religious writings. As Johnson sees it, until the time of Watts the dissenters had let their zealousness dictate their words, and their writings were "commonly obscured and blunted by coarseness and inelegance of style" (*Lives*, 3: 306).

Watts's writings, on the other hand, are praiseworthy for "his meekness of opposition and his mildness of censure" (*Lives, 3:* 308).

To see the reverse of this image, one might move from here to the life of another dissenting churchman, which can be taken as its antithesis, much in the manner of Hamlet's "Look here upon this picture, and on this." If Watts is the dissenter as saint, the "Life of Cheynel" presents a nearly demonic Puritan divine. Cheynel suffers from a lack of self-distrustfulness. Like Watts and Boerhaave, he is temperamentally resentful, but Cheynel lets his passion rule him. His actions are always precipitate, and he is totally self-assured. Whereas Watts accepted his position as a dissenter—he might have gone to Oxford or Cambridge on a scholarship had he conformed—Cheynel not only sided with the rebels, but used his position when the Puritans took over Oxford to have the degree that had been denied him for espousing Presbyterian doctrine presented and dated retroactively. When he arrived at Oxford he not only dismissed the old president, Dr. Baily, from his office, but broke down the door in order to evict him. Cheynel's "heat" is remarked throughout the biography and the personifications that Johnson uses to describe him take on a demonic life of their own. Where one action would be most humane, "Cheynel's fury prompted him to a different conduct."[42] This life, which was originally published in *The Student*, a periodical intended for undergraduates at Oxford and Cambridge, presents a lesson to the reader that appears in one of the early paragraphs: "A temper of this kind is generally inconvenient and offensive in any society, but in a place of education is least to be tolerated."[43] It is noteworthy that Cheynel is close to the traditional hero—a "fighting parson."

The men whom Johnson most admires endure trials and sufferings without complaint and maintain their virtues despite their troubles. They are sustained by their piety and display, in the words of *The Vanity of Human Wishes*, "Obedient Passions and a Will resign'd." Such men, let us note in defense of Johnson, whose supposed chauvinism and political and religious bigotry have become legendary, include Boerhaave, a foreigner, Watts, a dissenter, and Blackmore, a Whig. The men for whom he has the least sympathy in this context are those who subvert the established

order or indulge in social pride (a wishful subversion of order) or
self-pity. Cheynel and Milton are the foremost subverters of order
among his subjects. Swift, and to some extent Congreve, act in
ways unbecoming to their stations in life. Both Pope and Swift
portray themselves as though the world were conspiring against
them.

The Stoic element in Johnson's thought is firmly grounded in his
belief in God. In his biographies, Christian Stoicism (*"patientia
christiana,"* to use the phrase he borrows from Lipsius) is the
proper response to adversity, particularly sickness. It springs from
the sense of man's limitations. In one of his earliest productions,
the "Life of Boerhaave," he praises Boerhaave's "patience" while
bedridden and distinguishes it from that of the Stoics. It is "more
rational" because "it was founded . . . not on vain reasonings, but
on confidence in God."[44] In another early life he discusses the
behavior of Dr. Thomas Sydenham, who was subject to attacks of
the gout and suffered from kidney stones during the last thirteen
years of his life:

> These were distempers which even the art of Sydenham could
> only palliate, without hope of a perfect cure, but which, if he has
> not been able by his precepts to instruct us to remove, he has, at
> least, by his example, taught us to bear; for he never betrayed an
> indecent impatience, or unmanly dejection, under his torments,
> but supported himself by the reflections of philosophy, and the
> consolations of religion.[45]

The man whom Johnson admires faces sickness, adversity, and
death, as does Roger Ascham, with the "resignation and piety of a
true Christian."[46]

Savage, whom one could hardly think of as a Stoic, is credited
with "the Virtue of *suffering well.*"[47] But the *Life of Savage* is a
brilliantly balanced account of vices and virutes, and Johnson
immediately qualifies his remark by ironically bringing another
Stoic ideal to bear on Savage's behavior:

> The two Powers which, in the Opinion of *Epictetus,* constituted
> a wise Man, are those of *bearing* and *forebearing,* which cannot
> indeed be affirmed to have been equally possessed by *Savage;*

and indeed the Want of one obliged him very frequently to practice the other.[48]

Carey McIntosh's article, "Johnson's Debate with Stoicism," is full of careful discriminations as to Johnson's acceptance of stoical doctrine, but it misses the limitations of the scope of Stoicism in Johnson's thought. His conclusion, which asserts that "Johnson as moralist is less concerned with 'interpersonal relations' than with individual well-being,"[49] certainly overemphasizes Johnson's religious individualism. For Johnson, who like so many in his day thinks that "man" is synonymous with "social being," salvation is individual, but man must exist in society. And it is his business to help actively his fellow beings. Again, the Stoic *apathia* has nothing in common with the intellectual striving Johnson desiderates.

There is, however, a way of seeing the essential unity of the different kinds of actions that Johnson admires. For Johnson a primary fact about man is his mortality. Hence human time is of great importance to him. The difficulty of achievement in a world of flux was a problem to which he frequently returned. And he most admired men who took cognizance of the human condition by creating for themselves a sense of duration while at the same time recognizing their total dependence on the mercy of God. In this perspective we should notice that the radical difference between his praise of intellectual attainment and pious submission begins to evaporate. Early in this essay it appeared that Boerhaave, the scientist with a European reputation, and Boerhaave, the modest Christian Stoic, were almost coincidentally the same man. But his learning and his virtue share the same relationship to time. One might draw from the "Life of Boerhaave" a catalogue of temporal virtues. Boerhaave displays "steady adherence," "patience," "constancy." His intellectual pursuits are distinguished by "long and unwearied observation"; his behavior in sickness by "fortitude and steady composure of mind."[50]

The qualities that make a great poet are also dominated by a sense of the importance of time. In the definition of genius quoted earlier, the operative words, repeated a total of six times, are "still" and "always." Johnson throws his emphasis on the persevering qualities. No wonder he said, agreeing with Locke, that "the widest excursions of the mind are made by short flights frequently repeated."[51] The man of genius must continually snatch graces. The Romantics could admire far, far better things and single intense moments, but for Johnson the things that one can do day in, day out are more important. And he tends to think of accomplishment in terms of customary excellence.

Finally, we can see why the writer becomes a central hero for Johnson: "Statesmen and generals may grow great by unexpected accidents and a fortunate concurrence of circumstances, neither procured nor forseen by themselves: but reputation in the learned world must be the effect of industry and capacity."[52] And if the ideal of heroism described in Johnson's "Prologue to *Irene*" ("the virtuous mind / Daring, tho' calm; and vigorous, tho' resign'd") seems to be most nearly approached in such modest polymaths as Boerhaave and Watts, his very definition of genius is heroic and applies most fully by his own standards to Pope, Dryden, and Milton.

It is perhaps best to end with Milton, for if Johnson has little but scorn for his Republicanism, the conclusion of the *Life of Milton* surely describes the poet as hero:

> He was naturally a thinker for himself, confident of his own abilities and disdainful of help or hindrance; he did not refuse admission to the thoughts or images of his predecessors, but he did not seek them. From his contemporaries he neither courted nor received support; there is in his writings nothing by which the pride of other authors might be gratified or favour gained, no exchange of praise nor solicitation of support. His great works were performed under discountenance and in blindness, but difficulties vanished at his touch; he was born for whatever is arduous; and his work is not the greatest of heroick poems only because it is not the first. *(Lives,* 1: 194)

This is the *areté* of the poet. All the heroic qualities that Johnson denies Milton in his active life are absorbed into this portrait of the contemplative man. (The traditional dichotomy, however, may not be apt. The poet is in a sense active: his poem is characteristically for Johnson a "performance.") Here we see the destined task of the hero, the aspiration and endurance, the isolation and independence, the overcoming of limitations both physical and social—all lead to an almost unequaled human achievement. If Johnson's final presentation of Milton is not heroic, where, we may ask, is heroism to be found?

NOTES

1. Samuel Johnson, No. 99, *The Idler* and *The Adventurer,* ed. W. J. Bate, J. M. Bullitt, and L. F. Powell (1963) in *The Yale Edition of the Works of Samuel Johnson* (New Haven, Conn.: Yale University Press, 1958–), 2: 433. This edition will be cited hereafter as *Yale Works.* For the political consequences of these anti-heroic views, see Donald J. Greene's excellent article, "Samuel Johnson and the Great War for Empire," *English Writers of the Eighteenth Century,* ed. John Middendorf (New York: Columbia University Press, 1971), pp. 37–65.

2. Samuel Johnson, *The Poems,* ed. E. L. McAdam, Jr., with George Milne, in *Yale Works* (1964), 6: 15–16, ll. 1–7.

3. For my comments on the humanists I am indebted to C. A. Patrides, *Milton and the Christian Tradition* (Oxford: Clarendon Press, 1966), especially ch. 5, "Deeds above Heroic", pp. 149–52, and Robert P. Adams, *The Better Part of Valor* (Seattle: University of Washington Press, 1962).

4. Elizabeth Hughes translates his book as *Man and Ethics: Studies in French Classicism* (Garden City, N.Y.: Doubleday and Co., 1971) and entitles the chapter "The Destruction of the Hero" (p. 113).

5. See the essay by Arthur Lindley in this volume, pp. 195–204.

6. Samuel Johnson, "Prologue to *Irene,*" ll. 17–18, 9–10, *Poems, Yale Works,* 6: 111.

7. Samuel Johnson, *Johnson on Shakespeare,* ed. Arthur Sherbo, in *Yale Works* (1968), 7: 49.

8. Samuel Johnson, *The Lives of the English Poets,* ed. George Birkbeck Hill (Oxford: Clarendon Press, 1905), 1: 348–49; hereafter cited as *Lives* by volume and page in text.

9. Voltaire, *The History of Charles XII* (London, 1732), p. iii. While this anonymous contemporary translation leaves a good deal to be desired, it is as likely to have been known by Johnson as Voltaire's original. The "Discourse" first appeared in the second edition. I have chosen the fourth because it differs verbally in some interesting ways from the earlier editions.

10. Ibid., p. viii–ix.

11. Ibid., pp. 9–10.

12. Samuel Johnson, *Poems,* ed. McAdam, *Yale Works,* 6: 101, ll. 193–98.

13. Voltaire, *Charles XII,* p. 30.

14. Ibid., p. 15.

15. Howard Weinbrot notes the untenable suggestion by the Yale editors that these lines refer to Catherine the Great. See *The Formal Strain: Studies in Augustan Imitation and Satire* (Chicago: University of Chicago Press, 1969), p. 201 n.

16. Voltaire, *Charles XII,* pp. 232, 197. Cf. Voltaire's statement that "the Kam is by his own subjects called Emperor; but notwithstanding the Grand title, he is a meer slave of the Porte," p. 229.

17. While speaking of portraits in *Idler* No. 45, Johnson points out that more genius is displayed in historical pictures:

But it is in painting as in life; what is greatest is not always best. I should grieve to see Reynolds transfer to heroes and to goddesses, to empty splendor and to airy fiction, that art which is now employed in diffusing friendship, in reviving tenderness, in quickening the affections of the absent, and continuing the presence of the dead. (*Yale Works*, 2: 140)

Johnson nonetheless goes on to suggest as possible subjects for historical paintings the death of Epaminondas and Cromwell's dissolution of Parliament.

18. Samuel Johnson, "Memoirs of the King of Prussia," in *The Works of Samuel Johnson*, [ed. F. P. Walesby] (Oxford, 1825), 6: 474; hereafter cited as *Works*. Johnson's antimonarchical thrusts can be found earlier as well. In the "Life of Barretier" (1740), he claims that his subject "attained such a degree of reputation, that not only the public, but princes, who are commonly the last by whom merit is distinguished, began to interest themselves in his success" *(Works*, 6: 381).

19. Samuel Johnson, *Rasselas*, ed. R. W. Chapman (Oxford, 1927), p. 125.

20. Samuel Johnson, *Idler* No. 284, *Yale Works*, 2: 262.

21. John Dryden, "The Life of Plutarch" (London, 1683), most easily available in James L. Clifford, ed., *Biography as an Art* (New York: Oxford University Press, 1962), p. 19.

22. Samuel Johnson, "Sermon XX," *Works*, 9: 475.

23. Samuel Johnson, "Life of Boerhaave," *Works*, 6: 278.

24. Pomfret, Watts, Yalden, and Blackmore. See the first paragraph of the *Life of Watts*.

25. James Boswell, *Boswell's Life of Johnson*, ed. George Birkbeck Hill and L. F. Powell (Oxford: Clarendon Press, 1934–50), 3: 231; hereafter cited as *Life*. Cf. 1: 399.

26. See *Rambler* Nos. 77, 85, 129, 137, 150; *Adventurer* No. 111.

27. Samuel Johnson, *Yale Works*, 2: 401.

28. Cowley's phrase "Poet and saint" is applied, however, to Gilbert West in the scanty *Life of West*.

29. James Boswell, *Life*, 1: 425. And see Johnson's *Lives*, 3: 177 for an estimate.

30. Hester Lynch Thrale, *Thraliana: The Diary of Mrs. Hester Thrale (Later Mrs. Piozzi) 1776–1809*, ed. Katherine C. Balderstone (Oxford: Clarendon Press, 1942), 1: 377.

31. Samuel Johnson, *The Rambler*, ed. W. J. Bate and Albrecht Strauss in *Yale Works* (1969), 4: 362.

32. James Boswell, *Life*, 4: 235.

33. Ibid., 2: 263–64.

34. Quoted by Sir Arnold McNair, *Dr. Johnson and the Law* (Cambridge: Cambridge University Press, 1948), p. 4, from Philip C. Yorke, *Life and Letters of Lord Chancellor Hardwicke* (London, 1913), 1: 56.

35. Samuel Johnson, *Works*, 6: 429.

36. Samuel Johnson, "Life of Boerhaave," 6:277.

37. Samuel Johnson, *Life of Savage*, ed. Clarence Tracy (Oxford: Clarendon Press, 1971), p. 4.

38. Samuel Johnson, *Works*, 6: 290.

39. Ibid., p. 412.

40. Samuel Johnson, *Life of Savage*, p. 40.

41. Cf. Samuel Johnson, "Life of Boerhaave", *Works*, 6: 200.

42. Ibid., p. 424.

42. Ibid., p. 415. I cannot agree with Edward A. Bloom, who sees as the primary objective of this biography a covert attack on Methodism. See his *Samuel Johnson in Grub Street* (Providence, R.I.: Brown University Press, 1957), p. 114.

44. Samuel Johnson, *Works*, 6: 284.

45. Ibid., p. 412.

46. Samuel Johnson, "Life of Ascham," *Works,* 6: 518.

47. Samuel Johnson, *Life of Savage,* p. 126.

48. Ibid. I have adopted the readings of the first and last editions.

49. *ELH* 33 (1966): 336. Donald J. Greene has argued that Christian Stoicism is "a contradiction in terms," but I think that Johnson's use of specific Stoic thinkers for Christian ends would seem to warrant the tag ("Johnson as Stoic Hero," *JNL* 24 (June 1964): 8. For a useful account of Johnson's relationship to Stoicism, see Robert Voitle, "Stoicism and Samuel Johnson," *SP,* Extra Series, (1967): 107–27.

50. Samuel Johnson, *Works,* 6: 285, 284.

51. Samuel Johnson, *Rambler* No. 137, *Yale Works,* 4: 361.

52. Samuel Johnson, "Life of Boerhaave," *Works,* 6: 289.

Wars within Doors: Erotic Heroism in Eighteenth-Century Literature

PETER HUGHES

1

Eroticism is assenting to life even in death.

—Georges Bataille

IN Shakespeare's *Antony and Cleopatra* Pompey contrasts his own warlike zeal with Antony's lovestruck refusal to fight:

> My powers are crescent, and my auguring hope
> Says it will come to th'full. Mark Antony
> In Egypt sits at dinner, and will make
> No wars without doors.
>
> (2.1. 11–13)

Antony will only fight his wars—the wars of passion he wages with Cleopatra—within doors. These erotic wars, as I shall suggest in the first part of this essay, create a new kind of literary heroism that displaces in both English and French literature the older epic ideal of the warrior driven on by heroic fury. I shall then outline the stages through which heroic actions and styles are erotically transformed into oblique and allusive modes of expression. The transformations outlined in this second section are not offered as denials of the individual talent's freedom to imagine and innovate. They are on the contrary evidence for those central realities of our literary history—those cultural and linguistic conflicts, prohibited words and acts, without which neither expression nor imagination nor consciousness itself could exist.[1] And as the final section suggests, a reading of texts in both literatures leads from Racine's repression of the unconscious to Sade's enactment of the unspeakable, from allusions to the sword as a phallus in Wycherley's *The Country Wife* to their reversal in Cleland's *Fanny Hill,* where the phallus is described as a machine and even, in some grotesque examples, as a pikestaff or cannon.[2] We move from the class struggle of *Pamela,* whose heroine describes herself as a Lucretia threatened by Tarquin, a virtuous republican assaulted by lordly honor, to the war games of *Les Liaisons dangereuses,* whose hero enacts the sadism latent in sensibility. Our concern is a period and a governing mode of expression that moves from metaphor and symbolic statement through allusion and symbolic negation to the literal enactment of erotic possibilities.

In defining this period according to these transformations of the heroic, we find that it stretches from the mid-seventeenth century to the early years of the nineteenth. In any comparative study of English and French literature during this period, when their connections were intimate and self-conscious, we must reject concepts of period borrowed from outdated political history. We should instead begin to develop the implications for literature of modern proposals in historical theory, art history, and cultural anthropology. One such is Fernand Braudel's theory of *la longue durée,* which recognizes the prolonged influence of factors such as opinion, climate, and social change in what might otherwise seem like sudden historical events.[3] Another is Robert Rosenblum's balancing of iconography and style—those visual analogues of cultural structures and events—to discover and analyze remarkable metamorphoses in works of art produced during the decades that preceded and followed the French Revolution.[4] In another, a study with a direct bearing on this subject, Franco Venturi has shown that honor, the cultural and ethical principle of monarchy, was throughout this period opposed and finally overthrown by the republican principle of virtue.[5] That, as we shall see, is precisely what happened in the transformation of the heroic. Tragedy, epic, the heroic epistle—all literary modes based upon the principle of honor—are subverted and displaced by satire, history, and the novel (first composed of familiar letters)—all literary modes based upon the principle of virtue. And finally, modern studies of Vico,[6]

whose *Scienza nuova* (1725 and 1744) has remarkable affinities
with the writings of contemporaries such as Swift and Montesquieu, are beginning to reveal the role of language and critical history in subverting the grandiose dominance of the heroic
in European culture. The process by which the language of heroes
was subverted by the language of men produced the anti-heroic
tone of works such as Voltaire's *Histoire de Charles XII* and
Fielding's *Jonathan Wild;* the later process by which it was subverted by the language of gods accounts for the revival of Hebraic
prosody in Christopher Smart, the European phenomenon of
Ossian, the ecstatic rhythms of Diderot, and the demonic notions
of Burke concerning both the sublime and the French Revolution.
It might even be argued that the period's literary texts describe a
cycle whose final stages bear a certain resemblance to its beginning.
The language of love and duty in Jane Austen's *Mansfield Park* has
an ethical rigor that equals and parallels what one finds a century
and a half earlier in the Christian heroism of Corneille's *Polyeucte.*

The earliest and most neglected aspect of the phenomenon of
erotic heroism appears in romances such as Tasso's *Gerusalemme
Liberata* and Spenser's *The Faerie Queene,* both of which consciously express the cultural and ethical revolution we artificially
distinguish as the Protestant Reformation and the Catholic
Counter-Reformation. The great reformers of the sixteenth century, from Wittenberg to the Council of Trent, extended downward to the common people the moral consciousness and individual responsibility that had earlier been limited to theolo-
gians and lords, to saints and heroes.[7] Both sides sought to create
"a royal priesthood of the people." The differing forms that it
might take ranged from the Jesuit ideal of a *militia Christi* to the
Puritan ideal of a Kingdom of the Saints. But in all of its forms the
attempt was revolutionary. It attacked and sought to destroy the
tribal and amoral codes that still dominated Christian culture.
Lutheran treatises on faith and free will, like Jesuit treatises on
individual ethics (i.e., "casuistry") placed conscience and virtue
foremost in religion, politics, and literature. The reformers sought
to replace the chivalric ideal of honor by a popular ideal of truth,
the adulterous passions of medieval romance by faithful loves that
lead to and remain within marriage, and the vendetta or blood-feud
of noble honor by a crusading heroism that served as the ideal of

the individual Christian and might be embodied in groups as different as the Knights of Malta and Cromwell's New Model Army.

Spenser, who was as strongly influenced by Tasso as he was by Foxe's *Book of Martyrs,* expressed this attempt at heroic reform in his invocation at the beginning of the First Book of *The Faerie Queene:* "Fierce warres and faithfull loves shall moralize my song." We can recognize in Tasso's *Gerusalemme Liberata* a similar conjunction of Christian love and the crusading spirit. The passionate love of Rinaldo and Armida, for example, is to be fulfilled only after the end of the crusade:

> Sarò tuo cavalier quanto concede
> la guerra d'Asia e con l'onor la fede.
>
> (16. 54)

This is a promise made repeatedly by later heroes in the plays of Corneille and Dryden. It is an attempt to reconcile honor and virtue, and by so doing renew the traditional role of Europe's military aristocracy—a class that sought to recover through wars against Turks and heretics the mission celebrated in the *Chanson de Roland* and in Chaucer's description of his Knight. Heroes of these romances, like those of Shakespeare's tragedies, reveal new qualities of moral introspection and self-doubt that continue to mark later literary heroes. And by a paradox that is at the very center of the Catholic Reformation, this new labyrinth of choices and imaginings can only be escaped through the collective ceremonies and certainties of the Tridentine Church. As C. P. Brand has observed of Tasso's great poem,

> . . . two different themes of a religious nature occur in the *Liberata.* On the one hand there is the personal, intimate sense of mystery, loneliness and weakness which seeks for God as an explanation and consolation; and on the other is the consciousness of the collective force of the Church and the delight in its ceremonial and liturgy.[8]

This paradox, which leads to the eighteenth-century view that individual expression in both style and conduct depends upon shared standards—

> True ease in writing comes from art, not chance,
> As those move easiest who have learn'd to dance[9]

—has a companion in the impact on the heroic of the advent of printing.

In a number of brilliant articles, Elizabeth Eisenstein has traced the connections, some of which are causal, between a suddenly widespread availability of texts and books and what we call the Renaissance and Reformation.[10] Particular connections between printing and the heroic arise from a number of consequences of this development. Both the writer and the reader can now recover the heroic past and verify or disprove its texts and pretensions by reference to other books and to *the* Book of the Bible. The heroic poet must therefore, as Tasso argues at length in his two *Discorsi (dell' arte poetica* and *del poema eroico),* ground his work in history and moral truth. These considerations continued to weigh heavily on the poet and were the chief reasons behind Milton's decision a century later to abandon Arthurian romance in favor of the Book of Genesis as the source for *Paradise Lost.*

As literary models became more broadcast, self-conscious poetic rivalry became intense. The heroic role of the poet became an increasingly obvious feature of the heroic poem. Less obvious, but if anything more significant, is the poet's growing need to develop heroic stature out of his own introspection and that of his reader. Rinaldo's sojourn in the Gardens of Armida and Sir Guyon's in the Bower of Bliss have sources that go back through romance and epic to Odysseus's encounter with Circe. But nowhere in the heroic past do we discover so self-conscious a use of sources or so introverted a portrayal of beauty, pleasure, and guilt. The internal struggle provoked by love and lust equals for the first time in heroic literature the external struggle of combat and heroic fury. This transformation of the heroic is already apparent in early plays of Corneille such as *Le Cid* and *Polyeucte* and in Milton's repeated use of spiritual struggle or psychomachy as the mainspring of heroic action in *Comus, Samson Agonistes,* and the greater part of *Paradise Lost.* Corneille's concept of the "unity of peril" and Milton's taste for temptation have in common a balance between the unfulfilled desire or fear and the image it begets, between the military and erotic conflict, between the heroic model and the human spirit, the poet's memory and the poet's vision.

2

As they turned inward from the conquests of the sword and siege train to those of the phallus and erotic intrigue, the gallants and *gens d'épée* were compelled both by the necessities of peace and by those tendencies within their own code that had remained latent during the long wars of the sixteenth and seventeenth century. As Paul Bénichou has observed,

> In the world of the aristocracy the creation of heroic values went hand in hand with a very special elaboration of the amorous instinct. There is a general tendency in the spirit of chivalry to make love a spur to greatness. Amorous conquest, with its rivalries, its difficulties, and its glory, imitated military conquest and could demand the same virtues. The woman herself could challenge her suitors and, like Brunhild in the *Nibelungen,* give herself only to the man who could subdue her. Love then becomes the direct reward for strength and valor. But the amorous conquest ordinarily prefers to take other paths; a triumph of pure force over a woman in real life would scarcely please lovers of exemplary prowess and would be offensive to pride, which takes much greater satisfaction in gaining the consent of the loved one. Hence the primitive combat is replaced by a symbolic struggle in which the woman, before she yields to a man, requires that he cover himself with glory.[11]

That requirement, we might point out, gave the woman an articulate equality with her amorous warrior that she retained until the middle of the eighteenth century. And she retained it even though the only glory possible to her warrior was that conferred by her love. This limiting possibility provokes a second transformation of the heroic, one that appears in English Restoration tragedies, the late plays of Corneille, and the tragic psychodramas of Racine. In all of these works the external and physical world of heroism— battles, walls, Parthians—is overwhelmed by the internal and psychic world of desire.

Let us turn first to Corneille and to his last play *Suréna* (1674). This is a tragedy of remarkable grace and poignancy. It is also Corneille's own tragedy, the surrender of the Cornelian hero to the Racianian, the surrender of *gloire* to *tendresse.* The contrast between these two dramatists has become a byword in French literature. In his art criticism Diderot even takes the contrast as proof that the poet's style, like the painter's, is inimitable: "Jamais Racine n'eût bien rempli le canevas de Horaces; jamais Corneille n'eût bien rempli le canevas de Phèdre."[12] Diderot here opposes the most extreme contrasts—*Horace,* which sacrifices love to a fanatic's raison d'état, and *Phèdre,* which immolates reason and hope to frustrated passion. But even when one considers their conscious emulation of one another, Corneille in *Suréna* and Racine in *Alexandre,* the contrast between military and erotic heroism remains striking. In a remarkably personal and bitter passage in his poem *Au roi sur son retour de Flandre* (1671), Corneille welcomes the triumphant Louis XIV with the news of his own poetic defeat at the hands of Racine and his successful new tragedies of *tendresse.* His defeat represented one aspect of this cultural transformation, while Corneille's rejection by the audience of *la cour et la ville* represented another:

> A force de vieillir, un auteur perd son rang,
> On croit ses vers glacés par la froideur du sang;
> Leur dureté rebute et leur poids incommode
> Et la seule tendresse est toujours à la mode.
>
> (Ll. 37–40)

In *Suréna* Corneille attempts to make himself part of the new style. He succeeds in doing something greater than that; for *Suréna* is a great elegy for the military hero: it is a baroque funeral. And like the visual and rhetorical splendor of such a funeral, whose announced purpose was to show the tomb to the court, the *pompes funèbres* of Suréna's end show that the palace gate opens to death. Each insists we recognize that the end of so much military and amorous life is the solitary peace of death. As Bossuet told the audience who came to hear his panegyric for the great Condé and to see the lavish decorations constructed at Notre Dame for the occasion,

> princes et princesses, nobles rejetons de tant de rois, lumières de la France, mais aujourd'hui obscurcies et couvertes de votre douleur comme d'un nuage: venez voir le peu qui nous reste

d'une si auguste naissance, de tant de grandeur, de tant de gloire.[13]

Both modes of expression, of the actor and the preacher, depend upon a double paradox. If the hero's pride and glory are so great, why does he find it so easy to give them up? And if princely grandeur is all ashes and vanity, why should it be celebrated through such verbal and visual splendor? Both modes may be two masks of that eroticism central to all baroque art, which exploits to the full Bataille's formula: "eroticism is assenting to life even in death."[14]

Suréna himself is at first glance the perfect baroque hero. A great and eloquent prince of the Parthians, he was also the conqueror who inflicted upon the Romans the most crushing defeat in their history. And since the history of what Bacon called the "exemplar states" of Greece and Rome had a momentous significance for Corneille's contemporaries, they could feel more immediately than a modern audience the barbaric power and heroic fury of that catastrophe. The Roman legions annihilated and the severed head of the consul Crassus thrown down before the Parthian king as he sat with his court watching a recitation of the *Bacchae* of Euripides, and that severed head used in the performance, so legend has it, for the head of Pentheus—all this was part of the fear and wonder evoked by the name and glory of this Parthian warrior.[15] But Suréna consciously and fatalistically resigns all his *gloire* to *tendresse*. He gives all his fame to love, abandons even the final prize of the hero—his fame in the eyes of posterity. We recall how much this matters to earlier epic heroes, how afraid Roland and Oliver are that in time to come people may "sing bad songs" of them. But Suréna abandons all that: "Que m'importe / Qui foule après ma mort la terre qui me porte?" And he does not die by what were then the hero's weapons, the sword or the lance, but by arrows shot from an ambush he makes no attempt to avoid. Suréna's last speech before his farewell and the speech in which his death offstage is reported show in their allusive use of imagery a further step toward the style of internal allusion that characterizes this new heroism. He uses the veiled language of *tendresse* even as he protests his own strength:

La tendresse n'est point de l'amour d'un héros,
Il est honteux pour lui d'écouter des sanglots,
Et parmi la douceur des plus illustres flammes,
Un peu de dureté sied bien aux grandes âmes.
                                    (5.3. 1675–78)

This is impossible to translate literally because it is written in the code of tendresse. We should notice the keywords in that code, "sanglots," "flammes," "dureté." All of them are used here in a figurative or "galant" way, in the style of Madame de La Fayette's *La Princesse de Clèves*.[16] But a moment later, in Ormène's description of Suréna's death, they turn into a literal allusion to the way he died:

À peine du palais il sortait dans la rue,
Qu'une flèche a parti d'une main inconnue;
Deux autres l'ont suivi; et j'ai vu ce vainqueur,
Comme si toutes trois l'avaient atteint au coeur,
Dans un ruisseau de sang tomber mort sur la place.
                                    (5.5 1712–16)

The sound and homonym of *sanglots* suggest both Suréna's dying breath and the blood that drowns it; the *flammes* of love the burning pain of the arrows, whose hard *dureté* pierces his heart.

This technique of what might be called "buried metaphor" is also common in the plays of Racine. In his early *La Thébaïde*, for example, *sang* first refers to the blood-ties between brothers, but by the play's end this figurative usage has turned literal and refers to the blood spilt between and by Étéocle and Polynice. In *Bajazet* the word *noeud* is used thematically and figuratively for the knots that bind one character to another. But it finally comes to mean the literal knot of the garotte, the *noeud fatal* that kills Bajazet himself. And in *Phèdre* the word *monstre* that the heroine applies figuratively to herself (because of her incestuous passion for Hippolyte) becomes a literal sea-monster that kills him and mutilates his body. All of these examples of the reciprocity between the figurative and the literal in French literature show the tragic possibilities of erotic heroism.

In Racine's *Andromaque*, for example, Pyrrhus declares that the torments and violence of passion exceed even those of war. He claims that in loving Andromaque he has been treated more cruelly than even he, the son of Achilles, treated the conquered Trojans:

> Je souffre tous les maux que j'ai faits devant Troie:
> Vaincu, chargé de fers, de regrets consumé,
> Brûlé de plus de feux que je n'en allumé,
> Tant de soins, tant de pleurs, tant d'ardeurs inquiètes . . .
> Hélas! fus-je jamais si cruel que vous l'êtes.

(1.4. 318–22)

They show too a further step from the overt to the covert, from statement to negation that becomes increasingly characteristic of both English and French style during this period.

English literature of the Restoration seizes upon the comic as well as the tragic possibilities of erotic heroism, and the witty obscenity of much Restoration comedy and satirical poetry constitutes a third transformation. We should not, however, overlook the internalized heroism of Restoration tragedy. It is manifest in Otway's *Venice Preserv'd* (1682), for example, and in Dryden's *All for Love* (1677), which in its tone and style bears a certain resemblance to *Suréna*. Any one who has read Dryden's Preface to *All for Love* will remember his chauvinist heartiness on the subject of French poetry in general and *Phèdre* in particular. His comment on the crucial secret of Phèdre

> their *Hippolytus* is so scrupulous in point of decency, that he will rather expose himself to death than accuse his stepmother to his father; and my critiques, I am sure, will commend him for it: but we of grosser apprehensions are apt to think that this excess of generosity, is not practicable but with fools and madmen.[17]

shows that, "grosser apprehensions" or no, he misses the point of Racinian tragedy. But he grasped superbly the qualities that distinguish Cornelian tragedy, and *All for Love* is comparable in several respects to *Suréna*. Consider the parallel scene in Dryden that describes the last words and death of Antony. Like Suréna, he despises the imperial world of war and power. But he does so in ways that belittle as they reject the trophies of military heroism. In

Act 2 he orders the pagan gods to give this world to Octavius, but mocks the gift by comparing the Roman *orbis terrarum* to a child's toy:

> Give to your Boy, your *Caesar*
> This Rattle of a Globe to play withal,
> This Gu-gau World, and put him cheaply off:
> I'll not be pleas'd with less than *Cleopatra*.
>
> (2.1. 443–46)

At the end, even though Antony has resolved to die in what Shakespeare calls "the high Roman fashion" by falling on his sword, his thoughts before death are as introverted, resigned, and elegiac as Suréna's:

> For I'll convey my Soul from Caesar's reach,
> And lay down life my self. 'Tis time the World
> Shou'd have a Lord, and know whom to obey.
> We two have kept its homage in suspense,
> And bent the Globe on whose each side we trod,
> Till it was dinted inwards: Let him walk
> Alone upon't; I'm weary of my part.
> My Torch is out; and the World stands before me
> Like a black Desart, at th'approach of night:
> I'll lay me down, and stray no farther on.
>
> (5.1. 278–87)

Notice the increasing force of negation and denial in these lines. They are pervaded by a quietist desire to lie down in darkness and oblivion, by a verbal sequence that emphasizes not courage and fame, not the heroic person, but the soul, weariness, solitude, deserts, and night. It evokes not so much baroque *pompes funèbres* as the suicide's unmarked grave.

The comic rejection of glory and military heroism in Restoration literature has a contrasting vitality that expresses an important difference between English and French culture. It could be summed up in the contrast between Charles II and Louis XIV, between the ramshackle domesticity of St. James's Palace and the arrogant grandeur of Versailles. The increasing republicanism of the English constitution, memories of regicide and the cavaliers' defeat at the hands of "dirty people with no names," and a widespread desire for peace after the carnage of the Civil War and the jackboot theocracy of the Commonwealth—all of these were a contrast to the French world of ceremony, conquest, and absolutist rule. In *A Satyr on Charles II*, Rochester compares the whoring exploits of his sovereign with the campaigns of Louis XIV and declares with libertine obscenity that the one is a less destructive substitute for the other, but that both are forms of domination. In England, we are told,

> There reigns, and oh! long may he reign and thrive,
> The easiest King and best-bred man alive.
> Him no ambition moves to get renown
> Like the French fool, that wanders up and down
> Starving his people, hazarding his crown.
> Peace is his aim, his gentleness is such,
> And love he loves, for he loves fucking much.
> Nor are his high desires above his strength:
> His scepter and his prick are of a length.[18]

The English court aristocrats' rakish promiscuity increasingly separated them from the virtuous ways of their country cousins, whom the *Verney Papers* and the *Letters* of Dorothy Osborne show to have been a highly moral class. But it also prefigured the fate of the French *noblesse d'épee* in the eighteenth century, a fate that evoked in both cultures a vehement middle- and lower-class assertion of virtue to oppose this erotic conception of honor. Just as the Restoration rake was essentially an officer with no wars to fight, the fops and sparks had to substitute clichés and witticisms for armor and courage. They were confined, still wearing their swords, to the drawing room, while the concept of honor, as we can tell from the meanings of the word in *The Rape of the Lock*, was in court society primarily sexual. Erotic heroism had so fully replaced its military or even dueling forms that when Pinchwife in Wycherley's *The Country Wife* draws his sword and lunges at his wife, Sparkish is moved to sum up the new heroic morality: "What," says the fop, "drawn upon your wife? You should never do that but at night in the dark when you can't hurt her" (4.4).[19]

What this comic and erotic reduction implies is positive as well as negative. It is not only the end of heroic fury and the baroque tendency to *overdo* everything. It is also the beginning of that playful and civilized approach to style and conduct that characterizes the rococo and the century it flowered in. As Johan Huizinga overstates the point, "The whole of eighteenth-century literature seems to consist of play and play figures: abstractions, pallid allegories, vapid moralizings. That masterpiece of capricious wit, Pope's *Rape of the Lock,* could only have been penned when it was."[20]

Play, however, is a serious thing, and its reduced forms of mimesis are as much negations of unconscious fears as they are assertions of caprice. In its most literal and serious form, as in a play of Racine, it can embody a denial of the unconscious horror aroused in a decorous culture and in a Jansenist sensibility by unbridled or forbidden passion. And yet in *Phèdre,* for example, or in a similar work such as Pope's *Eloisa to Abelard,* the controlled denial through poetry of what is unbearable or obscene if stated openly becomes itself a mode of statement. It also becomes, through a psychological process comprehended in Freud's theory of repression, a way of drawing attention to what is consciously being mimed or even concealed. In its most highly developed literary form, this technique actually intensifies our sense of the reality behind the game, the unacknowledged fear or desire. This technique, which Francesco Orlando has discussed brilliantly in his *Lettura Freudiana della "Phèdre,"*[21] serves not only to portray the somber and scandalous aspects of erotic heroism in this period, but also to call attention to the psychic violence that underlies even the most polished eighteenth-century treatments of sex, politics, and religion.

In *Phèdre,* as Orlando has shown, the text offers an interlocked series of symbolic negations. The need for these arises from the incestuous and monstrous significance of the story, even though Racine consciously omitted Seneca's declaration that Hippolytus had actually raped Phaedra and even though their step-relations would not make their union genuinely incestuous. On the most basic level of negation, the use of one name conceals while it reveals the existence of another more scandalous or fearful name. When Phèdre speaks of the Labyrinth she represses the Minotaur, when she speaks of heroic ancestors she represses prehistoric monsters, and when, as we have seen, she speaks figuratively of a monster (herself), a real monster is repressed. In a number of passages Phèdre refuses to allow Hippolyte's name to be spoken in her presence. Even to Oenone, her nurse and confidante, Phèdre expresses herself through a series of refusals and euphemisms, each of which increases the sense of tragic horror:

Oenone: Et quel affreux projet avez-vous enfanté,
            Dont votre coeur encor doive être épouvanté?
Phèdre: Je t'en ai dit assez. Epargne-moi le reste.
            Je meurs, pour ne point faire un aveu si funeste.
Oenone: Mourez donc, et gardez un silence inhumain;
            Mais pour fermer vos yeux cherchez une autre
               main. . . .
Phèdre: Quel fruit espères-tu de tant de violence?
            Tu frémiras d'horreur si je romps le silence. . . .
            Quand tu sauras mon crime, et le sort qui m'accable,
            Je n'en mourrai pas moins, j'en mourrai plus
               coupable. . . .
            O haine de Vénus! O fatale colère!
            Dans quels égarements l'amour jeta ma mère!
Oenone: Oublions-les, Madame. Et qu'à tout l'avenir
            Un silence éternel cache ce souvenir.

                                             (1.3. 223–52)

The language of denials, as this passage shows, can be powerfully expressive. Notice in particular that Phèdre's oblique exclamation: "haine de Vénus" and "égarements" allude to the unnatural passion and bestiality that made her what she is, and what she (together with Racine her other creator) cannot bear "fille de Minos et de Pasiphaë."[22] What Racine had recoiled from in heroic legend, what Gay, Fielding, and Voltaire mocked in their anti-heroic works, is part of a revulsion from the pagan heroic in which the Reformation and the Enlightenment combined their voices. Their mockeries and criticisms of the heroic are summed up in Fontenelle's devastating questions:

Pourra-t-on croire qu'on puisse tirer quelque chose de bon de cet amas des chimères qui compose l'Histoire des Dieux et des Héros du Paganisme? Ne semblerait-il pas plutôt que pour l'honneur du genre humain, la mémoire de ces impertinences devrait être abolie à jamais?[23]

The suppression that Fontenelle urges upon the eighteenth century was carried out with mixed success and results. The epic itself, except in expensive translations, began to lose its readers and its cultural influence in face of widespread disbelief and disapproval. It retreated into the academic study or library, where it took on the pedantic extravagance mocked in Pope's *Dunciad,* which itself, as William Kinsley has pointed out,[24] is a mock-book. Tragedy, which depended upon the same pagan sense of fate and heroic fury criticized in the epic, fell back on erotic heroism and then disappeared. In his Prologue to Addison's *Cato,* Pope supported its attempt to break away from love or *tendresse* and make its subject the traditional story of "a brave man struggling in the storms of fate, / and greatly falling with a falling state!" (ll. 21–22),[25] but *Cato* and its successors were upholding a lost cause. The tragic play and the tragic hero, considered as literary and ethical models, went into total eclipse in the course of the eighteenth century. Until roughly 1750 an aspiring writer might be expected to turn out a tragedy in the classical manner: an *Oedipe* or *Henriade* for Voltaire, a *Cato* for Addison, even an *Irene* for Johnson. But by the end of the century it had been displaced by the novel, whose opposed versions of the erotic hero and heroine we shall turn to in a moment.

One heroic mode of writing that escaped the attacks of the late seventeenth and early eighteenth century was the heroic epistle. It had indeed undergone a revival during that period, and Pope had not only the classical source of Ovid's *Heroides* for *Eloisa to Abelard* but also the more recent English examples by Oldmixon, Crauford, Lady Winchilsea, and L'Estrange, the last of which were translations of the *Lettres portugaises.* His most immediate source was of course John Hughes's translation (1713) of the French letters of Abelard and Eloisa. In a thematic and cultural sense, all of these contemporary examples of the heroic epistle represent the taste and interest of well-born women. In an Ovidian and proper sense such letters are always written by a heroine to a man who has abandoned or deserted her. They offer, therefore, an heroic role to a woman of honor, a role to balance those for men in the heroic plays of the period and in narratives such as Fénelon's *Les Aventures du jeune Télémaque*. But in a stylistic sense, Pope's *Eloisa to Abelard* parallels in English the allusive techniques of negation we have just considered in Racine. The extended contrasts Eloisa draws between her passion and the chastity of her convent, in which she becomes the light and flame of her melancholy cell, and the interweaving of sacred and profane love, resemble the obliquity of Racine's heroic style. But the parallel is even closer than that, for many passages taken from *Eloisa to Abelard* could be read as free translations from Racine. One such passage may bring home the full significance of the parallel:

> Come *Abelard!* for what hast thou to dread?
> The torch of Venus burns not for the dead;
> [Cut from the root my perish'd joys I see,
> And love's warm tyde for ever stopt in thee.]
> Nature stands check'd; Religion disapproves;
> Even thou art cold—yet *Eloisa* loves.
> Ah hopeless, lasting flames! like those that burn
> To light the dead, and warm th' unfruitful urn.[26]

The lines surrounded by square brackets appeared in the first edition of 1717, but after the edition of 1720 they disappear. The reason seems obvious: they were thought to be too direct a reference to the castration of Abelard and its physical consequences. Less obvious but more revealing is Pope's recognition that they are out of place in the oblique and repressed narrative of the poem. They affirm in the midst of denial and use the names and paraphrases for phallus and semen that are otherwise not found in the poem and that appear nowhere in Racine. The antitheses and opposites, the encoded language—"The torch of *Venus* burns not for the dead"—are a superb parallel in English to the Racinian technique of negation. In both poets it is a technique by which the passion underlying erotic heroism may be at once punished and celebrated.

3

It was, however, in and through the novel that the eighteenth century came to know a new kind of erotic heroism based upon middle-class virtue rather than aristocratic honor. In a reversal of earlier transmissions of heroic ideals and styles, it arose in England and had its greatest influence abroad in France. In the *Esprit des lois* (1748), Montesquieu maintains that while honor is the principle of a monarchy, the principle of a republic is virtue. And while the French *philosophes* could oppose their own absolutist monarchy by pointing to the republican example of the ancient Italian communes of Venice and Genoa or to the states of Holland and cantons of Switzerland, their most vital and impressive example, as we know from Voltaire's *Lettres philosophiques*, was England. More clearly than the Jacobites and Tories, they could see the reality behind the royalist trappings. "La république d'Angleterre," as one Frenchman put it in 1771, "se cache derrière le trône."[27] It was through the works of the English republicans, above all through Shaftesbury's *Characteristicks*, that the republican ideal of virtue became widely known in France. They saw from the start that this ideal had revolutionary implications for both politics and literature. Diderot, who did so much to popularize the theories of Shaftesbury, responded with the same enthusiasm to the novels of Richardson. In his *Éloge de Richardson* of 1761 he perceived the violence implicit in this ideal of self-sacrifice:

> Qu'est-ce que la vertu? C'est, sous quelque face qu'on la considère, un sacrifice de soi-même. Le sacrifice que l'on fait de soi-même en idée est une disposition préconçue à s'immoler en réalité.[28]

Diderot drew together these implications and added to Richardson's status as a great French novelist, which he had become through Prévost's translations,[29] a role in inspiring that religion of virtue that became an important part of the ideology and liturgy of the French Revolution. What struck French readers so forcibly about Richardson—apart from the English grossness and pietism that Prévost removed in his ruthlessly shortened translations—was the revelation of bourgeois life and morality. If the Reformation extended downward from the lords temporal and spiritual the need for individual faith, prayer, and ethical choice, the novels of Richardson transmitted to all three estates an heroic

ideal of middle-class virtue that was consciously opposed to aris-
tocratic honor. In so doing they advanced the cause of both
Enlightenment and Revolution. The revolutionary heroine
Marianne is the daughter of Pamela and Clarissa.

The crass undertones of *Pamela*'s subtitle, *Virtue Rewarded*,
have sometimes obscured both the ethical and erotic character of
the novel's central conflict, a conflict between the lascivious
gentlemen Mr. B. and the heroine Pamela, a girl of modest birth
whose only dowry is her virtue. So much is obvious. It is less
obvious, but equally important, to recognize that virginity, which
is as much Pamela's virtue as it was earlier Belinda's honor, really
did have a value and a price for the middle classes.[30] Even more
important in the transformation of the heroic is the fact that Mr. B.
is at once the seducer and savior of Pamela, at once the villain and
hero of the novel, while Pamela is simultaneously its heroine and
victim. The duplicity of this might be described as an analogy to
the technique of symbolic negation considered earlier in Racine
and Pope. It might also be described as characteristic of erotic
heroism, whose code allows for repeated changes of wicked
seducer into devoted lover, scheming temptress into innocent
virgin. It is a far cry from the old heroic certainties of Oliver and
Roland. It is not so far removed, however, from *Tristan and Isolde*,
in which the violence and duplicity of passion are the reality
behind its heroic theme of love and death.[31] The closest parallel to
the interplay of roles in *Pamela*, however, appears in pornographic
and sadistic narratives that enact sexual fantasies. The shifting and
at times ambiguous encounters of Fanny Hill with her various
protectors and seducers is one example, those of Sade's Justine are
another. I do not make these comparisons lightly. As what were
once external conflicts are internalized in eighteenth-century erotic
literature, the playful analogy between love and war apparent in
The Rape of the Lock turns first serious and then vicious.

Its serious phase dominates *Pamela*, and what emerges is a
miming, through erotic encounters between honor and virtue, of
what is virtually a class struggle. This becomes clear early in the
novel in two separate scenes. In the first of these Mr. B. repeats his
earlier offer of her late lady's fine clothes. This time, however, he
offers her the accoutrements of a *belle*, all of the clothes needed to
mark Pamela as either a haughty lady or a fallen woman:

> He called me up to my late lady's closet, and, pulling out her
> drawers, he gave two suits of fine Flanders laced head-clothes,
> three pair of fine silk shoes, two hardly the worse, and just fit for
> me (for my lady had a very little foot), and the other with
> wrought silver buckles in them; of white fine cotton stockings,
> and three pair of fine silk ones; and two pair of rich stays.
>
> (Everyman ed. 1: 8)

This is a reversal of the epic arming of the hero: it is the attempted
disarming of the heroine. Mr. B. then compliments her in a way
that both of them recognize as a challenge to an erotic encounter:

> I believe I received them very awkwardly; for he smiled at my
> awkwardness, and said, Don't blush, Pamela: dost think I don't
> know pretty maids should wear shoes and stockings?

The Pamela who reports this is the narrator who a moment before
shrewdly noted the condition and size of some pairs of shoes.
While she fends off Mr. B.'s advances, Pamela, as Marceline says
of Susanne in *Le Mariage de Figaro*, is "as innocent as an old
judge." And the conflict of virtue with honor becomes increasingly
social and political. Surprising her in the summer-house soon
afterward, Mr. B. cries out,

> I tell you I will make a gentlewoman of you, if you be obliging,
> and don't stand in your own light: and so saying, he put his arm
> about me, and kissed me! (1: 12)

Pamela briefly swoons, but recovers herself quickly enough to
reject this proffered social contract by pointing to the ideal social
distinction between them that in practice does not exist:

> You have taught me to forget myself and what belongs to me,
> and have lessened the distance that fortune has made between us,
> by demeaning yourself to be so free to a poor servant. Yet, sir, I
> will be bold to say, I am honest, though poor: and if you was a
> prince, I would not be otherwise. (1: 12)

The clearest focus of Pamela's class hatred is not, however, the
ambiguous Mr. B. It is the fine ladies who urge on his seductive

plans. When one of them, a Lady Towers who is "called a wit" insults her virtue "with a free air," Pamela reports bitterly, "I know what I could have said, if I durst. But they are ladies—and ladies may say anything" (1: 38). We should reflect on this suggestion that ladies are as corrupted by gallant manners as their lords. It implies that the independence they gained during the eighteenth century had made them accomplices rather than judges in the trials of erotic heroism. It also helps to explain why, in a later revolution dominated by virtue, they were sent to the guillotine along with their men.

In *La Nouvelle Héloïse*, the most significant novel of the century and probably the most widely read, Rousseau repeats Pamela's accusations and makes them even more damaging. Rousseau, who was deeply influenced by Richardson's displacement of male and military honor by the triumph of female and erotic virtue, transforms that influence in a remarkable way. He divides the celebration of virtue between Saint Preux, his hero and alter ego, and his heroine Julie. A virtuous hero, which to Fielding was a comic possibility, thus becomes a serious fact. And the *Tristan* motif, which usually involved adultery and death, is transformed into a chaste *ménage à trois*—Julie's husband like a sword between them—that lasts until Julie dies while caring for her sick child. Saint Preux attacks the military code in language and conduct that governed upper-class sexual relations among the French and perhaps, as a manuscript variant suggests, among the English:

> Ôtons le jargon de la galanterie et du bel-esprit, quel parti tirerons nous de la conversation d'une Espagnole, d'une Italienne, d'une Allemande? Aucun, et tu sais, Julie, ce qu'il en est communément de nos Suissesses. Mais qu'on ose passer pour peu galant et tirer les Françoises de cette forteresse, dont à la vérité, elles n'aiment guère à sortir, on trouve encore à qui parler en rase campagne, et l'on croit combattre avec un homme tant elle sait s'armer de raison et faire de nécessité vertu.[32]

Rousseau mocks this military slang of gallantry by using it against itself. And in a later part of this passage, he (or is it Saint Preux?) points to the true significance of this reciprocal code. Although apparently a sign of women's power, it was in reality a sign of their debasement. It was a code in which they could only speak as accomplices and by which they could be silenced as victims.

The full truth of Rousseau's remarks about this late stage in the erotic code of honor emerges in a reading of Choderlos de Laclos's *Les Liaisons dangereuses*. Although attempts have been made to treat *Les Liaisons dangereuses* as a puzzle or roman à clef, it can be understood better as the culmination of the changes we have been considering. It was both an answer to the moralizing that Richardson had brought into the novel and a retort to the sentimental treatment of erotic heroism in the novels of Crébillon fils. These novels deserve more attention than they usually receive. Crébillon's *Lettres de la Marquise de M*** au Comte de R**** was published in 1732.[33] It precedes—and is a mirror-reversal of—Richardson's *Pamela*. Its conclusion is not virtue rewarded but honor punished, and its narrative grows out of the heroic transformations that concern us here. The hero of his best-known novel, *Les Égarements du coeur et de l'esprit* (1736–38), sums up the military aristocrat's view of love as the amoral equivalent of war in one gracefully sinister paragraph:

> L'idée du plaisir fut, à mon entrée dans le monde, la seule qui m'occupe. La paix qui régnait alors me laissait dans un loisir dangereux. Le peu d'occupation que se font communément les gens de mon rang et de mon âge, le faux air, la liberté, l'exemple, tout m'entraînait vers les plaisirs: j'avais les passions impétueuses, ou pour parler plus juste, j'avais l'imagination ardente, et facile à se laisser frapper.[34]

Crébillon's hero Meilcour speaks here of his *loisir dangereux* in times of peace. Laclos's Valmont turns this into *liaisons dangereuses* and erotic intrigues that are comparable to full-scale warfare.

Although *Les Liaisons dangereuses* depends upon the language and tactics of *galanterie*, its most remarkable stylistic feature is a total self-consciousness. What Phèdre could not bring herself to say, Valmont and Madame de Merteuil do with others and then recount fully in letters to one another. Madame de Merteuil urges him to lay trophies at her feet like the *preux chevaliers* or valiant knights of the past, and Valmont declares that he is Alexander the Great and she is his empire. But the trophies she asks are the ruin

of the virtuous Présidente de Tourvel, together with a full account
of the siege and assault, and Valmont means Alexander's empire
after his death, for she is now in the arms of his less heroic
successors. There is a strong element of voyeurism in Madame de
Merteuil's proposal that they report their conquests by letter, as
well as a streak of mental sadism:

> Par cet arrangement, d'une part, je deviendrai une récompense
> au lieu d'être une consolation, et cette idée me plaît davantage:
> de l'autre votre succès en sera plus piquant, en devenant lui-
> même un moyen d'infidelité.[35]

What this results in is therefore a double betrayal, both of their
victims and of one another.

The theatrical aspects of their conquests and the zeal of their
supposed victims to lead themselves into temptation, give a his-
trionic and imaginative power to the campaigns and intrigues.
Madame de Merteuil seduces a certain chevalier who is clearly
eager to be seduced by luring him to her *petite maison* by a
tortuous route. While her lackey sets out a dinner table and a bed,
Madame de Merteuil dresses in what she describes as *le déshabillé
le plus galant:*

> Après ces préparatifs, pendant que Victoire s'occupe des
> autres détails, je lis un chapitre du *Sopha,* une Lettre d'Héloïse et
> deux Contes de La Fontaine, pour recorder les différents tons
> que je voulais prendre. (P. 30)[36]

After they make love hastily—on the ottoman, she tells Valmont,
which was the scene of their breaking off—she acts out with the
chevalier a number of fantasies. In one of these, she reports to
Valmont, she regards him "comme un Sultan au milieu de son
Sérail, dont j'étais tour à tour les Favourites différentes."

Valmont's campaign to seduce *la Présidente de Tourvel,* who has
revealed interest of a sort by having Valmont followed everywhere
by a spy, begins with a brilliant use of virtue to defeat the virtuous.
Setting out across the fields with the excuse that he is going
hunting—that ancient substitute for war—Valmont first toys with
the idea of shooting his opponent's and victim's spy, but then
thinks of a better use for him and continues on to an impoverished

hamlet nearby. Making sure that the spy is at hand to report his generosity, he saves a peasant family from ruin with a gift of fifty-six livres. Then, while the peasants prostrate themselves before him as an "image de Dieu" and he sardonically allows that he has not done too badly as the "Héros d'un Drame," Valmont tastes the pleasures of virtue.

> J'avouerai ma faiblesse; mes yeux se sont mouillés de larmes et j'ai senti en moi un mouvement involontaire, mais délicieux. J'ai été étonné du plaisir qu'on éprouve en faisant le bien; et je serais tenté de croire que ce que nous appelons les gens vertueux, n'ont pas tant de mérite qu'on se plaît à nous le dire. (P. 48)

The pains of honor destroy the lives or hopes of all the conspirators and conquerors at the end of *Les Liaisons dangereuses*. Valmont is killed in a duel, the Chevalier d'Anceny returns to the Knights of Malta, the ingenue of the story is immured in a convent, and Madame de Merteuil, mutilated by smallpox and utterly ruined, flees the country. All of this only confirms the collapse of erotic heroism manifest in Valmont's astonishing performance, in his fusion of virtue and vice, honor and shame, into the single sensation of firsthand and vicarious *plaisir*.

Laclos's novel, by consuming both humor and virtue through the appetites of sensibility, reveals both the dark side of the Enlightenment and the brighter vision of the Romantics. The Enlightenment, which was above all else the application to man and society of the angelic and demonic discoveries of the seventeenth century, was responsible for the sinister aspects of ethical liberty and unbridled imagination that we find in *Les Liaisons dangereuses*, in Sade, and in Blake. La Mettrie, for example, provides what might stand as a gloss to Valmont's sentiments—and to those of the depraved Franciscans in Sade's *Justine:*

> Since the pleasures of the mind are the real source of happiness, it is perfectly clear that, from the point of view of happiness, good and evil are things quite indifferent in themselves and he who obtains greater satisfaction from doing evil will be happier than the man who obtains less satisfaction from doing good. This explains why so many scoundrels are happy in this life and shows that there is a kind of individual felicity which is to be found, not merely without virtue, but even in crime itself.[37]

The long process by which the heroic mode had been transferred from war to love and sensation, from heroic fury to tendresse and sadism, here comes to an end. But its end is in a sense the completion of a cycle. By the last decades of the eighteenth century the corruption of morals had become a commonplace subject in both English and French culture. In England Shelley offered an erotic cure for that corruption ("The secret of morals is love"). The heroic quest continued inward to the imagination, out of which the romantic movement created a new visionary heroism. In France literature was abandoned for action. The concept of honor fell with the monarchy, and the heroic possibilities of love were displaced by war, which with the guillotine had become an arm of republican virtue. The indirections and symbolic negations of eighteenth-century literature yielded to direct statement. As the revolutionary leader Saint-Just defined the alternative to virtue in one of the most direct of these statements: "Un gouvernement républicain a la vertu pour principe; sinon la terreur." That terror takes us back to a world of pity and fear, a world of fate and heroic fury—which is where this discussion began.

NOTES

1. John Traugott both shows and insists upon this willful freedom in his study of a particular aspect of the larger question that concerns me here: see "The Rake's Progress from Court to Comedy: A Study in Comic Form," *SEL* 6 (1966): 381–407. For the historical significance of clashes between levels of expression see Friedrich Heer, *The Intellectual History of Europe* (Cleveland, Ohio: World Publishing Co., 1966); for their linguistic importance, Emile Benveniste, *Problèmes de linguistique générale* (Paris: Gallimard, 1966), esp. pp. 119–31; for the creative as well as coercive power of prohibition and taboo, Michel Foucault, *L'Ordre du discours* (Paris: Gallimard, 1971), Mary Douglas, *Purity and Danger* (New York: Praeger, 1966), and above all, Georges Bataille, *Eroticism*, trans. Mary Dalwood (London: J. Calder, 1962).

2. In "Fanny Hill and Materialism," *ECS* 4 (1970): 21–40, Leo Braudy proposes links between Cleland's descriptive language and La Mettrie's theories of "l'homme machine." But one may open Cleland's work almost at random and find that the allusions gathered magnetically around this machine image refer instead to military and sacrificial violence. One such "fierce erect machine," for example, provokes in a few pages the following terms: "victim," "uplifted stroke," "dispatching thrust," "the effect of a fire to a train," "undermost combatant," "venture to come to a close engagement with [the enemy]." To a modern reader much of this language is no more than weakly figurative: to a contemporary it would have been martial jargon of the sort Trim puts to such obscene good use in *Tristram Shandy*.

3. Braudel outlines this concept in his "Histoire et sciences sociales: la longue durée," *Annales E.S.C.* 13 (1958): 725–53.

4. Robert Rosenblum, *Transformations in Late Eighteenth-Century Art* (Princeton, N.J.: Princeton University Press, 1967).

5. Franco Venturi, *Utopia and Reform in the Enlightenment* (Cambridge: At the University Press, 1971), esp. "Kings and Republics in the Seventeenth and Eighteenth Centuries," pp. 18–46.

6. For a sense of the range of current Vichian research, see Giorgio Tagliacozzo and Hayden V. White, eds., *Giambattista Vico: An International Symposium* (Baltimore, Md.: Johns Hopkins University Press 1969).

7. John Bossy, "The Counter-Reformation and the People of Catholic Europe," *Past and Present* 47 (May 1970): 51–70.

8. C. P. Brand, *Torquato Tasso: A Study of the Poet and His Contribution to English Literature* (Cambridge: At the Cambridge University Press, 1965), p. 96.

9. Alexander Pope, *Essay on Criticism,* in *The Poems of Alexander Pope,* Twickenham ed., vol. 1, *Pastoral Poetry and An Essay on Criticism,* ed. E. Audra and Aubrey Williams (London: Methuen and Co., 1961), p. 281, ll. 362–63.

10. See in particular her "The Advent of Printing and the Problem of the Renaissance," *Past and Present* 47 (November 1969): 19–89 and "L'avènement de l'imprimerie et la Réforme," *Annales E.S.C.* 26 (1971): 1355–82. These now form parts of chs. 3 and 4 of Elizabeth Eisenstein, *The Printing Press as an Agent of Change,* vol. 1 (Cambridge: At the University Press, 1979).

11. Paul Bénichou, *Man and Ethics: Studies in French Classicism,* trans. Elizabeth Hughes (Garden City, N.Y.: Doubleday, 1971), p. 24.

12. Dennis Diderot, *Salons de 1759, 1761, 1763,* ed. Jean Seznec (Paris: Flammarion, 1967), p. 132.

13. Jacques Bossuet, *Oraisons funèbres,* ed. J. Truchet (Paris: Editions Garnier frères, 1961), p. 407.

14. Georges Bataille, *Eroticism,* p. 11.

15. Malcom A. R. Colledge, *The Parthians* (London: Thames & Hudson, 1967), p. 42.

16. My approach to heroic style as an allusive code has been supported by Jacques Guicharnaud's comments on the "style galant," which I came upon after this essay was written. In distinguishing it from the "style honnête" of Tartuffe, he observes, " 'Le style galant' qui évite de blesser l'honnêteté, est un voile transparent; on accepte de lire comme si le voile était opaque. En fait, il consiste seulement à nommer le concret par l'abstrait." *Molière, une aventure théâtrale* (Paris: Editions Gallimard, 1963), p. 153.

17. John Dryden, *"Of Dramatic Poesy" and Other Critical Essays,* ed. George Watson (London: J. M. Dent & Sons, 1962), 1:224.

18. John Wilmot, *The Complete Poems of John Wilmot, Earl of Rochester,* ed. David M. Vieth (New Haven, Conn.: Yale University Press, 1968), pp. 60–61.

19. The reduction of heroic exploits from bold deeds to bold words can be seen earlier in the play in Sparkish's refusal to take offense when insulted by Harcourt as "a bubble, a coward . . . a wretch below injury" and his zeal to avenge his damaged honor when Harcourt ridicules his claims to be a wit: "How! did he disparage my parts? Nay, then, my honour's concerned, I can't put up that, sir, by the world—brother, help me to kill him—[Aside] I may draw now, since we have the odds of him—'tis a good occasion, too, before my mistress—" [Offers to draw] ((2.1).

20. Johan Huizinga, *Homo Ludens: A Study of the Play-Element in Culture* (Boston: Beacon Press, 1962), p. 187.

21. Francesco Orlando, *Lettura Freudiana della "Phèdre"* (Turin: G. Einaudi, 1971).

22. In his remarkable book, *La Violence et la sacré* (Paris: Editions B. Grasset, 1972),

René Girard discusses the recurrence of these patterns in Greek tragedy: see especially his chapter "Du Désir mimétique au double monstrueux," pp. 201–34.

23. Bernard le Bovier de Fontenelle, *Essai sur l'histoire,* in *Histoire des Oracles,* Bibliothèque 10/18 ed. (Paris: Union Générale d'Editions 1966), p. 163. Such attacks by the *philosophes* on the pagan gods and on what Voltaire called "le chaos de l'antiquité" often should also be read, as Lester Crocker has pointed out to me, as camouflaged attacks on "l'Infâme," on Christianity and its superstitions.

24. William Kinsley, "The *Dunciad* as Mock-Book," *HLQ* 35 (November 1971): 29–47.

25. Pope, *Poems,* Twickenham ed., vol. 6, *Minor Poems,* ed. Norman Ault and John Butt (London: Methuen & Co., 1964), p. 96.

26. Alexander Pope, *The Rape of the Lock and Other Poems,* ed. Geoffrey Tillotson (London: Methuen and Co., 1962), ll. 257–62, and variant couplet, Twickenham ed., vol. 2, pp. 340–41. In his note to line 258 ff., Tillotson suggests, "Pope may have withdrawn this couplet because of Concanen's citing it as an instance of his pruriency (*A Supplement to the Profound,* 1728, p. 15)." That may well have been part of the reason. Pope's revisions and justifications show him to have been alternately bold and squeamish in making and unmaking obscene and blasphemous allusions. But in favor of a more purely aesthetic motive one might point out that in the poem's other direct reference to Abelard's castration—"Barbarian stay! that bloody stroke restrain" (l. 103)—the 1717–20 reading for "stroke" is the more carnal "hand." Through such revisions Pope moves from the physical and direct toward the pathetic and oblique.

27. For this quotation and this section's opening comments I am indebted to Venturi, *Utopia and Reform,* pp. 70–73.

28. Denis Diderot, *Oeuvres,* Pléiade ed. (Paris: Librairie Gallimard, 1962), p. 1061. In his study of *exemplum virtutis* subjects in Revolutionary art (*Transformations,* pp. 50–106), Robert Rosenblum notes the role of Richardson's novels in popularizing such didactic art (p. 50) and the continuing influence of Diderot, apparent in Gérard's claim of 1793 that "the arts should 'faire haïr le vice, adorer la vertue en charmant les yeux'" (p. 85). In a remarkable analysis of several paintings and statues, Rosenblum shows how those who sacrificed their lives in the cause of republican virtue and liberty could be represented through the sacred images of Christian martyrdom. This emerges very clearly from his discussion of David's *Death of Marat,* in which etherial light, a *Pietà* treatment of the body, and a hint of stigmata about its wounds, transform "the victim of a sordid bathtub murder into an icon of a new religion" (p. 83). But when one turns to a work such as David's *Death of Bara* (or Viala?) the eroticism punished by republican virtue—yet latent in its ideals of self-immolation— gives the painting great power and makes it a strange transformation indeed. For although Rosenblum offers impressive parallels from sacred art, including a Counter-Reformation Saint Cecilia and a *Restauration* Tharsicius, he does not comment on a striking difference. The other martyrs are clothed and austere, but David's republican boy-martyr is nude and sensual. He is also androgynous: his flowing hair, glossed-over genitals, rounded lines of legs and thighs, combine to make the painting seem the portrait of a violated girl.

29. Georges May, "The Influence of English Fiction on the French Mid-Eighteenth Century Novel," in *Aspects of the Eighteenth Century,* ed. Earl R. Wasserman (Baltimore, Md.: Johns Hopkins University Press, 1965), pp. 265–80.

30. Christopher Hill, "Clarissa Harlowe and her Times," *EC* 5 (1955):315–40. And see Robert Folkenflik, "A Room of Pamela's Own," *ELH* 39 (1972): 585–96.

31. See John Carroll, "Lovelace as Tragic Hero," *UTQ* 42 (1972): 14–25, esp. 18–19, for a perceptive discussion of the "military metaphors and allusions" that permeate *Clarissa* and

of Lovelace's self-image as a "Great Man" and conqueror. And see Arthur Lindley, "Richardson's Lovelace," in this volume.

32. Jean-Jacques Rousseau, *Oeuvres complètes,* Pléiade ed. (Paris: Librairie Gallimard, 1961), 2: 275. The manuscript copy Rousseau sent to the maréchale de Luxembourg adds "quelquefois même d'une Angloise" but subtracts "d'une Espagnole" (p. 275n.).

33. See the valuable critical "Présentation" by Ernest Sturm in L. Picard's edition of the *Lettres* (Paris: Editions A. G. Nizet, 1970). Among other points of agreement with my approach, Sturm recognizes in the literary language of the period the continuing transformation of heroic conflicts into sexual encounters. He also traces these changes back through the "longue durée" proposed here to the same starting point in the mid-seventeenth century.

34. Claude Prosper Jolyot de Crébillon, *Les Égarements du coeur et de l'esprit,* ed. Etiemble (Paris: 1961), p. 10. In his introduction (p. xviii), Etiemble stresses the specifically military character of the novel's erotic activities: "Rompus au siège des places fortes, que faire pour eux en temps de paix, qu'assiéger et forcer les belles qui se voulaient destinées aux fantaisies des guerriers (écoutez-les un peu parler de ces robins, noble pourtant, qui osent les courtiser)." Only the *noblesse d'épée* can take part in these fantasies; the *noblesse de robe* are excluded.

35. Pierre Ambroise François Choderlos de Laclos, *Oeuvres complètes,* Pléiade ed., ed. Maurice Allem (Paris: Librairie Gallimard, 1951), p. 45.

36. The range of works is revealing—from the purity of Eloise's letters to the obscenity of Crébillon's *Sopha.*

37. Julien Offray de la Mettrie, *Anti-Sénèque, ou discours sur le bonheur,* in *Oeuvres philosophiques* (Berlin, 1764), 2: 166, trans. and quoted in James A. Leith, "Peter Gay's Enlightenment," *ECS* 5 (1971): 169.

Richardson's Lovelace and the Self-dramatizing Hero of the Restoration

ARTHUR LINDLEY

RICHARDSON'S Lovelace is a continually self-generating character: one who reinvents his identity from moment to moment, casting himself into different roles according to his situation. He is, as Gillian Beer has suggested, "an existential hero."[1] Though we tend to think of this type as modern or at least post-Romantic, it is at least as old as Falstaff in English literature. It is a staple but little-noticed element of eighteenth-century fiction. As Martin Price notes, for example, Defoe's narrators are constantly surprising themselves, finding that each situation redefines them by dramatizing some unsuspected element in their characters.[2] Smollett's Roderick Random hardly exists except as a series of reactions: a center of nervous energy generating a series of performances. The most ambitious and self-conscious example of this type in the period is Richardson's dark redaction of a Dryden hero: Lovelace.

Lovelace casts all his experience into the mold of dramatic form; it is characteristic of him to externalize an internal conflict by projecting its elements onto the people around him and by managing their conflict.[3] Thus, the struggle between good and evil in his soul becomes the struggle between Clarissa and himself; the war between himself and his conscience becomes his contention with Belford. Lovelace responds to every situation as literary material: fantasizing it, staging it, discussing and re-discussing it, exploring its dramatic and rhetorical possibilities.[4] His relation to any given situation constantly changes. His most ardent attacks on Clarissa are followed by his most ardent recriminations, which in

195

turn are followed by spasmodic avowals of reform, by fantasies—like the rape of Anna—which deflect his impulses into other channels, by mock-serious discourses on the history of evil and, finally, by denunciations of Belford for criticizing him. He is, however demonic, an experimenter of the emotions, who views the siege of Clarissa as a test of his theories about women. ("Knowledge by theory only is a vague, uncertain light," he tells Belford, like a Royal Society man lecturing Swift [3:64].)[5] He is a playwright manqué who says he has read "the story of the Prodigal Son . . . and one day . . . will write a dramatic piece on the subject" (2:88). Clarissa in one of her shrewder moments calls him a "perfect Proteus" (2:82).

One can perhaps see this quality in action by examining a specific passage in detail. Here is Lovelace telling Belford what will happen if they kidnap the Howes and, by the by, kill Hickman:

> Let me indulge a few reflections upon what thou mayst think the *worst* that *can* happen. I will suppose that thou art one of us; and that all five are actually brought to trial on this occasion: how bravely shall we enter a court, *I* at the head of *you*, dressed out each man, as if to his wedding appearance! You are sure of all the women . . . on your side. What brave fellows! What fine gentlemen! There goes a handsome man! meaning *me*, to be sure. Who could find it in their hearts to hang such a gentleman as that! whispers one lady, sitting perhaps on the right hand of the Recorder (I suppose the scene to be in London). . . . All will crowd after *me*; it will be each man's happiness . . . to be neglected.
>
> But then comes the triumph of triumphs. . . .
>
> Enter the slow-moving, hooded-faced, down-looking plaintiffs. And first the widow, with a sorrowful countenance, though half-veiled, pitying her daughter more than herself. . . .
>
> Next comes the poor maid—who perhaps has been ravished twenty-times before; and had not appeared now, but for company-sake; mincing, simpering. . . .
>
> But every eye dwells upon Miss! See, see, the handsome gentleman bows to her!
>
> . . . . See her confusion! See! She turns from him! Ay! that's because it is in open court, cries an arch one! While others admire her. Ay! that's a girl worth venturing one's neck for!
>
> Then we shall be praised—even the judge, and the whole

crowded bench, will acquit us in their hearts; and every single man wish he had been me!—the women, all the time disclaiming prosecution, were the case to be their own. To be sure, Belford, the sufferers cannot put half so good a face upon the matter as we. (2: 422)

The passage is a remarkable example of both naively self-gratifying fantasy and highly self-conscious performance. Characteristically, Lovelace is using fantasy to externalize an impulse, here the urge to violate Anna and the social order. The fantasy is projected as a dramatic speech, full of calculated asides, about a dramatic event. The fact that he poses it in dramatic terms imposes a high degree of particularity, forcing him, for example, to imagine specific voices in a crowd and to visualize each gesture of the performance. Thus, an imaginary and improbable scene acquires the same propping of realistic detail that "actual" scenes in *Clarissa* possess. Realism, Lovelace knows, is a two-handed engine. It can be used, not only to establish fictive reality, but to flout it. In his letters, the imaginary rapes are always more circumstantial than the real one.

The scene Lovelace has chosen is that most theatrical of public ceremonies, an open trial, at which he can move the mob by the example of his behavior. Here and elsewhere, he assumes as literally as Pamela does that social rank and prestige are a function of one's ability to act out the values of society. "The world," as Dryden puts it, "is governed by precept and example."[6] Lovelace will edify his courtroom as Pamela does her congregation.[7] The difference is simply that Lovelace assumes the aspirations to be malignant and the performances cynical.[8] The representative characters in his scene belie their feelings in their manner. He always presumes—consciously, at least—on the falsity of appearances and the corruption of institutions. Thus, we have here his ironic treatment of the sincere embodiments of grief faced down and defeated by the pretense of courtesy: "See her confusion. . . . Ay! that's because it is an open court! cries an arch one!" Needless to say, Lovelace imagines an audience that, like his judge, is basically a projection of his own attitudes. (His syntax, stripped of transitions, tends to blur the distinction between speakers.) He is generally unable to imagine moral alternatives to himself. Nothing short of rape will convince him that Clarissa's chastity is not a pretense, like his gentility. He does not, in other words, acknowledge independent centers of consciousness.

This scene is imbued with an ambiguity of tone characteristic of his letters. It is, of course, a performance dramatizing the deceptiveness of performances. Like the whole kidnapping project, it both is and is not to be taken seriously. It is for Belford's—and Lovelace's—entertainment, but it is never quite disavowed as a real plan. Like the outrageous egotism, the violence and cynicism of the letter are both avowed and disavowed. Imagining rape is, after all, a step toward doing it, one whose importance is emphasized by its placement midway in the book and midway between the abduction of Clarissa and her rape. Moreover, the scene dramatizes assumptions about the lawlessness of society that Lovelace takes with ultimately fatal seriousness. He is, of course, a real kidnapper.

Lovelace's literary talents and tactics give him an illusion of control over his impulses. They allow him to make his least realistic fantasies deceptively convincing. They allow him, in addition, the vanity of presuming he knows all the levels of reality and can use them as he wishes. His illusions have, however, the unfortunate tendency to come true, as his pretended sickness becomes a real one. He is "a better mimic . . . than I wish to be" (4: 434). Thus, the rape of Clarissa is at first merely her deception and abduction, a kind of concrete metaphor, which later becomes the fantasy of abducting Anna, then an obsessive possibility and finally the thing itself. He is, as we have observed, an improvisor who invents his character as he goes. He is also a poetizer, who always thinks of sex in metaphors (usually those of battle or the hunt) and ultimately rapes her to fulfill the metaphors. He thinks of the act in literal terms only after he has done it, his announcement of which is striking precisely for its abandonment of rhetoric: "The affair is over. Clarissa lives" (3: 196). We can see the survival of the imagery in his presumption that she might have died, which ironically becomes the truth. He is, in short, the most elaborate of eighteenth-century warnings against the dangers of the imagination.

At the same time, he is an obsessive exegete. The literal is for him inextricably mingled with the metaphoric; the historical and the literary, with the abstract and the anagogical. "It would be the pride of my life to prove, in this charming frost-piece, the triumph of nature over principle, and to have a young Lovelace by such an angel" (4: 38). Clearly, the woman's individual identity is here subsumed in abstraction and metaphor. Even the imaginary child is only a small version of the speaker. Indeed, Clarissa has hardly any literal reality to him. Within eight pages she is "an angel" or she is "Queen Dido" (4: 30) or "The Queen of Scots" (4: 31) or "a woman whom I once had bound to me" (4: 33) or "Lucrece" (4: 38), but never simply herself. He is Aeneas, Queen Elizabeth to her Mary, the force of nature, Tarquin, but never himself.[9]

What happens to Lovelace is, to a considerable extent, that he becomes lost in his roles and metaphors. His fate is Volpone's.[10] He traps himself into acting parts, the implications of which he cannot initially see, but which he is compelled to follow out to the end because they dramatize elements in himself—destructiveness, the death wish, misogyny—which are irresistible when released. His self-ignorance is of the most self-conscious kind. His art is "*Imposture*, as the ill-mannered would call it" (3: 304). Assuming that he can approach life as esthetic material, not significantly different from the mass of allusion and quotation in which he immerses every project and event, he sees himself as a potential literary object who wonders, for example, "What a figure shall I make in rakish annals" (3: 144). All his plots, like the staged threat that precipitates the elopement, are theatrical devices. Naturally, he presumes that literal reality is as malleable as language or dramatic action. Since he always views Clarissa in metaphors, he assumes that she must eventually be what he has called her. He resists for a remarkably long time the discovery that she does not fit his general concept of womanhood, that she is intractably somebody else. His shock at the discovery is as much comic as tragic: "by my soul . . . this dear girl gives the lie to all our rakish maxims. There must be something more than a name in virtue" (3: 261).

He has, in fact, an almost childlike faith in the power of his will to shape reality. Nothing short of Clarissa's death will convince him that she cannot be made into what he wants. He boasts constantly of his devotion to analyzing other minds, women's especially, but is nearly always wrong about Clarissa and, in larger matters, about everyone around him. When she insists on dying, he seems half to believe he can will her out of it: "nor shall she die," he tells Belford, "Nobody shall *be* anything" (4: 89).[11] Like Almanzor, the hero of *The Conquest of Granada*, he builds a protean identity on the foundation of an obsessed will, one which habitually denies that anything can be beyond its power.

Like Falstaff, he assumes that he can play with identities while retaining his own. He is wrong. The protean, theatrical concept of self erodes his self-control and commits him to concretizing every impulse, to playing it out. The idea of rape grows into the fantasy, which grows into the fact. You can go one way but not the other.

It seems clear that Lovelace's place in the moral structure of the novel is determined by his assumptions about identity and that these are the logical correlatives of the modes of expression available to him. If he confuses language with fact, that is perhaps because he must constantly translate the one instantaneously into the other. He is solipsistic for the same reason that Dryden's heroes are. Like them, whom he admires, he is preoccupied with the expression of his own will, a center of ego that serves him in place of a stable identity, with reducing it to verbal formulas and confirming those by symbolic action. Both Lovelace and Almanzor are persuaded that they possess an absolute and private self, divorced from social alliances and "free as nature first made man, / Ere the base laws of servitude began" (*1 Conquest of Granada*, 1.1). Each insists on his freedom to put on and take off social roles without admitting any personal alteration. Almanzor never changes sides without insisting that everyone has changed except him (see *1 CG*, 3.1 and 4.1). They assume that their character exists solely in their formulation of it and that they can make that formulation by pure self-scrutiny. Both uphold an ideal of absolute clarity: the persuasion that they can express everything in their minds. Almanzor boasts of being

> so plain,
> That men on every passing thought may look,
> Like fishes gliding in a crystal brook.
>
> (*1 CG*, 4.1)

This striving and this trust in self-expression give rise to Richardson's famous prolixity and to the frequently ludicrous self-consciousness with which Dryden's characters formulate themselves. Abdalla is required at one point, for example, to say: "To sharp-eyed reason this would seem untrue; / But reason I through love's false optics view" (*1 CG*, 2.1).

I would argue, in fact, that Lovelace's character is built on an elaborate and ironic analogy to Almanzor, of whom Dryden says, "I designed in him a roughness of character, impatience of injuries, and a confidence of himself, almost approaching to an arrogance."[12] The parallels, given Lovelace's addiction to Dryden, seem too clear to be accidental. Each professes the domination of passion by self-conscious will; each learns the impotence of verbal self-consciousness by watching himself fall in love against his will. Each enters the social scene as a "brave unknown" (*1 CG*, 1.1), an heroic outsider who introduces himself by a victory in combat, though the ironic distance between Almanzor's defeating the bull and Lovelace the bullish James Harlowe measures the difference between the two works. If Almanzor is superior to all around him in the military virtues, Lovelace is equally superior in their domestic equivalents; he is handsomer, cleverer, braver, wealthier, nobler, and of vastly better address than anyone in Clarissa's world, and for Lovelace, as for Almanzor, one's virtues are the weapons by which one enforces one's will. Each is made the most dangerous man around by the combination of his abilities and his self-proclaimed exemption from the social order. "Since," Boabdelin tells Almanzor, "no power above your own you know, / Mankind should use you like a common foe" (*1 CG*, 1.1).

Like Almanzor, Lovelace imagines himself free from social constraint, able to follow the bent of his heroic will. "The minds of heroes their own measures are, / They stand exempted from the rules of war," Almanzor puts it (*2 CG*, 4.2). Both identify their will with nature and see themselves engaged in an allegorical combat with social convention; the formulation makes Dryden's hero a "noble savage" (*1 CG*, 1.1) and makes the rape of Clarissa a "triumph of nature."[13] For each, his will is the functional center of reality, the only thing that seems to him really to exist. Standing outside the formulation, Belford identifies it as merely "SELF . . . an odious devil" (4.9). This will is shaped into identity by verbal analysis and the testing of verbal formulas in action. Lovelace sees himself (or nature) as the resident playwright in the theater of the world. This curiously theatrical view of the world is at the core of his egotism. It is also the source of his proteanism, which depends on the presumption of the moral equivalence (to him) of all roles.

For most of the novel, Lovelace is divided between a species of moral relativism, which argues the right to do "small" evils from the general corruption of the world, and a species of man-icheanism, which convinces him that he is involved in a contention of devils and angels. The former encourages him to presume on free will and the disconnection of character from any stable principle of behavior except appetite. The latter encourages him to believe that he is acting out an abstract conflict. It gives him the kind of moral and psychological fixity which he has, in one sense, sought throughout the novel. The identification of himself as a devil and Clarissa as an angel supplants earlier, more tentative formulations of their relationship, such as nature versus principle. The stable identity he finds is, ironically enough, one which requires his self-destruction, since it is based on a recognition that his actions have consequences, that they are not merely theatrical, and that the rape of Clarissa and her death are incurably real.[14] As the mock-trial scene indicates, he has previously had little or no sense of consequences. This discovery of their existence is enough to drive him temporarily mad.

It may be useful to think of Lovelace as a late example of a type central to seventeenth-century literature: the devil as a player of parts, or more specifically, one who baffles himself by his own mimetic skill, who loses his identity by immersing himself in theatrical performances. Falstaff, Volpone, Don Juan, Milton's Satan, Lovelace—all depend for their corruptive power on their theatrical abilities, their capacity to imitate and persuade, to take on other identities.[15] All come to identify themselves with that power. Their capacity for evil is a function, in other words, of their protean character, their lack of a stable self, while their damnation is a response to that: a freezing of identity into a fixed role. The imitation snake is made a snake in earnest. The final role is epiphanic, a demonstration of the essence underlying the various roles and performances, but it is also reductive and ambiguous, since so much of the character is involved in his disguises. The multiplex self overflows his moral niche. The appeal of virtuosity subverts the condemnation of evil. In the case of Almanzor, the protean virtuosity and the superiority to social role, are allowed to stand virtually uncriticized, though they are finally reconciled to restraint and the Christian social order.

Of course, Lovelace is never merely a devil. The choice of that role is self-limiting. It is a semiconscious renunciation of the other elements in his character. It denies his strong, if temporarily defeated, conscience and the other elements that plague him before and after the crime. He chooses to identify himself exclusively with the plurality of his traits. The decision represents an effort on his part and on Richardson's to get back to the stability of timeless categories, an effort we can also see in the progressive allegorization of Clarissa in book 4.

Lovelace's position in the novel is, undeniably, more ambiguous than his ultimate damnation would suggest. He *does* have his virtues. He *is* victimized to an extent by Clarissa's impenetrable reserves, which make it difficult for her and impossible for him to know how her mind lies. If he is the product of Richardson's intense distrust of the imagination and the liberties it takes with firm reality, he is also the active embodiment of the author's narrative imagination. He controls the shape of the majority of the novel's scenes, from the abortive duel with young Harlowe to the fatal duel with Morden. As such, he is clearly a surrogate for his author, a point reinforced by his frequent identification of himself as a would-be author. One is, in fact, tempted to impose a Burkeian reading on the novel by arguing that it dramatizes Richardson's relation to the "amoral" implications of his own method, its ability to subvert easy or even confident judgments. Certainly, after the *Pamela* controversy, Richardson was strongly aware of the latent ambiguity of the dramatic novel. Certainly also, *Clarissa* is built on the contrast between self-clarifying and self-confusing modes of externalizing identity, between the ordered ritual in which Clarissa approaches her death and the madness in which Lovelace approaches his.

NOTES

1. Gillian Beer, "Richardson, Milton, and the Status of Evil," *RES* 19 (1968): 267.

2. Martin Price, *To the Palace of Wisdom* (Garden City, N.Y.: Doubleday & Co., 1965), pp. 265–66.

3. The relation of Lovelace's role-playing to his downfall is analyzed in an excellent essay by John Carroll, "Lovelace as Tragic Hero," *UTQ* 42 (1972): 14–25. Carroll sees Lovelace's acting as primarily a tool rather than a mode of vision or an idea of self. Lovelace "uses his

. . . Protean nature to bind others to his scheme" (p. 22). He uses historical allusions "to justify his own cruelty" (p. 18). I would argue that they are the very means of his existence as he conceives it, means forced upon him by the epistolary mode that forces him to constant literacy and the perpetual revelation of character. I am concerned chiefly with ontological and psychological issues, Carroll with moral and thematic ones.

4. Morris Golden, *Richardson's Characters* (Ann Arbor, Mich.: University of Michigan Press, 1963), pp. 17–27, discusses Lovelace as a fantast, but does not talk about the characteristically dramatic terms in which the fantasies are presented.

5. All references to *Clarissa* are to the Everyman edition, 4 vols. (New York: E. P. Dutton & Co., 1962). Emphasis is that of the original.

6. John Dryden, *Three Plays,* ed. George Saintsbury (New York: Mermaid Dramabooks, 1957), p. 3. Subsequent references to *The Conquest of Granada* are by act and scene in the text.

7. Samuel Richardson, *Pamela,* ed. William M. Sale (New York: W. W. Norton & Co., 1958), p. 519.

8. The function of example and self-dramatization in *Pamela* is analyzed in my unpublished doctoral dissertation, "Samuel Richardson and the Novel of Soliloquy," Rutgers University, 1973, pp. 53–84.

9. The range of allusions in *Clarissa* is catalogued by Richard Cohen, "Literary References and Their Effect upon Characterization in the Novels of Samuel Richardson," monograph (Bangor, Me.: Husson College Press, 1970). See also Carroll, "Lovelace as Tragic Hero," p. 18.

10. Both also have their fantasies come true. Both feign a sickness they later contract. Both are brought down by rape. Both are satanic figures whose satanism is linked to their mastery of disguise. Whether the parallels are calculated or not I cannot say, but see below, p. 202.

11. Cf. Almanzor, *2 Conquest of Granada,* 4.3: "She is not ill, nor can she be; / She must be chaste because she's loved by me."

12. Dryden, "Of Heroic Plays: An Essay," in *Three Plays,* ed. Saintsbury, p. 5.

13. Almanzor in his famous speech of introduction also identifies his will with a nature that stands outside social law:

> I alone am king of me.
> I am as free as nature first made man,
> Ere the base laws of servitude began,
> When wild in woods the noble savage ran.

(1 CG, 1.1)

14. Carroll, "Lovelace as Tragic Hero," p. 23.

15. The relation of Lovelace to Milton's Satan is analyzed by Beer, "Status of Evil," pp. 261–70. On Lovelace and Don Juan, see Carroll, "Lovelace as Tragic Hero," pp. 24–25.

Gothic Heroes

HOWARD ANDERSON

THE Mysteries of Udolpho . . . is in my opinion one of the most interesting Books that ever have been published. I would advise you to read it by all means, . . . and when you read it, tell me whether you think there is any resemblance between the character given of Montoni in the seventeenth chapter of the second volume, and my own. I confess, that it struck me, and as He is the Villain of the Tale, I did not feel much flattered by the likeness."[1] The intensity of M. G. Lewis's response to Mrs. Radcliffe's novel is well known; still, we can assume he is more playful than serious in urging upon his mother the congruity of his own identity and Montoni's.[2] The passage (written by the man soon to become Monk Lewis, the artist inseparable from his creation) amounts almost to a prescient parody of the readiness to merge all gothic novels into The Gothic Novel, to fuse every gothic hero in The Gothic Hero.[3]

This impulse is the less surprising since many novelists in the last years of the eighteenth century drew at random on the characteristics of Manfred, Montoni, Ambrosio, and Schedoni to formulate their own recipes for the mass production of excitement. The lines of distinction get blurred not only between Montoni and Ambrosio, but between one gothic work and another. But while the male protagonists that Walpole and Radcliffe and Lewis create do of course have qualities in common, including at times an ability to induce excitement, their differences should receive as much attention as their similarities. The differences that seem to me most worth exploring determine the varying ways in which the men in these novels approach being protagonists of education novels: what sort of change, or development, or learning is possible for men in these books? This subject can make most sense when it includes recognition of the fact that what constitutes "men" is divided, fragmented, split among different characters (usually a young man and a mature one) in terms that seem at first mutually exclusive. And finally, what change we see—whether it amounts to permanent growth or mere inconsistency—will depend upon the writer's methods of presenting character.

When Ann Radcliffe looks at men in *The Mysteries of Udolpho*, she sees stability. Emily St. Aubert starts out rather too susceptible to indulgence in "the pride of fine feeling, the romantic error of amiable minds"; her experience at Udolpho and Chateau le Blanc provides for careful articulation of her progress to mental and emotional discipline.[4] No such development is observable in either Valancourt or Montoni. Radcliffe's approach to both men is pictorial. We first encounter Valancourt as a figure in a mountain scene, and though an account of his imminent change and development seems promised, what finally is provided is summary, and in any case the change turns out to have been illusory. Montoni is a part of the rugged terrain and brooding castle from which he emerges. Both men remain essentially a part of a landscape in which only the sensibility of a young woman moves.

The intentions of Walpole and Lewis are quite different. Their men are characterized by neither the unchanging integrity of Emily's lover nor the monolithic malignity of her enemy. Montoni does indeed occasionally allow a moment's weakness to cross his visage, but for Walpole's Manfred and Lewis's Ambrosio (and for Raymond, as well) such inconsistency is a central fact of character. Equally important, these men are presented to us from the inside and are undergoing experience which—whether they learn anything from it or not—is meant to leave them decisively different by the time their stories end.

Such a vision of masculine possibility as embodied in Manfred was insufficient to challenge Ann Radcliffe, but Ambrosio stirred her to respond. When she turned to imagining Vivaldi and Schedoni in *The Italian*, it was with a willingness to incorporate into her pictorial vision an articulation of inner forces that she had earlier preferred (or been able?) only to suggest. To read these four novels in the context of one another is to find them marked by

opposing conceptions of the nature and possibilities of men—
conceptions that manifest themselves in essentially different modes
of characterization.

1

Walpole's *The Castle of Otranto* is often referred to as a
blueprint from which later gothic works derive their plans; its
subtitle, "A Gothic Story," invites such a conclusion. The hero-
villain, Manfred, in particular, along with the castle itself, play
roles whose power is felt in many later novels. And no wonder:
compared to any of his novelistic predecessors, Manfred is a
dangerous hero whom we encounter as mysterious. Or better, as
strange. For Manfred's behavior from the first is not so much
brooding and inscrutable as it is erratic, irrational, unexpected.
The opening of the novel places him in a domestic scene whose
interruption by a supernatural surprise leads to responses on
Manfred's part that no one—least of all his bewildered family—is
prepared for. When his son is crushed by the giant helmet, the
servants convey "the disfigured corpse into the hall, without
receiving the least direction from Manfred. As little was he attentive to the ladies who remained in the chapel: on the contrary,
without mentioning the unhappy princesses his wife and daughter,
the first sounds that dropped from Manfred's lips were, Take care
of the lady Isabella."[5] Daunted, but determined to be (as usually
expected) of service, his wife and daughter keep trying to comfort
him, not comprehending that Conrad—formerly the apple of his
eye—has been replaced by a new set of concerns.

Not entirely new: Walpole does assert that in fact Manfred's
interest all along has been in the dynasty, rather than in its
individual components. But the point still holds; Manfred continues to appear not so much passionately determined as frantically
active. Having decided to marry Isabella and produce another heir
to Otranto (even though it means all the awkwardness of a
divorce), he lets her slip out of his hands and out of the castle. Next
he is uncertain what to do about Theodore: he is furious at him for
helping Isabella escape, but he can't help admiring his courage in
admitting it (p. 30). And for every reference to Manfred's cruelty

and his steely courage, there is another to his shame at his conduct, his sliding back to soft feelings for his wife, and to his "heart capable of being touched" (see pp. 34, 24, 62, 35, 55, 81).

These inconsistencies seem to be signs of Walpole's effort to make Manfred a complex figure, dangerous but not unadmirable. That objective is apparent in a passage early in the novel where he is described as being "not one of those savage tyrants who wanton in cruelty unprovoked. . . . his temper . . . was naturally humane; and his virtues were always ready to operate, when his passion did not obscure his reason." Manfred's characterization does become a little richer through the placement of this passage in a context where his virtues appear to be very close to those of the young Theodore, who is his more consistently noble rival and enemy through the story. But while linking Manfred and Theodore does result in ennobling the villain, it also tends to demystify his nature: "the circumstances of fortune had given an asperity to his temper, which was naturally humane" (p. 30).

As the plot thickens, Manfred becomes more erratic: "Ashamed of his inhuman treatment of a princess, who returned every injury with new marks of tenderness and duty, he felt returning love forcing itself into his eyes—but not less ashamed of feeling remorse towards one, against whom he was inwardly meditating a yet more bitter outrage, he curbed the yearnings of his heart, and did not dare to lean even towards pity. The next transition of his soul was to exquisite villainy" (p. 35). He is particularly unimposing when we find him asking for pity from Frederic and his knights. He weeps, and then—inventing a figure of rhetoric somewhere between a whine and a sacrilegious boast—tells them that in him they see "a man of many sorrows."[6] He again edges toward the absurd after the banquet scene when we find him "flushed with wine and love" (p. 103).

Manfred's unsteady behavior does not finally invest him with complexity enough to tease us out of thought, as Walpole seems to have intended. Rather, for all Walpole's attempt at a terrifying exploration of the dark cavern of his hero's mind, what Manfred has of impressiveness abides in what Maurice Lévy calls "l'énergie farouche et aveugle."[7] It is his energy that holds our attention and makes it impossible quite to condescend to him—not the turnings of his mind or the richness of what he learns from his experience.

The Castle of Otranto conforms to what Misao Miyoshi defines as the gothic dualism: remorse following passion.[8] But though that rhythm provides a link between this book and some very great education novels, what Manfred discovers about himself and what he makes of the discovery does not matter much. The *Castle of Otranto* points the way to a gothic hero fully psychologized and fully transformed by his experience, but it was not a way that Walpole was himself able to take.

2

Ann Radcliffe did not for a long time take that direction, either, though her reasons may have been more fully a matter of choice than were Walpole's. It is not surprising that she stayed in closer touch with the minds of women than of men; she looks out at the heroes and villains of her early novels from inside the consciousness of her heroine. To speak of *The Mysteries of Udolpho* as representative of her early practice, Montoni's terrifying power lies precisely in his impenetrability, and Valancourt's only interestingly ambiguous behavior is presented in a summary report that turns out to be false.

The stress on the "manliness" of their appearance as each is introduced implies what the presentations of the two very different men have in common.[9] Valancourt is exemplary in his manners, habits, and sentiments, he reads the right books (p. 35), and he has the right feelings about scenery: "a frank and generous nature, full of ardour, highly susceptible of whatever is grand and beautiful, but impetuous, wild, and somewhat romantic. Valancourt had known little of the world. His perceptions were clear, and his feelings just; his indignation of an unworthy, or his admiration of a generous action, were expressed in terms of equal vehemence. St. Aubert smiled at his warmth, but seldom checked it, and often repeated to himself, 'This young man has never been at Paris' " (p. 41). The stultifying generalizations in the description make us pay attention to St. Aubert's particularizing comment, and indeed it is repeated often enough to build our interest and our hopes concerning what Valancourt will learn about himself (and what we will learn about him) when he finally does get from the provinces to the city.

But Valancourt is not destined to be Julien Sorel. Radcliffe plays with the theme that was to preoccupy the great novelists of the nineteenth century as she allows an acquaintance of Valancourt's to recount to Emily a sordid story of her lover's fall into betrayal and dishonor in Paris. But the account is merely a synopsis (and edited, at that, for the heroine's ears), briefly told, from the point of view of a remote observer. And in the end it turns out not to be true. Insofar as we see inside Valancourt at all, he remains simple—divided only by the most conventional and perfunctorily stated conflicts: he could not come to Udolpho to help Emily because of duty to his regiment (p. 292). His stay at Paris has presumably taught him that La Vallée is a better place to live, but compared with Emily's painful progress toward that truth, his is unconvincing—or better, unrealized.

Montoni is more fully developed, but we have even less privileged access to his mind. If Valancourt really requires fuller inner treatment to make him an adequate counterpart to Emily (whose imagination, stimulated by Udolpho, will find him at best merely soothing), Montoni maintains himself sufficiently by what appears on his exterior: "A man about forty, of an uncommonly handsome person, with features manly and expressive, but whose countenance exhibited, upon the whole, more of the haughtiness of command, and the quickness of discernment than of any other character" (p. 23). This is how he is first described, and while the passage contains what can be called psychological description, it is characteristic of Radcliffe's representation of her central male figure in stressing the look that implies certain dominant inner qualities. She presents throughout what is essentially a portrait of Montoni. Another early passage defines Emily's response to him as the result of what she discerns in his appearance: "His visage was long, and rather narrow, yet he was called handsome; and it was, perhaps, the spirit and vigour of his soul, sparkling through his features, that triumphed for him. Emily felt admiration, but not the admiration that leads to esteem; for it was mixed with a degree of fear she knew not exactly wherefore" (p. 122).

That fear is rightly understood by most readers to be sexual, but it is important that it is sexual at a remove: nothing we see of Montoni suggests simple lust. His motive, in fact, is defined as greed, and he is sexually predatory toward Emily only to the extent that she is a pawn to be traded for property. This has the effect of making him the more sinister; being the only man at Udolpho (among the socially acceptable) who does not have more immediate designs on the heroine clearly places him out of the common run of humanity. The Byzantine convolutions of his sexuality give him depths that mere greed would not have. Beyond that, greed—or ambition, or any of the associated general terms with which Radcliffe begins to get at Montoni's motivation—is not enough to describe the depths so formidably suggested in the scenes where she captures his restlessness and his arrogance. The restlessness is perhaps best caught in the passage about his gambling that Lewis referred to in his letter to his mother (see n. 1). His vigorous arrogance is here: "Montoni displayed his conscious superiority, by that decisive look and manner, which always accompanied the vigour of his thought, and to which most of his companions submitted, as to a power, that they had no right to question" (p. 288). And these expressive attitudes elicit the response we share with Emily: "O could I know . . . what passes in that mind; could I know the thoughts, that are known there, I should no longer be condemned to this torturing suspense" (p. 243).

There are very few instances in which "what passes in that mind" is described, and even fewer that reveal ambiguous feelings; there is one, however—when Montoni feels pity for Emily and then shame for having felt it (p. 366). But the depths implied by his peculiar heroic stance are sufficiently frightening—he does not have to be complicated as well. If he is in this monolithic sense a simple character, so also his experience is simple in that so far as we know he never changes, discovers nothing. Montoni's end is conveyed in a description even more disappointingly brief than the story of Valancourt's days in Paris: he is arrested, poisoned—it is all done in a few sentences (pp. 521–22, 569). If, as Victor Brombert suggests, heroic experience measures freedom and morality,[10] that measurement is registered entirely in its ostensible victim—Emily—who thereby becomes the beneficiary of her suffering. Montoni sees nothing at the end that he did not see at the beginning. Compared to Emily, both he and Valancourt are people to whom nothing ever happens—a form of self-victimization that Henry James takes up without entirely intending to in Gilbert Osmond, and which he treats directly in *The Beast in the Jungle* and *The Jolly Corner*. Miyoshi's gothic dualism of passion and remorse is absent from this book. Valancourt sheds some tears when he fears he has acted unworthily, but they turn out to have been unnecessary. For Montoni—who had refused to feel pity, and who disputed about Hannibal while ignoring the sublime Alps— there are no tears.

3

Ambrosio and Raymond in *The Monk* are a pair quite different from the others. They are young—there is no such thing as *established* character in *The Monk*—and the experience of both is distinctly and specifically educational. For the first time we have men who indeed measure freedom and morality, and to a considerable extent, register what they have seen. When we discover at the end that there has been all along a blood relation between the two, the fact serves to suggest that their common problems extend roots into their common past.

Those common problems are sexual in their origins; Lewis's heroes suffer as fully and directly for their sexuality as did Radcliffe's heroines, though of course differently. And what they undergo comes with corresponding directness. The narrative of Ambrosio's story stays very close to his consciousness, tracing its turnings attentively; and Raymond's long account of his love affair is told in the first person. The effects are not pictorial as in Radcliffe, but psychological, and the psychological interest is furthered by unprecedented attention to the formative forces at work in Ambrosio's early life. No earlier novelist, not even Richardson, had traced the causes of his hero's perversity as Lewis does.

In fact, it may come as a surprise to find that in a novel usually considered richly realistic, Richardson had provided only the sketchiest outline of the origins of Lovelace's demonic feelings toward women. And if we are accustomed to thinking of gothic novels as "romances" and of gothic heroes as Northrop Frye's "stylized figures which expand into psychological archetypes,"[11] we will be even more suprised to find how much Lewis has to say about how Ambrosio came to be the kind of person he is. The destructively adulatory attention that Ambrosio gets from his fellow monks is often touched on early in the book, but it is when he has fallen for the first time into the ready arms of Matilda—and is about to embark on his self-consuming search for ultimate sexual satisfaction—that Lewis provides a detailed account of what the monastery has done to pervert Ambrosio's originally noble nature:

> Had his Youth been passed in the world, He would have shown himself possessed of many brilliant and manly qualities. He was naturally enterprizing, firm, and fearless: He had a Warrior's heart, and He might have shone with splendour at the head of an Army. There was no want of generosity in his nature. . . . His abilities were quick and shining, and his judgment vast, solid, and decisive. With such qualifications, He would have been an ornament to his Country: That He possessed them, He had given proofs in his earliest infancy, and his Parents had beheld his dawning virtues with the fondest delight and admiration. Unfortunately, while yet a child He was deprived of those Parents. . . . The Abbot, a very Monk, used all his endeavours to persuade the Boy, that happiness existed not without the walls of a Convent. He succeeded fully . . . his Instructors carefully repressed those virtues, whose grandeur and disinterestedness were ill-suited to the Cloister. Instead of universal benevolence, He adopted a selfish particularity for his own particular establishment: He was taught to consider compassion for the errors of others as a crime of the blackest dye: The noble frankness of his temper was exchanged for servile humility; and in order to break his natural spirit, the Monks terrified his young mind, by placing before him all the horrors with which Superstition could furnish them: They painted to him the torments of the Damned in colours the most dark, terrible, and fantastic, and threatened him at the slightest fault with eternal perdition. . . . While the Monks were busied in rooting out his virtues, and narrowing his sentiments, they allowed every vice which had fallen to his share, to arrive at full perfection. He was suffered to be proud, vain, ambitious, and disdainful: He was jealous of his Equals, and despised all merit but his own: He was implacable when offended, and cruel in his revenge.[12]

Lewis may owe something to Godwin in this passage, but neither Walpole nor Radcliffe had gone into detail about the social forces that could help account for their villains. Neither goes further than to assume the enormous influence of social ambition in the lives of men. Lewis particularizes what society has done to Ambrosio, describing his education as a trap constructed to separate him from all that was best in his potential; the confining monastery becomes the apt symbol of one side of himself erected to imprison another aspect of his being.

Most important, Lewis reveals the extent to which Ambrosio has incorporated the values inculcated by his education. Alien as monastic standards are to what he was originally, Ambrosio has absorbed them so fully that they are now a great part of him; he is in fact the head of the monastery, its chief embodiment.[13] It is precisely because Ambrosio cannot reject the standards of the monastery that the ensuing explosion in his personality occurs. In Manfred and Montoni, the individual will chains itself to the past in the unquestioning service of social prestige and power. Lewis's contribution is to put the service very much into question, but it is no less enslaving for that. Ambrosio at thirty suddenly glimpses the ecstatic possibilities of individual fulfillment through sexual experience. But, unable to imagine foregoing the status and respect attendant on his position in his world, he cannot even want to break free. His terrible self-destruction is not caused by revolt against the established order; indeed it may be said to happen because he does not revolt enough. The sexual insatiability at the center of his rapid downward spiral in the second half of the book results from the inadequacy of sexual pleasure to assuage the guilt created by tension between his lives of license and of order. This is only another way of describing the tension between his attempts to live in a new world and an old at once. We are told repeatedly that the Monk's need for the respect of his community grows in proportion to his failure to deserve it,[14] and his sense of that failure leads him to the pursuit of stronger, more intense, and violent anodynes. Artaud's perception that Ambrosio's essential engagement is in an attempt to break the physical and moral boundaries to "le mouvement naturel de l'amour"[15] needs to be adjusted by the recognition that he does not attempt to break, but rather to circumvent, the perverse cultural boundaries upon which much of his identity continues to depend.

There is no suggestion in the novel that Ambrosio's psychic dilemma could be solved by revolt or escape. The tedious, touching story that Elvira tells about her attempt with her husband

(Ambrosio's father, though we may not yet know it) to avoid the wrath of his own aristocratic father suggests in fact the impossibility of simply replacing old worlds with new ones. Gonzalvo had married beneath him, against his father's will; when the two escape to Cuba, their love, strong as it is, proves insufficient to supply the place that the old land had occupied in Gonzalvo's life. The poem he wrote to express his unhappiness ("The Exile")[16] is nearly unreadable, but it summarizes Lewis's message on the limitations of trying to find freedom by running away. The novel's long subplot centering on Raymond de las Cisternas reinforces the same theme in rich psychological detail.

Raymond's grand tour through France and Germany parallels Ambrosio's encounter with the social world; each constitutes in its own way the last step in the education of the young man. If the Grand Tour was classically intended to allow investigation of foreign courts, Raymond's is a good deal more a sentimental journey; like Ambrosio's his education as an adult really begins when he encounters a woman. It is important that she is an old woman—too old to interest him, anyway, though not too old to be herself interested. Before his story ends he discovers that he must deal not only with this unappealing lady, but with one who has been around much, much longer. In fact, Raymond's heroic task is precisely Ambrosio's: he must recognize that the most apparently free and individual human impulses have lines of liaison with other people and with the past; he has to reconcile his spontaneous acts with the world of which he is a part. Raymond finally survives this test as Ambrosio does not, but in the process he is driven to the edge of madness and of death.

When Raymond chivalrously saves the Baroness Lindenberg from murderous robbers, the lady falls in love with him, invites him to her castle in Bavaria, and despite the fact that she is married begins a vigorous courtship that he is too naive to comprehend. When he does wake up, he is in love with the baroness's young niece and assumes that a polite explanation of his feelings will suffice to extricate him from the older woman's unwanted embrace. He is wrong, of course: her feelings have been engaged and are by now under neither his control nor her own. She will not agree to let him marry Agnes, and to elude her the two optimistic young people decide to harness local superstition. Agnes will dress in the costume of the Bleeding Nun who is said to have haunted the castle for a hundred years, and when the terrified gate keeper opens to let the "ghost" out, she and Raymond will elope together in his waiting carriage.

The results are predictable: the real ghost joins Raymond in the carriage, gathering him in an embrace even harder to break than the baroness's. What follows is a tale of psychological possession—of his long and laborious effort to rid himself of her haunting presence, to reunite himself with Agnes, and later still to redeem Agnes from the ghastly vault in which she is buried alive. Its interest lies in the suggestiveness of its description of the reasons why autonomous and spontaneous expression of sexual passion is impossible in the world of *The Monk*. The Bleeding Nun, who gets a grip on Raymond when he tries to love where he pleases, turns out herself to have been a woman whose unbridled sexual passions led to murders, and finally to her own. This embodiment of carnal violence—the convent could not hold her long—had been, furthermore, a member of Raymond's own family; the same blood flows in their veins (and hence, not incidentally, in Ambrosio's). It is only by locating her unburied corpse and carrying it to burial in their family vault that Raymond can exorcise her haunting presence. Until he performs that symbolic act of reconciliation between her violent individualism and her family he languishes nervous, sleepless, unmanned.

Having done so, he locates Agnes, and though she has by now taken the veil at her family's insistence, he manages a fatal meeting with her in the convent garden that results in her pregnancy. What the Bleeding Nun has taught about the dangers of attempting sexual freedom is then repeated as another bitter old woman—this time the convent's mother superior—prevents the fulfillment of Raymond's love by consigning Agnes to a living death in a subterranean cell. Raymond's agitation when he cannot find her, followed by another long bout of hysterical illness, leads him again near madness and death. At the very least, we can say that the two assertions of his sexuality lead to paralysis from which he is saved only by sheerly fortuitous turns of events. Miyoshi's gothic dualism of passion and remorse reaches its apogee in *The Monk:* both Ambrosio and Raymond exemplify fully this fluctuation of feeling. It is represented in each in such careful and prolonged detail as to constitute the rhythm of the book. Furthermore, the careful attention on the one hand to nuances of feeling, and on the other to the placement of these passions in a context of both environment and heredity, make Lewis's heroes the richest embodiments of a kind of heroism whose origin Maurice Lévy traces to the novels of Sophia Lee—a hero "sensible et malheureux, victime à la fois de ses passions et du Destin."[17]

4

The rhythm of Radcliffe's *The Italian* is very different: it ends with the wedding of Vivaldi and Ellena, where there is no expression of that regret for what has been lost that pervades the long-delayed weddings in *The Monk*. Furthermore, Schedoni counters Ambrosio's "dread" of death by taking his into his own hands: he poisons himself, and his last expression is a shriek of exultation. Yet to read *The Italian* is to know that *The Monk* was the most interesting book Ann Radcliffe read after she had finished writing *The Mysteries of Udolpho*. In Vivaldi and Schedoni she manages, without at all abandoning the striking visual presentation of her heroes, to combine with it greater psychological range and complexity. These two characters are larger than Radcliffe's other men because she imagines much more their inner experience, she allows that inner experience more contradiction and reversal (if not permanent change), and—particularly in their long mutual confrontation with the Inquisition—she endows the two men with characteristics that link them, hero and villain, in ways that are both admirable and human.

It is a new departure of real importance for Radcliffe to begin her narrative with an exploration of her hero; it is even more important that as the book continues we remain as often with Vivaldi or Schedoni as with Ellena. Vivaldi is described as partaking of the characteristics of his parents, and though he is nobly devoid of their more serious limitations, the ambiguities of his nature are sufficient to provide a real basis for his later problems in achieving that marriage which he considers his "most sacred right":[18] "his pride was as noble and generous as that of the Marchese; but he had somewhat of the fiery passions of the Marchesa, without any of her craft, her duplicity, or vindictive thirst for revenge. Frank in his temper, ingenuous in his sentiments, quickly offended, but easily appeased; irritated by any appearance of disrespect, but melted by a concession, a high sense of honor rendered him no more jealous of offence, than a delicate humanity made him ready for reconciliation, and anxious to spare the feelings of others" (p. 8).

It is exactly Vivaldi's high sense of his own honor that makes him so determined to marry as he chooses, and it is his quickness to take offense that fixes the indomitable Schedoni as his most dangerous opponent in accomplishing that end. In setting himself in opposition to the idea that "you belong to your family, not your family to you" (p. 30), Vivaldi aligns himself with the assertive individuals that Lewis's heroes try to be, far more than with Radcliffe's passive Valancourt. And like Ambrosio and Raymond, he is sometimes inconsistent and self-indulgent. His romantic propensity to find pleasure in fanciful superstition makes him rather like an early Radcliffe heroine, and its effects are double-edged: his curiosity about the supernatural is an element of his sensitivity and openness to experience, but it contributes to his being locked up at Paluzzo while Ellena is being carried away to a mountain convent (p. 78).

Vivaldi comes to life, then, as something more than a "manly figure" like Valancourt, lending human interest to a sublime mountain landscape. But though in the end he confronts the villain of the piece (as Valancourt never does) and contributes importantly to his destruction, Vivaldi is otherwise no match for Schedoni. The book contains two extended descriptions of the villain's character and his past (pp. 34–35, 226–28). The first, while more detailed than anything comparable in *The Mysteries of Udolpho*, carries on brilliantly Radcliffe's visual artistry: the evocation of depths through description of surfaces is epitomized in Schedoni's face, which "bore the traces of many passions." The second passage provides the historical information that culminates in Schedoni's choosing to transform his identity from aristocrat to monk, summed up in his taking a new name. And there are innumerable other passages that provide on the one hand the suggestive hiero-glyphs of Schedoni's character (the description of his cell is one sort of example) and on the other analysis of his inner feelings and motives (e.g., pp. 102, 52).

But the novel's greatest accomplishment lies in the portrait—visual *and* psychological—of its evil genius, first as he awes the heroine by his mysterious appearance on the barren shores of the Adriatic, and then late at night, when he stalks the confines of her room, struggling to prepare himself to kill her (pp. 220–40). Caught between rocks and waves, we see Schedoni through Ellena's terrified eyes; she is both terrified and confused—for he appears apparently from nowhere, and then, when she appeals for help to the monk, she is confounded by his aloofness and hostility. It is a stunning nightmare scene that would be sufficient in itself to explain the attraction the gothic novel has had for the surrealists. In it, Schedoni lives fully as an ambiguous nature—the dangerous religious—observed.

The interior scene is quite different. We follow Schedoni to the small upper room where Ellena is asleep (the description is heavy with *Othello*), and we follow his mind as it discovers "an emotion new and surprising" that he tries vainly to suppress so that he can get on with the business at hand (p. 228). "Had it been possible to shut out consciousness, he would have done so," but his consciousness grinds on, pushing him to discoveries and awarenesses altogether unlike anything Radcliffe had imagined for Montoni (p. 225). Schedoni's misgivings, his strange forebodings, his unaccustomed paralysis, culminate in the discovery that he has in fact almost killed his own daughter. It does not, I think, finally matter that he is mistaken—she is only his niece—nor that after being so thoroughly shaken he shortly returns to his old ambitions, only now with the aim of ensuring Ellena's marriage to the wonderfully eligible Vivaldi, rather than preventing the match. It is less important that he is very soon again "willing to subject himself to any meanness however vicious, rather than forego the favorite ambition" (p. 251). The fact remains that he has been shaken: Schedoni is a greater novelistic achievement than Montoni because we have been there when something happened to him and have been convinced of it with him. In these scenes on the stormy Adriatic he is at once an austere force of nature and a vulnerable human being.

His appearance before the Inquisition manifests the same combination of superiority and victimization in the face of powers beyond even his own. None of these scenes rises to the dramatic or visual power of those by the shore, but Radcliffe's description of

Schedoni being hounded and trapped while at the same time taking command of his own fate (and being certain to bring his betrayer down with him) is not radically anticlimatic. Most important, her attribution of some of the same characteristics to both Schedoni and Vivaldi as they face the relentless Inquisition has the effect of making each seem an instance of the same humanity: where Vivaldi displays "grandeur of mind," Schedoni remains "firm and even tranquil, and his air dignified" (pp. 305, 355). And certainly Ann Radcliffe is showing Monk Lewis how a man should die when she allows Schedoni even at the last to conquer "for a moment, corporeal suffering," and speak for himself in firm tones (p. 404).

Surely it is better, then, not to let the fact that all of these writers divide their masculine worlds among roughly similar casts of characters lead us to ignore what individuates those characters. Walpole, Radcliffe, and Lewis have in common a view of the past as possessing and imprisoning good and bad "heroes" alike. "Are there really *ghosts?*" asks Francis Russell Hart in his valuable essay on gothic characterization, and he replies that the answer of the gothic as a genre is that "*We* are ghosts."[19] The past lives on, paradoxically and terribly, in a whole range of men who try precisely to free themselves from it, to assume individual freedom. Yet, again, each character is related to that haunting past in his own way, and their common effort to transcend it should not prevent attention to Walpole's, Radcliffe's, and Lewis's ways of realizing the terrors that haunted English literature through a revolutionary generation, and which survive into our own.

NOTES

1. Lewis F. Peck, *A Life of Matthew G. Lewis* (Cambridge, Mass.: Harvard University Press, 1961), pp. 208–9. The passage from *The Mysteries of Udolpho* is as follows:

Montoni had been otherwise engaged: his soul was little susceptible of light pleasures. He delighted in the energies of the passions: the difficulties and tempests of life, which wreck the happiness of others, roused and strengthened all the powers of his mind, and afforded him the highest enjoyments, of which his nature was capable. Without some object of strong interest, life was to him little more than a sleep: and, when pursuits of real interest failed, he substituted artificial ones, till habit changed their nature, and they ceased to be unreal. Of this kind was the habit of gaming, which he had adopted, first, for the purpose of relieving him from the languor of inaction, but had since pursued with the ardour of passion. In this occupation he had passed the night with Cavigni and a party of young men, who had more money than rank, and more vice than either. Montoni despised the greater part for the inferiority of their talents, rather than for their vicious inclinations. Among these, however, were some of superior abilities, and a few whom Montoni admitted to his intimacy, but even towards these he still preserved a decisive and haughty air, which, while it imposed submission on weak and timid minds, roused the fierce hatred of strong ones. He had, of course, many and bitter enemies; but the rancour of their hatred proved the degree of his power; and, as power was his chief aim, he gloried more in such hatred, than it was possible he could in being esteemed. A feeling so tempered as that of esteem, he despised, and would have despised himself also had he thought himself capable of being flattered by it.

Ann Radcliffe, *The Mysteries of Udolpho,* ed. Bonamy Dobrée (London: Oxford University Press, 1970), p. 182. The passage occurs in vol. 2, ch. 3, which in the first edition is misnumbered XVII—hence Lewis's reference.

2. His mother may have been best prepared to find her son in Montoni's substitution of "artificial" pleasures when "pursuits of real interest failed." She had already had several of what would prove an endless stream of letters from country house parties.

3. Devendra P. Varma, *The Gothic Flame* (London: Arthur Barker, 1957), p. 215, distinguishes the genealogies of three types of gothic villain, and Maurice Lévy's *Le Roman "Gothique" Anglais, 1764–1820* (Toulouse: Association des publications de la Faculté des lettres et sciences humaines, 1968), is often very good in describing the strongest traits of the villains of the writers studied.

4. Radcliffe, *The Mysteries of Udolpho,* p. 79.

5. Horace Walpole, *The Castle of Otranto,* ed. W. S. Lewis (London: Oxford University Press, 1964), p. 17. Further page citations are in the text.

6. This scene, verging on the comic, is the best example in *The Castle of Otranto* of the gothic hero as false-rhetorician, with borrowings from Mark Antony and Satan. It can be compared with Ambrosio's efforts to seduce Antonia in *The Monk,* which also comes close to being funny through the obvious artifice of the argument.

7. Lévy, *Le Roman "Gothique" Anglais,* p. 101.

8. Misao Miyoshi, *The Divided Self: A Perspective on the Literature of the Victorians* (New York: New York University Press, 1969), p. 53.

9. Radcliffe, *The Mysteries of Udolpho,* pp. 23, 31. Further page citations are in the text.

10. Victor Brombert, "The Idea of the Hero," in *The Hero in Literature,* ed. Brombert (Greenwich, Conn.: Fawcett Publications, 1969), p. 13.

11. *Anatomy of Criticism* (Princeton: Princeton University Press, 1957) p. 304.

12. Matthew G. Lewis, *The Monk,* ed. Howard Anderson (London: Oxford University Press, 1973), pp. 236–37.

13. When we realize that the monastery is itself geographically and socially at the center of the city, we must see its values as epitomizing those of the larger culture; it is important to notice the parallel between Ambrosio's sadistic destruction of Antonia in the vaults and the populace's treatment of the nuns and the mother superior, which takes place at the same time in the streets above.

14. The parallel with Falkland in *Caleb Williams* is particularly apparent here.

15. Cited by Lévy, *Le Roman "Gothique" Anglais,* p. 365.

16. Lewis, *The Monk,* pp. 215–17.

17. Lévy, *Le Roman "Gothique" Anglais,* p. 183.

18. Ann Radcliffe, *The Italian,* ed. Frederick Garber (London: Oxford University Press, 1968), p. 40. Further page citations are in the text.

19. Francis Russell Hart, "The Experience of Character in the English Gothic Novel," in *Experience in the Novel,* ed. Roy Harvey Pearce (New York: Columbia University Press, 1968), p. 99.

Notes on Contributors

ROBERT FOLKENFLIK, the editor, has published *Samuel Johnson, Biographer* (Cornell) and edited Swift's *A Tale of a Tub* (Joseph Simon). He has recently completed *Self and Society in the Eighteenth-Century Novel,* and his articles on Johnson, Pope, Fielding, Richardson, Smollett, Gibbon, and others have appeared widely. He has held a National Endowment for the Humanities Fellowship and a Guggenheim Fellowship.

J. W. JOHNSON is the author of *The Formation of Neo-Classical Thought* (Princeton) and has edited *Utopian Literature* (Random House) and several textbooks. He is currently writing a critical biography of the earl of Rochester.

LARRY CARVER is at work on a study of patriarchy in Restoration Literature. His articles have appeared in *The Huntington Library Quarterly* and *Papers on Language and Literature.* He is editing the Restoration play *Sodom* (with J. W. Johnson).

W. B. CARNOCHAN is the author of *Lemuel Gulliver's Mirror for Man* and *Confinement and Flight: An Essay on English Literature in the Eighteenth Century* (both California). He has edited Etherege's *Man of Mode* for the Regents Restoration series (Nebraska).

ROBERT D. HUME has published *Dryden's Criticism* (Cornell) and *The Development of English Drama in the Late Seventeenth Century* (Clarendon). He has edited (with Arthur Scouten) a recently discovered Restoration play, *The Country Gentleman* (Pennsylvania) and a *Festschrift* for Scouten, *The London Theatre World 1660–1800* (Southern Illinois).

C. J. RAWSON has published *Henry Fielding* in the Profiles in Literature series, *Henry Fielding and the Augustan Ideal under Stress* and *Gulliver and the Gentle Reader* (all Routledge & Kegan Paul). He has also edited a book of Swift criticism for Sphere. He serves as general editor of the Unwin Critical Library (Allen & Unwin) and coeditor of *The Modern Language Review* and the *Yearbook of English Studies*.

PAUL HUNTER is the author of *The Reluctant Pilgrim*, a study of Defoe, and *Occasional Form*, a study of Fielding (both Johns Hopkins). He has edited *Moll Flanders* (Crowell) and several anthologies (Norton).

PETER HUGHES has edited volume 8 of *The Journals and Letters of Fanny Burney* (Clarendon), coedited *The Varied Pattern: Studies in the Eighteenth Century* (Hakkert) and published widely in learned journals. He is publishing on the semiotics of allusion and has been a fellow of the Cornell Society for the Humanities.

ARTHUR LINDLEY has recently completed a book-length study of Richardson. His poetry appears in various journals and magazines.

HOWARD ANDERSON is the coeditor of *The Familiar Letter in the Eighteenth Century* (Kansas) and *Studies in Criticism and Aesthetics* (Minnesota). He has edited Matthew Lewis's *The Monk* in the Oxford English Novels series and *Tristram Shandy* for the Norton Critical Editions series. His articles on Sterne and other eighteenth-century novelists have appeared in *Studies in English Literature, PMLA, Philological Quarterly,* and elsewhere.

Index